THE MARKETING
OF IDEAS
AND SOCIAL ISSUES

General Editor

Steven E. Permut

Yale University

Praeger Series in Public and Nonprofit Sector Marketing

THE MARKETING OF IDEAS AND SOCIAL ISSUES

Seymour H. Fine

PRAEGER

PRAEGER SPECIAL STUDIES • PRAEGER SCIENTIFIC

Library of Congress Cataloging in Publication Data

Fine, Seymour H
    The marketing of ideas and social issues.

    Bibliography: p.
    Includes index.
    1. Marketing—Social aspects—United States.
2. Marketing—Social aspects—United States—
Case studies.   I. Title.
HF5415.1.F55   303.4   81-850
ISBN 0-03-059277-1   AACR1

Published in 1981 by Praeger Publishers
CBS Educational and Professional Publishing
A Division of CBS, Inc.
521 Fifth Avenue, New York, New York 10175 U.S.A.

© 1981 by Praeger Publishers

456789 052 987654

Printed in the United States of America

FOREWORD
Philip Kotler

We are coming to recognize that there is a marketplace of ideas just as there is a marketplace of goods. In this marketplace, purveyors of ideas—lobbyists, publicists, charismatic leaders, change agents—promote ideas to influence the attitudes and behavior of target audiences. They use modern channels of communication and distribution to reach their audiences. They approach their task from a variety of perspectives, but rarely a marketing one. In this book Seymour Fine describes how ideas and issues can be more effectively disseminated through the use of modern marketing concepts and tools.

Marketing ideas goes far beyond their promotion. Anyone who wishes to influence others must research the target audience; understand their perceptions, attitudes, and needs; develop and test effective communication concepts; and use the most cost-effective distribution channels. Ideas, according to Fine, can be managed like any other commodity.

Although the suggestion that marketing planning could be applied to ideas and issues was made some years ago, only a few writings have appeared to date. Most are specialized to a particular area of social marketing, such as family planning, antismoking, or better environment. Fine is the first person to write a book on the general principles of social marketing, and he is to be congratulated.

The reader will find much stimulating material in this book—a book that shows a high standard of scholarly research and an adept pen. The reader will not only emerge convinced of the contributions that a marketing point of view can make to the effective dissemination of ideas but also be sensitized to the role of the four Ps (product, price, place, and promotion) in this endeavor. While it is hard to evaluate the first book written on any new subject, I am sure that Fine's work will gain recognition as a major and enduring contribution.

Some readers may be squeamish about "idea marketing," as if it can only be used to persuade people to act against their best interests. This is not the philosophical position of social marketing. Social marketing is an effective way to promote ideas that serve the best interests of people—better nutrition, physical exercise, conservation, environmental protection—to the point where people might act on what they believe and really want to do. True, bad ideas can also be promoted, and are being promoted all the time, with or without the aid of modern marketing concepts. We have to assume that all ideas enter a marketplace where consumers of ideas are exposed to multiple claims and counterclaims and in the end are intelligent enough to know which ideas best serve their interests.

PREFACE

The objective of this work is to investigate meeting grounds where the theory and practice of marketing overlap with processes of dissemination of ideas and social issues. The marketing of ideas and issues—concepts—is an important process not only to those who are in the business of proposing and diffusing concepts, such as freedom of the press, nudism, consumer cooperatives, or "Join the Peace Corps." (A more complete list appears in Table 1.1.) It is also useful in the marketing of conventional goods and services, for which ideas are used in the design of promotional messages.

In the very early stages of the work it became apparent that the subject being explored here is nothing more or less than the study of propaganda; the marketing of ideas and social issues is not very different from the spreading of propaganda. This realization sent the writer scurrying back to the drawing board wondering whether what was about to be written had already been well covered under the propaganda rubric. The danger of reinventing the wheel is always a threat that niggles at the spirit of a writer. A computerized search in fact revealed no less than 224 references on the subject of propaganda. But a review of that literature led to the conclusion that while propaganda was indeed well covered, none of the writings seemed to approach the topic from a formal marketing viewpoint—the goal of the present work. What resulted was a reinforced decision to proceed as though nothing had ever been written on the subject—a zero-based approach. The work takes as given the rich fundamental concepts of marketing, examining their applicability to the adoption and dissemination of ideas and social issues whether or not such processes are, or have ever been, taken as the spread of propaganda.

Another reason for adopting this philosophy is that the word propaganda suffers from pejorative connotation, just as indeed the term marketing occasionally does. Propaganda is frequently associated with politically inspired and malevolent inculcation of ideas into the minds of those opposing the established order, in other words, brainwashing. *Webster's New World Dictionary*, in fact, states that the word is "now often used disparagingly to connote deception or distortion" (2nd ed., p. 1138). A zero-based approach assumes innocent-till-proved-guilty status for both terms, propaganda and marketing.

In assembling material for a book, unless one's scope is delimited in advance, the temptation to digress is difficult to curb. The scope here is confined to ideas that stand by themselves as products. Considered beyond the area of discourse are those ideas underlying conventional products and that are used in the marketing of those products. For example, motorcycle helmets are discussed within the context of highway safety, but safety as an attribute in the marketing of helmets is outside the book's domain.

On the other hand, sometimes the relationship between an idea and a product is quite remote and indirect. A case in point is that of a shoe producer sponsoring the idea of nature hikes or group walks through historic places. The adoption of the idea of walking, while ultimately increasing shoe consumption, is sufficiently independent of the direct promotion of footwear so as to be considered an idea on its own. By contrast, the idea of shoe comfort is a product attribute and is ordinarily included as part of the actual promotion of shoes. In this example, the idea of nature hikes is within the scope of this study, while the idea of shoe comfort is not.

Moreover, in this book ideas and social issues are differentiated from social change. While social change usually results from the dissemination of ideas and issues, it is excluded from this study, except briefly in Chapter 1, to provide a context for ideas. There exists a large and rich body of literature on the subject of social change (for example, Etzioni and Etzioni-Halevy 1973; Zaltman and Duncan 1977) that could not possibly have been enhanced by inclusion of the topic in this study. The scope of the book is schematized below:

Scope of the book:
    Ideas per se, that is, ideas unrelated to actual products
    Social issues and causes (concepts)
Outside the book's scope:
    Ideas directly underlying specific products
    Social change

At least four classes of readers have been kept in mind: (1) the college student, looking forward to career formation, who is concerned with the apparent dilemma of reconciling altruistic ideals with current negative myths about the business world; (2) the social cause advocate who is already marketing ideas and perspectives on social issues and who hopefully will take delight in seeing these activities described in a somewhat structured way; (3) marketers of goods and services who may recognize broader areas for applicability of the tools of their trade; and (4) those involved in pursuits in which marketing approaches may be usefully introduced for the first time. It is hoped that it will prove valuable, too, to students and workers in other fields such as politics, human services, and a broad spectrum of institutional endeavors.

Part I of this study introduces the notion of an idea sector. Its three chapters deal, respectively, with the nature of ideas, the rationale for a marketing approach, and sponsors or initiators of ideas. In Part II marketing strategy is discussed by following the time-honored four Ps model—product, price, promotion, and place (channels of distribution)—in Chapters 4, 5, 6, and 7, respectively. Part III presents a real-world application (Chapter 8), then considers consumers of concepts (Chapter 9), and finally market segmentation (Chapter 10). The promotion chapter introduces the communication model, treating the objective, the message, and the effect of a communication. The channel, source, and receiver of the message are the subjects of Chapters 7, 3, and 9, respectively. Throughout, topics are introduced as they apply to conventional commodities, and then transfer is made to the realm of concepts taken as products.

Each of Chapters 3, 9, and 10 contains an empirical study. Chapter 3 reports on a survey that was administered to institutions sponsoring ideas. Chapter 9 describes another survey whose purpose was to examine consumer behavior in the adoption of ideas. The reporting of these studies, for purposes of this volume, has been reduced to the simplest terms and should be entirely comprehensible to the lay reader. By contrast, Chapter 10, highlighting a proposed methodology for market segmentation research, contains a heavy complement of statistical details. It may be perused lightly by the reader not accustomed to research jargon, or may be omitted completely without loss of continuity.

Ben Enis (1973) pointed out that the marketing literature has been characterized by two classes of scholarship. One consists of "extremely provocative and interesting . . . works (that) have been relatively generalized and abstract." The other is "significant empirical work . . . insightful and rigorous . . . (but) specialized and narrow" (p. 60). This book attempts to bridge the theory/practice gap, first by postulating concepts such as a presence of an idea sector, then testing those concepts with data, and finally presenting a real-world application.

I wish to express my sincere appreciation to the many persons who were helpful in this book's preparation. I am particularly grateful for valuable insights provided by Russell Belk, William Novelli, Steve Permut, Jagdish Sheth, and Gerald Zaltman. Susan Barrett, Morris Holbrook, and Michael Rothschild read all or portions of the manuscript and offered sage suggestions, as did Charles Nanry who also contributed most of Chapter 6. It would be nice if it were otherwise, but alas, I alone must shoulder the blame for any errors. I acknowledge with thanks the indefatigable research assistance or Roberta Goodzeit, Joanne Lattanzio, and Sandeep Tungare. Typists should be mentioned first, but I accede to tradition and last but not least thank Maureen Greeley and Adele Hartig for their skill at translating hieroglyphics into keyboard miracles.

To my wife, Adell, I owe much of my inspiration, particularly in regard to humanistic and altruistic ideas. I here express my deepest appreciation for her constant encouragement and patience during the long periods of time during which the project abstracted me from our otherwise close 32 years together. Furthermore it was she who inspired our sons to teach their father that the Fine home should be a free marketplace for all sorts of ideas. My wife also set an example for us to become a socially conscious family; Paul followed his mother into social work, Michael is in social medicine, while I chose social marketing.

One must meet Philip Kotler as I did, only once, to appreciate his rare combination of warmth and scholarship. Yet it is frustrating to have a Kotler in one's discipline! It almost seems as though whenever one wishes to reduce some marketing thought to writing, research reveals that Kotler has already written it, and better. The present volume is a case in point; social marketing is so clearly his subject that in writing about it one feels intrusive and presumptuous. So it is only fitting that this book is respectfully dedicated to Philip Kotler.

CONTENTS

GLOSSARY

Because words might sometimes take on differing connotations, it is well to begin with a brief glossary of terms associated with ideas as employed in this book.

Advertising. Nonpersonal promotion of goods, services, or commercial ideas by an identified sponsor who pays for message delivery.

Attitude. A predisposition or general orientation toward something (it is wrong to develop nuclear energy).

Belief. The mental acceptance of something as true or real, more basic than an attitude (the development of nuclear energy will endanger the human race).

Diffusion. Dispersion or spread of knowledge across a population.

Gossip. Small talk with or without a known basis in fact.

Idea. Previous experience collected and organized into a new pattern.

Infusion. Inculcation, indoctrination, or instillation of information into one or more people.

Interest. A feeling of concern about something.

Law. Ideas established as enforceable public policy.

Lobbying. Pressure upon lawmakers by organized effort.

Opinion. One's view on an impending issue, for example, on which is the better of two alternatives (nuclear energy should not be developed).

Propaganda. Systematic dissemination of ideas to further a cause.

Public opinion. The aggregate of individual opinion.

Public relations or publicity. The promotion of rapport, goodwill, or image. Usually the carrier (medium) is not paid, nor is the sponsor identified.

Rumor. Information that is neither substantiated nor refuted, including gossip, grapevine, scuttlebutt.

INTRODUCTION

Every idea gained is a hundred years of slavery remitted.
—Richard Jefferies, *The Story of My Heart*

A marketing transaction is one in which some product offering is exchanged for a payment. But ideas are also offerings and are exchanged in marketlike transactions; the dissemination of ideas is a marketing process.

Picture a retail shop with all sorts of merchandise on display—cans of tuna fish on the shelves, floor samples of furniture, cameras neatly arranged in showcases, or attractive garments hanging on racks. Before arriving at the shop, these goods were designed, manufactured, packaged, wholesaled, delivered, and priced. At various times information about them was communicated to prospective buyers. In short, these products were produced and marketed. The marketing process culminates in physical transfer of the item from retailer to ultimate user.

In another kind of retail establishment the product offering consists of one or more services. These are provided, performed, or rendered by the marketer for the benefit of, or directly to, the customer.

In this book the reader is asked to consider yet a third category of transactions, different from the exchange of physical goods or rendered services. In these exchanges the offering is an idea or a social issue or a cause—a concept. Concepts are conceived, initiated, sponsored, advocated, promulgated, disseminated, and adopted by methods that resemble the marketing process. Products in this category are intangible and abstract. For that reason it is not always easy to imagine them as marketable or as ever being marketed.

This book's mission is to assist the reader in stretching his or her imagination to the point where abstract products are seen in essentially the same light as conventional products. One important aim is that advocates of societally beneficial ideas and issues will find new and increased efficacy in their efforts to educate their chosen publics—their target audiences. If adopting a marketing orientation in the dissemination of societally beneficial ideas will facilitate the spread of those ideas, then the purpose of this book will have been well served.

Idea dissemination has frequently been referred to as "social marketing." But social marketing also appears in literature addressing such topics as public policy, consumerism, and social responsibility; it is thus a catch-all phrase. Accordingly, a more precise name for the dissemination of ideas and social issues is "idea marketing" or "concept marketing," and all three of these expressions will no doubt be seen as the subject becomes more popular. All are employed throughout this book.

Why market ideas? Why a methodology for treating concepts as products? And why a free marketplace? One can think of at least two alternatives. One is that there be no social change at all, and no resolution of controversy—hardly a palatable solution. Another is that idea adoption be mandated by government edict. But the marketing process offers a more orderly and democratic alternative toward social change than that which comes about from some other possible methods, repression or violence for example. To be sure, ideas are transmitted in many ways, such as mores, laws, traditions, and so on. But in a choice between marketing and coercion it is certainly more consistent with the notion of a free society that an idea be offered to, rather than forced upon, people. For a customer enjoys the right of refusal to buy. "Free individual choice is a vital protection against tyranny" (Kelman 1965, p. 35), or as H. G. Wells is said to have quipped, "He who raises a fist has run out of ideas." Because he can be turned down, the marketer must be certain, a priori, that the product will truly benefit the customer, who, if dissatisfied, often has the privilege of going to a competitor the next time:

> When men have realized that time has upset many fighting faiths, they may come to believe even more than they believe the very foundations of their own conduct that the ultimate good desired is better reached by free trade in ideas—that the best test of truth is the power of the thought to get itself accepted in the competition of the market, and that truth is the only ground upon which their wishes safely can be carried out. That at any rate is the theory of our constitution. (Oliver Wendell Holmes [1919] in *Abrams* v. *U.S.*, 250 U.S. 616, 630)

When diverse factions employ marketing attempts to manipulate public opinion, then individuals may choose which points of view they wish to buy.

An inequity lies in the advantage enjoyed by the better endowed faction. Such differential advantage is characteristic of any marketplace, whether for goods or for concepts. Yet it is less unethical that a large corporation outadvertises a fledgling firm than that a well-funded candidate, for example, spends more on a campaign than his or her opponent having less resources. That question has not been overlooked by the Congress.

This book is timely. It is difficult to imagine a period in history when restrictions on the spread of ideas have been so relaxed, at least in the United States. Government, church, and family are as liberal as they have been at virtually any other time. Many ideas and issues considered blasphemous only a few decades ago are freely and openly exchanged in the marketplace. One witnesses a freer proliferation of concepts as minority groups, women, and children are becoming emancipated from their former inferior roles. Moreover, as literacy rates rise, the number and concern of participants in idea transmission increase. New communication technology facilitates the spread of ideas, good as well as bad, across vast regions on a scale unprecedented in history. So it is time for the trade in ideas, as perceived by Holmes, itself to be discussed more freely.

It will be argued in these pages that a marketplace does indeed exist for ideas and issues. To the various sectors within the economy—private, public, non-profit, services—one proposes the addition of an idea sector, an industry of ideas. The idea sector encompasses a large variety of "products" (see Table 1.1) and includes a long list of institutions engaged in the marketing of these products. These five sectors are not mutually exclusive, for the exchange of ideas, like services, can fall within the purview of any or all of private, nonprofit, and public organizations. That is, ideas are fostered by profit-making businesses and the nonprofits, as well as government.

The book's chapters are sequenced to suit the reader having little or no familiarity with marketing theory. Those with some grounding in the subject might first peruse Chapter 8 which illustrates with a real-world application the theoretic development of the earlier chapters.

PART I

1

THE NATURE OF IDEAS AND SOCIAL ISSUES

Man is not a circle with a single centre;
he is an ellipse with two foci.
Facts are one, ideas are the other.
                    —Victor Hugo, *Les Miserables*, vii

An idea is taken for granted in the scheme of things. Someone exclaims, "I've got an idea!" What is it that he has? From where did he get it? How was it transmitted? How might it spread to others? What will be the effect of the acceptance of the idea? These are some of the questions dealt with in this book. In this first chapter the nature of an idea is developed, contextualized, and shown to be a most timely topic. To pave the way for this book's argument that ideas are exchanged in marketlike transactions, the aim of this chapter is to present an idea as a dynamic and vital entity.

An early theory of ideas was postulated by Plato, who saw ideas in two modes or realms of being:

> One is the world of phenomena, in space and time, the world of "sights and sounds," as he called it, which is characterized by impermanence and change. However, lying behind the world of phenomena is the world of Ideas or Forms, and for Plato this is the true realm of reality. In contrast to the phenomenal world, the realm of ideas which is non-spatial and non-temporal, is characterized by being permanent, unchanging, and eternal. (Bryson 1948, p. 30)

Thus, long before modern advertising, Plato attached greater importance to ideas than to objects by recognizing that ideas underlie all tangibles: "Things and qualities in the time-space world are more or less close reflections of the abstract ideas at the heart of a total reality which is thus given more than spatial and temporal dimensions" (Bryson 1948, p. 30).

While Plato argued that ideas are real things in themselves, Aristotle took an opposing view. Although he agreed that ideas have potential for concreteness, Aristotle believed that they are ethereal and only become real when actualized into actions or tangible objects. The arguments in this book follow Plato. Aristotle's ideas, which underlie actual products, are, as stated in the Preface, beyond its scope.

ORIGINATION, MATURATION, AND ADOPTION OF IDEAS: A MICROPROCESS

An idea is something one thinks, knows, or imagines. It is more likely to be a vague impression—a passing fleeting phenomenon—than a clear conclusion. In fact, once some meaning becomes definite, it can no longer be considered an idea but is then an accepted belief. (On the other hand, the fact that ideas are less enduring than beliefs does not imply that either is more marketable than the other. Both can be considered as "items" within the context of this book.) This section borrows heavily from John Dewey's *How We Think* (1910, pp. 72-110), and all quotations are from that work. Dewey's essay "The Origin and Nature of Ideas" appears in Appendix A; his central thesis on ideas is summarized here in the following three key points:

1. An idea originates from the presence and awareness of a felt difficulty, discrepancy, or problem. The problem might appear suddenly or it might arise at some stage in an evolving process. Whichever the case, "The situation in which the perplexity occurs, calls up something not (otherwise) present to the senses." This "something" is only a suggestion, a suggested solution to the problem:

> The suggested conclusion so far as it is not accepted but only tentatively entertained constitutes an idea. Synonyms for this are supposition, conjecture, guess, hypothesis, and (in elaborate cases) theory.

2. The idea is subjected to reasoning, defined as

> The process of developing ... the *implications* of any idea with respect to any problem. ... As an idea is inferred from given facts, so reasoning sets out from an idea.

The state of the observed problem is usually in the form of confused facts. Therefore ideas initially inferred are very tentative, wild conjectures, remote suggestions; reasoning is required to shape ideas into beliefs and conclusions.

3. Finally, one acquires a belief and draws a conclusion by corroborating or verifying the conjectured idea.

The reasoning process is a two-way movement from partial, fragmentary, and often confused facts to an idea and then back again to facts (not merely the

FIGURE 1.1

The Idea Within the Context of the Problem-Solving Process

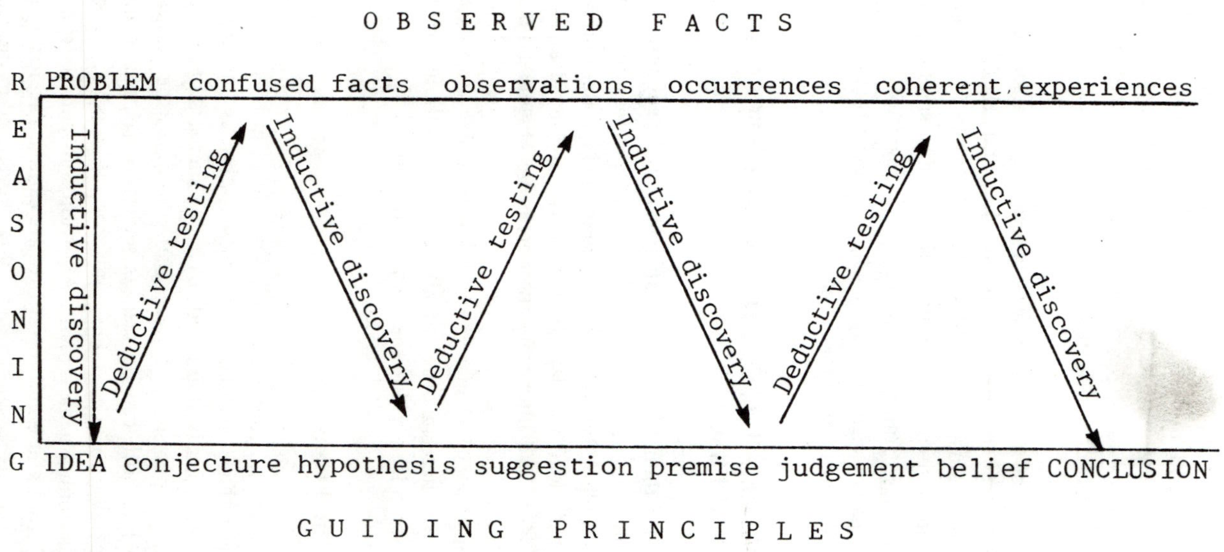

OBSERVED FACTS

R PROBLEM confused facts observations occurrences coherent experiences

Inductive discovery

Deductive testing

Inductive discovery

Deductive testing

Inductive discovery

Deductive testing

Inductive discovery

G IDEA conjecture hypothesis suggestion premise judgement belief CONCLUSION

GUIDING PRINCIPLES

Source: Constructed by the author.

original facts but also new particulars). The first leg of the trip is heuristic, intuitive, inductive. The second leg reinforces, orders, and synthesizes the original data by connecting them with one another as well as with additional facts to which the data have brought attention. The trip is never back and forth just once, but continuous. With each circuit, the original facts and the inferred ideas are strengthened into premises and, in turn, into final beliefs or conclusions (see Figure 1.1).

In Figure 1.1 the downward paths represent inductive discovery or inference of principles based on observed facts. The upward paths are deductive movements in search of verification of those principles with reference to the observations.

A simple illustration of the process is seen in the reasoning of a pipe smoker who is contemplating the idea to cut out the habit. He enjoys his pipe but is plagued by cinder damage to clothing, badgering from family members, and so forth—a problem. Inductively, he infers that to stop smoking would be a good thing to do. He tries it out and soon feels some degree of nervousness; he begins to overeat and gains weight. Unhappy with the new affliction, he concludes that it might be less damaging to smoke than not to smoke.

FROM PROBLEMS TO SOCIAL ISSUES TO SOCIAL CHANGE: A MACROPROCESS

Apart from their place in human reasoning, ideas reside in yet another context, the phenomenon of social change. In the reasoning process, an idea stems from a problem directly affecting an individual. But in the realm of social change, it is a societal problem that gives rise to the idea. At the individual (micro) level, ideas lead ultimately to conclusions (Figure 1.1). Societally, that is, aggregatively (macro), mass adoption of an idea frequently brings about social change. Although social change is outside this book's scope (see Preface), it is mentioned briefly here in order to introduce the notions of social issues and causes, which are indeed within the scope of the book.

Social Issues and Causes

Social issues and causes are ideas that are of interest to many individuals within a society. They are ideas to begin with, but assume issue status as they spread, or are sufficiently important, by some standard or other, to warrant the attention of many persons. A further distinction must be drawn between issues and causes. While both can be seen as societal ideas, issues are controversial; causes are generally not. One takes a position on an issue, but simply adopts a cause, such as joining a movement. Abortion and gun control are issues; the prevention of child abuse and forest fires are causes. Yet, for simplicity of exposition in this book, issues and causes will be considered in the same vein; no loss of clarity should result from the merger.

On the other hand, ideas are taken as quite distinct from issues and causes. An idea occurs to, is conceived by, or is espoused by an individual, while an issue emerges and is diffused within a group; it is a movement to be fostered, advocated, supported, or suppressed by a group. An idea is of personal interest; an issue or a cause is in the public interest. The impulse to adopt an idea, as with most tangibles and services, stems from self-serving motivation. But interest in a social issue is motivated by desire to help others as well. "With the exception of a few health-oriented social action campaigns (for example, "Stop Smoking"), most social changes advocated are to benefit other persons more than the receiver (of the message)" (Brembeck and Howell 1976, p. 340). The distinction is reminiscent of, and parallel to, C. Wright Mills's "private troubles vs. public issues." Thus the idea of using seat belts is quite individual until it becomes apparent that widespread adoption of that idea benefits society as a whole—for example, by easing the strain on hospital facilities as the number of serious injuries is decreased, by lessening insurance costs, and so on—at which point seat-belt use becomes an issue while at the same time remaining an idea. Again, physical fitness is an idea that quickly becomes a social cause in time of national emergency.

So, in terms of group process, ideas frequently become social issues as they "catch on." Ideas precede and probably induce social change. Social cause advocates such as public and not-for-profit institutions are aware of this "bubble-up" process in which the spread of ideas among a great many people often produces the issues that are subsequently espoused by change agents.

The adoption of innovative ideas is closely related to the formation of values, attitudes, beliefs, interests, opinions, and viewpoints on issues, all of which can, for simplification and present purposes, be broadly classed as beliefs. A belief is a mental acceptance of the validity of an idea. It is the totality of beliefs possessed by an individual—one's "belief system"—that determines the position one takes on an issue, which, in turn, often prompts participation in social action. Finally, implementation of social action brings about social change. At the macrolevel, then, the process from societal problems to social change includes ideas, issues, and causes.

Combining the micro- and the macroprocesses, what emerges is the following model:

> Problems
> Reasoning
> Ideas
> Beliefs
> Social Issues and Causes
> Social Action
> Social Change

The marketer of concepts is to social change what the pharmacist is to human health. C. M. Arensberg and A. H. Niehoff (1964) refer to new ideas as the "medicine of social change" (p. 6). As Figure 1.1 is a microview depicting the place occupied by ideas in an individual's reasoning process, the macroschema above presents ideas in a broader framework, as precursory to social issues and social change.

SOME CONCEPTS AND THEIR ATTRIBUTES

The nature of ideas and issues—concepts—is such that they share certain common characteristics, and these are taken up in this section. But first some popular concepts are listed in Table 1.1. The ideas, causes, and issues dealt with in the remainder of this book are drawn from that list. Some of its entries are not precisely ideas or issues but rather organizations, for example, the United Way, or tactics, such as VD hot line. These departures from strict consistency serve to make the list more consonant with custom and usage. The United Way is better known than the concept of volunteerism or nongovernment social service; VD is hardly an idea but the hot line is.

By no means is Table 1.1 to be considered a complete list of concepts; readers will no doubt find popular ideas and issues that were omitted. But it should, at a glance, serve to equip one's imagination with the breadth of "items" mentioned daily in the media, taken for granted in ordinary conversation, and yet to be considered as products in this book.

Under the rubric "characteristics of innovations," several writers have isolated and discussed attributes possessed by ideas. (They are attributes of ordinary products as well.) These are the dimensions along which one can measure ideas, the yardsticks to be employed in comparing one idea with another. As such, they are analogous to physical characteristics—width, strength, taste, color, durability—by which ordinary products are evaluated. They are defined in this section, and in Chapter 4 they are used "to position" ideas, that is, to compare them with other ideas with which they are in competition.

The following definitions are taken from Everett Rogers and F. F. Shoemaker (1971):

> *Relative advantage* is the degree to which an innovation is perceived as better than the idea it supersedes. The degree of relative advantage may be measured in economic terms, but often social prestige factors, convenience, and satisfaction are also important components. It matters little whether the innovation has a great deal of "objective" advantage. What does matter is whether the individual perceives the innovation as being advantageous. The greater the perceived relative advantage of an innovation, the more rapid its rate of adoption.
>
> *Compatibility* is the degree to which an innovation is perceived as being consistent with the existing values, past experiences, and needs of the receivers. An idea that is not compatible with the prevalent values and norms of the social system will not be adopted as rapidly

TABLE 1.1

Some Current Ideas and Social Issues

55-mph speed limit	Gay rights
200-mile fishing limits	Gun control
911 emergency number	Handicapped, employ the
Abortion rights	HMO
Affirmative Action	Health, value of
Alcoholism control	Legalized gambling
Banking innovation	Literacy
Birth defects	Litter prevention
Blood donation	Mainstreaming
Blue laws	Manpower programs
Buy American goods	March of Dimes
Cancer research	Marriage
Care packages	Mass transportation
Consumer cooperatives	Mental health
Car pooling	Metric system
Child abuse	Military recruiting
Child adoption	Minimum wage
Capital punishment	Motorcycle helmet, use of
Crime prevention	Museums
Credit purchasing	Nature conservation
Divorce	Nuclear energy
Draft registration	Nudism
Drilling, offshore	Nutrition
Drinking age	NYC
Drug abuse control	Obesity prevention
Drunk driving	One dollar coin
Education, continuing	Outdoor living
Energy conservation	Peace
Equal Rights Amendment	Peace Corps
Euthanasia	Pet care
Exporting	Physical fitness
Fair housing	Police, support of
Family planning	Politics
Fashion trend	Poetry
Fire prevention	Pollution control
Fluoridation	Population control
Foreign aid	Prayer in schools
Forest fire prevention	Prison reform
Foster parenthood	Product safety
Franchising Fraternal organizations	Productivity in industry
Free enterprise	PTA
Freedom of the press	Recycling wastes
Fund raising	Redlining

(continued)

13

TABLE 1.1 (continued)

Reforestation	Tax reform
Religion	Tax shelters
Safety	Tourism
Save Chrysler	Two-dollar bill
Save the Whales	UNICEF
Scouting	Union label, buy
Seat belt use	United Way
Shoplifting control	Urban planning
Smokending	VD hot line
Social security	Vegetarianism
Social welfare	Veterans' rights
Solar energy	Vivisection
Space program	Voter registration
Subsidies, government	Wife abuse prevention
Suicide hot line	Women's rights

Source: Constructed by the author.

as an innovation that is compatible. . . . An example of an incompatible innovation is the use of the IUD (intrauterine contraceptive device) in countries where religious beliefs discourage use of birth control techniques.

Complexity is the degree to which an innovation is perceived as difficult to understand and use. Some innovations are readily understood by most members of a social system; others are not and will be adopted more slowly. For example, the rhythm method of family planning is relatively complex for most peasant housewives to comprehend because it requires understanding human reproduction and the monthly cycle of ovulation. For this reason, attempts to introduce the rhythm method in village India have been much less successful than campaigns to diffuse the loop, a type of IUD, which is a much less complex idea in the eyes of the receiver. In general those new ideas requiring little additional learning investment on the part of the receiver will be adopted more rapidly than innovations requiring the adopter to develop new skills and understandings.

Trialability is the degree to which an innovation may be experimented with on a limited basis. New ideas which can be tried on the installment plan will generally be adopted more quickly than innovations which are not divisible. . . . Essentially, an innovation that is trialable represents less risk to the individual who is considering it.

14

Observability is the degree to which the results of an innovation are visible to others. The easier it is for an individual to see the results of an innovation, the more likely he is to adopt. For example, a technical assistance agency in Bolivia introduced a new corn variety in one town. Within two years the local demand for the seed far exceeded the supply. The farmers were mostly illiterate, but they could easily observe the spectacular results achieved with the new corn and were thus persuaded to adopt. In the United States a rat poison that killed rats in their holes diffused very slowly among farmers because its results were not visible (pp. 22, 23).

INCREASE IN CONCERN WITH IDEAS

From Inner- to Other-Directedness

As a society enters the postindustrial stage of development, personalities change from what David Riesman called inner-directed to other-directed (1950). Emphasis shifts from material to intrinsic concerns, from tangible possessions to ideas. This section attempts to substantiate the argument that such a phenomenon is indeed occurring in the United States, for if it is, then the study of concepts takes on added significance.

A trend appeared early in the 1970s as a rise in ideological concern became apparent in purchase decisions regarding actual tangibles. Highlighting the admixture of materialistic and psychological satisfaction or utility inherent in most goods, Etienne Cracco and Jacques Rostenne argued that "The ratio of physical utilities over purely psychic types is diminishing rather rapidly" (1971, p. 32). They described a socioecological product whose development strategy "would take into account that quality of life is a substitute for quantity of material welfare" (p. 33). Promotion appeals for many products began to emphasize ecological attributes.

E. B. Weiss (1972) observed that a shift in emphasis seemed apparent from taste to nutrition of foods, from texture to flammability of fabrics, from power to safety in automobiles, and from suds to pollution factors in cleansers. He reported a back-to-nature trend as having "created an enormous boom for flowers and plants, and reshaping marketing programs for cosmetics" with Revlon featuring milk treatments, Rubenstein promoting Herbessence cosmetics, and Clairol introducing a Herbal Essence shampoo. Noting that "The young generation obviously is less interested in possessions per se," he further pointed to increased sales of disposable products.

It soon appeared that people were increasingly "buying" nonmaterial products and societal welfare, such as the ideas of physical fitness and pollution control. An obvious signal was the trend apparent in the socialization of health-care services as practices moved from individual, to group, to Health Maintenance Organization, and so forth: "An affluent society tends to become less concerned with tangible goods and material possessions. It tends to become more interested in such thrusts as ecology and cultural inventories" (Lazer and Kelley 1973, p. 489).

In the Foreword to *The New State of the Economy* (Allvine and Tarpley 1977), Philip Kotler wrote:

> Americans will have to pay more attention to resource conservation, social costs, and quality-of-life considerations than they have in the past. Formerly, we were all happy riding our merry Oldsmobile, mowing our suburban laws, complaining about "ring-around-the-collar," eating our meat-and-sweet rich diets, and ignoring the poor and the disaffiliated at home and abroad. Now we recognize that no suburb is an island, that everyone's fate is connected, and that a distant military or political development has the potential for painfully disrupting our sheltered lives. (p. xiii)

In the book the authors succinctly speak of reformulation of the American Dream such that our society will have "to expect less in order to have more" (p. 153).

One might have expected that, as the decade drew to a close, plagued with soaring inflation, people would preoccupy themselves with the acquisition of material things, as indeed was the case in many quarters. Yet outside the retail tangibles shops, interest continued in the ideational. For example, the futurist Alvin Toffler sees "large numbers of workers (are) involved in moving intangible symbols and information rather than physical goods" (1980, p. 25). Toffler predicts a shift of many jobs from the plant or office to the home where people can work on, and with, intangibles. The airwaves and print media abound with examples of the promotion of ideas, providing a seedbed of altruism upon which social marketing is nourished. For example, a radio spot quotes scripture, admonishing that whales were intended to be fruitful and multiply ("Save the Whales" 1979):

> The materialistic American dream, while dominant, is not universal. Young adults show a concern for the quality of life as well as material success. They would like to see a restructuring of social values so as to stress simplicity, independence of technology, and conservation in a larger sense (Millstein, in Lovelock and Weinberg 1978, p. 287).

Voluntary Simplicity

Closely related to a shift away from materialism is a trend in which individuals depart from complicated lifestyles toward what has been termed "voluntary simplicity" (Leonard-Barton and Rogers 1980). Voluntary simplicity is characterized by enthusiastic participation in backyard vegetable growing, consumer cooperatives, hiking, bicycling, car pooling, nature conservation, family planning, outdoor living, and utilization of solar energy. Such devotees are likely to be strong supporters of such social issues as prison reform, product safety, reforestation, pollution control, gun control, and equal rights. As this trend continues, more people will purchase secondhand clothing and knocked-down furniture and will attempt to repair rather than replace defective objects.

SUMMARY

In this chapter ideas and social issues were defined, contrasted, and then for expository purposes coalesced into single terms, concept or innovation. To prepare for their treatment as products, innovations were presented as having certain attributes, a notion to be revisited in Chapter 4. The possibility was explored that Western society might be experiencing a shift in emphasis away from material objects toward the the direction of things more intangible, altruistic, and ideational.

It is more than half a century since Chief Justice Holmes alluded to a marketplace for a free trade in ideas. Yet as of this writing no structure seems to have been established in which that trade is to occur. It is hoped that the marketing treatment of concepts as suggested in these pages will be a start in that direction—the postulation of an idea industry, an idea sector. To that end, Chapter 2 introduces the role and function of marketing in the dissemination of innovations.

2

A MARKETING APPROACH
TO IDEAS AS PRODUCTS:
SOCIAL MARKETING

Marketing theory is too good to be wasted only on ordinary products.
—paraphrased

It was pointed out in Chapter 1 that ideas arise out of problem situations. This chapter attempts to show that many exchanges of concepts are marketing processes and are therefore, by definition, methods for the resolution of problems. This is the marketing approach to ideas. The chapter begins with a few "first principles" about marketing as a form of human exchange. Next ideas and social issues are introduced as particular types of products, and the concept of social marketing is discussed. A typology is developed classifying all "items" that are exchanged, and finally a partial list is given of several transactional processes by which social products are marketed.

MARKETING

Marketing is a process of planning and movement of a product offering from the supplier of that offering (the marketer) to those who are to use it. Marketing is often equated with selling, advertising, packaging, display, promotion, public relations, propaganda, and so on. It is erroneous to say that marketing is any one of these, because marketing is all of them. The marketing process is incomplete unless all of its functions are performed, functions that fall under four general headings—product, price, promotion, and place—the time-honored

The portion of this chapter describing a product typology was presented at the annual conference of the American Academy of Advertising, April 21, 1979.

four Ps model (McCarthy 1975). In turn, each of these four Ps subsumes specific functions, some of which are listed below:

Product
    Design
    Information
    Branding
    Packaging
    Classification and standardization
    Warrantee
    Postsale service, repairs

Price
    Financing
    Credit terms
    Concessions and discounts
    Nonmonetary sacrifices

Promotion
    Advertising
    Personal selling
    Promotional special events
    Public relations, image creation

Place
    Channels of distribution
    Storage
    Quantity breaking
    Delivery
    Inventory management
    Point-of-sale display

Thus, to reiterate: in order for marketing to be thoroughly accomplished, all of the above functions must be performed explicitly or implicitly, either by the marketer or by other parties to the transaction. If any are omitted or even poorly executed, an incomplete and usually ineffective process results.

Marketing functions within the four Ps model are generally considered to be within the marketer's control. The marketer can, and does, manipulate the amount and direction of resource allocation for determining how to design the product, what price to charge, where to promote, and how and when to make delivery. Other factors, however, are beyond the marketer's control, for example, economic conditions, government regulation, labor union activity, and consumer demand. (Whether or not consumer tastes are also controlled or at least shaped through advertising is a debate to be postponed for the present. Indeed, the position is taken here, in what follows, that consumers' wants and needs reign supreme.)

The Marketing Concept

The marketing concept is the philosophy that the consumer's interest is the starting point, if not the major focus, from which all planning takes place. This is also called consumer orientation. (The central thesis of this book, the concept that concepts are marketed using the marketing concept, is a tongue twister and every effort has been taken to assign unambiguous usage of such words as idea, concept, notion, and so on, so that their intended meaning will be clear from the context in which they are employed.) A consumer-oriented marketer plans strategy by first inquiring into the needs and desires of the clientele. Then and only then are the four Ps considered. By contrast, producer orientation dictates a policy that says, in effect, "I wish to market product X, now let me find people who wish to buy it." All too often a market for X simply does not exist.

Idea marketing, too, can be either consumer or producer oriented. Marketers, having ascertained consumers' felt needs and wants, disseminate ideas in such a manner that those ideas become available for adoption by interested individuals. This is called "pull" marketing because it is based on the premise that informed consumers seek out or pull at the product offering on their own initiative. Producer-oriented idea marketers engage in the opposite or "push" marketing, which is alternatively termed "high-pressure" or simply "persuasion."

The Marketing Approach as Problem Solving

One of the characteristics by which one discipline can be distinguished from another is the particular philosophy or method customarily employed by each discipline in solving problems. While most fields of endeavor employ a number of problem-solving techniques, some methods are typically associated with certain disciplines. Pure scientists usually experiment. Philosophers prefer inductive reasoning, while physicists and mathematicians lean toward deductive methods. Medical practitioners use diagnosis, and attorneys rely on an experiential approach or what is called case law. Economists look to utility theory, emphasizing the most efficient allocation of scarce resources that will maximize human welfare. Utility theory includes the ideas of preference and taste as determinants of welfare, and these ideas are borrowed from economists by marketers in framing their own special way to solve problems. Marketers' unique approach to solving problems is to attempt to match products with peoples' wants and/or needs. A product is developed to satisfy a need identified by the marketer (usually through marketing research upon a target population).

A major difference between the economist's approach and that of the marketer stems from the former's assumption of rationality in man—the economic man concept—under which individuals are said to be able to evaluate and choose what is required in order for them to achieve optimal satisfaction. Economists assume that individuals seek an "optimal bundle" of products, optimal in the sense of utility maximization, and that preferences are based on reason. This notion would support John Dewey's observation (1910) noted in Chapter 1 that ideas reside in a reasoning process. Economic man, faced with a dilemma, deliberately and rationally sets out to ponder, develop, and nurture one or more ideas as part of the problem-solving process.

Marketers, however, view people differently. In fact, they assume limited rationality in individuals. They are aware that consumer choice decisions are complicated phenomena—the complex man theory—and are based upon emotion, at least as much as on reason. To assume rationality acknowledges the presence of needs but not wants. During the time since Dewey wrote, theories by Freud, Lewin, Skinner, and others have argued that decision making, including idea adoption, rests more importantly upon emotional phenomena—perceptions, values, attitudes, group influence, and personality—than on reason. (These factors are addressed in Chapter 9.)

Rationality moves a person to choose a flat table rather than a rough stone upon which to place a sheet of writing paper. But the particular style of table selected is largely a matter of emotion. Marketers believe that people are influenced not just by reason but by a great many other factors as well, leading ultimately to the satisfaction of needs and wants, and that the satisfaction of utility is not ordinarily maximized but merely "satisficed" (Newell and Simon 1972), that is, satisfied with something "good enough," rather than optimally. Thus, while economists assume the existence of bundles of goods and theorize about utility that consumers derive from these goods, marketers investigate the properties inherent in product offerings that are capable of providing utility and then set out to provide those products most likely to satisfy. The assumption of rationality is relaxed.

The marketing approach implies specification of a product to be engineered in a manner so as to resolve some problem facing target consumers. For example, the product of the ASPCA is humane and responsible pet ownership. One way to market that product is to appeal to people's loneliness, their need for affection, and the mutual caring and companionship between master and pet. The marketing approach also involves consideration of several key questions. These are listed below with references to corresponding chapters of this book:

1. What is the product? (Chapter 2)
2. What are some other products of the same general type? Familiarity with these will facilitate understanding of the "cash crop." (Chapter 2)
3. In what type of transaction is the product exchanged? (Chapter 2)

4. What must be decided about strategies for design, pricing, communication, and distribution? (Chapters 4, 5, 6, and 7)
5. How marketing oriented is the sponsoring institution? (Chapter 3)
6. Who are the customers? Why do they purchase? (Chapter 9)
7. How do they differ one from the other? (Chapter 10)

IDEAS AS PRODUCTS: SOCIAL MARKETING

If marketers solve problems by offering tangible goods and services, then by extension human difficulties are susceptible to resolution by the introduction of innovative ideas if these can be delivered employing the marketing approach. It is an affirmative response to the question posed by Wiebe (1952): "Why can't you sell brotherhood and rational thinking like you sell soap?" There does not seem to be much difference between Dewey's observation that ideas stem from problems and the marketing view that products originate out of consumers' needs and desires. Ideas are to problems what products are to needs and desires. Each is capable of resolving or satisfying some situation; ideas solve problems, while products satisfy needs and desires.

To be sure, not all ideas will solve problems. Just as some products can be faulty and then exacerbate rather than satisfy needs, the same may be said regarding "bad" ideas. Similarly, the implementation of a social issue, which is controversial by definition, may be pleasing to some while creating difficulty for others (Belk 1980).

Deriving Benefits from Product Offerings

The notion that concepts may be viewed as products in the marketing sense is also rooted in two theories more recent than Dewey's. One is the "bundle of attributes" hypothesis of the economist K. J. Lancaster (1966), who argued that it is not the actual products that render utility to individuals but rather that satisfaction is derived from attributes inherent in those products. Later, an important paper by R. I. Haley (1968) introduced the notion that benefits perceived by consumers from the goods they purchase could constitute important criteria for segmenting markets.

When people purchase goods and services, their acquisitions bring certain benefits or satisfactions enjoyed through ownership of these goods or use of these services. But utility is also obtained from the adoption of ideas and social issues. If it can be shown that products and concepts share similar attributes, then one could surmise that the adoption of innovative ideas could, under certain circumstances, provide substitute utility, that is, could yield benefits otherwise derived from the acquisition of goods and services. Benefits ordinarily derived from material things could be obtained from abstract things such as ideas. To determine whether this premise makes any sense, one could examine the characteristics ordinarily inherent in tangible products and services and compare them with those possessed by innovations. If these two sets of characteristics can be shown to be either similar or reasonable substitutes one for the other, then the premise is supported.

For example, one may ask: "Can you compare the pleasure derived from wearing a new jacket with the feeling of satisfaction obtained from the completion of a course in some subject at a university? The jacket gives the wearer instant gratification, but benefits derived from the course may not come until much later—perhaps upon graduation or when the material learned in the course proves useful in a job setting. Thus one sees a time factor in considering the nature of utility.

In addition to time utility, economists by similar logic describe place utility, form utility, and possession utility. One could attempt to test the similarities and the differences of benefits derived as measured by these different kinds of economic utility. Finally, one may speak of a "quality utility." While a single jacket might not satisfactorily substitute for a college course, a warehouse full of jackets whose sales could render the owner financially secure might indeed be a more satisfactory product.

As another example, does religion as a form of exchange offer satisfaction to compensate for deprivation endured by the poor? Some form of assurance that the shaping of one's destiny is outside his or her control might be considered a substitute for material wealth: "I do not have enough food to feed my children so I take some solace in the assurance that an almighty power will look after my family." Indeed, religious institutions increasingly are looking to marketing to stem the tide of diminishing attendance (Austin 1980).

What, in the first place, are the sources of utility? What is it that satisfies people? Is it the case that ideas and social issues possess capabilities for imparting utility to individuals, utility that those individuals otherwise obtain through the acquisition of tangible products and services? If so, possibly one could replace an automobile agency with a social service agency or a real-estate broker's office with a government agency espousing physical fitness. This leads one to ponder the question that the adoption of ideas designed to assist the individual in making better use of his or her own resources could at least partially replace the need to amass material resources provided by others. Are ideas substitutes for things?

These rhetorical and problematic questions must remain open. However, it seems clear that people in postindustrial societies are confronted with an increasing volume of concepts whose adoption or nonadoption they must decide. That reality sparked the suggestion among some marketing scholars of the 1960s to broaden the scope of marketing to include ideational products.

The Scope Broadening Debate

The scope broadening debate, over how broad the scope of marketing should be, is well documented and will not be elaborated upon here. One might add that marketing is not the only discipline whose scope is broadening and whose boundaries are grey areas. Social workers perform psychotherapy and attorneys may legally serve as real-estate brokers. The American Institute of Architects has modified its rules to permit its members not only to design but also to build. A spokesperson from the profession commented: "The notion of the architect becoming actively involved in construction as well as design is not new, it began with Michelangelo and Bramante in Rome" (*New York Times* 1978, p. 16).

Strangely, while academicians argue whether the dissemination of social cause is or is not marketing, the U.S. government annually pays over $100 million to media and agencies to promote such issues as energy conservation, and third world nations employ Madison Avenue firms to spread nutrition and population control information, with eminent success. Like Nero, academicians fiddle with the "broadening" debate while the world burns with its many forms of suffering amenable to amelioration through social promotion.

Social Marketing: Two Meanings

The term social marketing seems to have earned for itself two different definitions (Luck 1974). Writers have applied the expression in one sense to mean the social responsibilities of marketers primarily in response to the pressures of consumer advocacy and government regulation. Within this meaning the emphasis is on economic benefits to business and social benefits to society that result from the adoption of socially responsible business policies by corporate enterprise. For example, a great number of firms have recently embarked on projects to help rebuild inner cities. Others search for programs of societal concern to which they may give monetary and other forms of support. One of many works emphasizing this meaning of social marketing is a book by William Lazer and Eugene Kelley (1973). Another, focusing on environmental conservation factors, is that of Donald Perry (1976). However, most writers agree with Andrew Takas (1974), who applies the expression societal marketing to the foregoing usage.

The second meaning ascribed to social marketing is the applicability of marketing thought to the introduction and dissemination of ideas and issues. That connotation was propounded by Wiebe in 1952 and later given impetus by Kotler, Levy, Zaltman, and others. (Fox and Kotler [1980] present a ten-year synopsis of social marketing.) The present work obviously falls within this second meaning of social marketing, for which a frequently cited definition is "the design, implementation, and control of programs calculated to influence the acceptability of social ideas and involving considerations of product planning, pricing, communication, distribution, and marketing research" (Kotler and Zaltman 1971, p. 5).

A BROADENED TYPOLOGY OF PRODUCTS

The broadened scope of marketing implies that product offerings could be anything considered to be of value by the parties to the transaction. What are the actual items that are marketed? What "things" do individuals exchange? Quite apart from the common characteristic shared by all commodities, that is, that they must have perceived value to the participants, how do different offerings compare with each other? If virtually anything and everything is subject to negotiated exchange, it is useful to categorize formally the enlarged domain of products in some orderly arrangement. That is the undertaking of this section.

A typological model is developed and proposed as an integrative framework for the analysis of all types of offerings. (The author begs license for using the term typology rather loosely. Strictly defined, a typology must provide exhaustive and mutually exclusive categories. The model proposed in this chapter somewhat violates that definition and hence might more accurately be called a quasi-typology.) It will thus serve too as a basis for analysis for those particular commodities highlighted in this book. It will pinpoint the position that concepts have within the entire gamut of products (Fine 1979b).

Even with conventional goods, a model that classifies product types is useful in framing, analyzing, and comparing marketing strategy, in suggesting new venture directions, and as a benchmark for assessing one's own product mix against that of the competition. However, for such a model to be useful, it must be sufficiently broad to encompass the entire set of choices—the "evoked set"— facing consumers. That set of alternatives contains not only goods and services but concepts as well. The typology advanced in this chapter permits marketers to position products against competing offerings, including those constituting exchange types different from their own. Kotler (1972) was an early proponent of the notion of classifying nontraditional products:

> A typology of marketing activity can also be constructed on the basis of the product marketed. Under the broadened concept of marketing, the product is no longer restricted to commercial goods and services. . . . A product classification of marketing consists of goods marketing, service marketing, organization marketing, person marketing, place marketing and idea marketing. (p. 51)

What is probably the first product categorization model partitions products as either convenience, shopping, or specialty goods (Copeland 1923). Other schemes are based on product characteristics (Aspinwall 1962; Miracle 1965; Shostack 1977), production and cost factors (Beckman, Davidson, and Talarzyk

1973), psychophysical aspects (Ramond and Assael 1974), and the Standard Industrial Classification (SIC) established by the government. None of these, however, considers social products, that is, ideas and issues. One wonders whether product typologies that omit social innovations as exchange types are still useful. Kotler's three stages of marketing consciousness model (1972) did account for social products and provided a three-category classification device, as did Ben Enis's model (1973), which classified on organizational goals and audience types. Shelby Hunt (1976) also took social marketing into consideration. However, he apparently did not intend his model to apply to products, per se, rather specifying it as useful in classifying "approaches to the study of marketing and all the problems, issues, theories, models, and research" (p. 22). By contrast, the model presented here deals with the actual product offerings designed to be marketed.

The Typology

The model is based on the assumption that all goods, services, and concepts may be classified on two dimensions: the profit-making nature of the transaction, and the degree of tangibility of the item.

Profit Making vs. Nonprofit Marketing

An obvious point of departure is provided by a dichotomy of all exchange processes as being either for profit or not for profit. This concept enjoys wide usage and denotes whether or not the seller in the marketing process intends to gain a profit over costs in the transaction. (The legal requirement is, of course, that an institution be incorporated as a nonprofit organization and/or obtain federal tax exemption status from the Internal Revenue Service.) The notion ignores consideration of profits accruing to the purchaser. Thus, a transaction in which the idea of private religion is adopted is profitable to the marketer, for example, Reverend Ike. But here, as in all market transactions, profit in the form of psychological utility to the purchaser is usually omitted from the definition, except perhaps by implication. If the case were otherwise, that is, if nonpecuniary profits entered into account, then there would be no such concept as a nonprofit transaction; all exchanges would be considered profit making. For an exchange takes place if, and only if, all parties benefit, or profit, as a result of the exchange. A blood donor profits financially if paid in cash for his or her blood; if a volunteer, the compensation takes the form of personal satisfaction, which is surely beneficial or profitable to the donor (Titmuss 1972).

In the present chapter accepted usage will be followed, and a transaction will be considered profit making only if it is characterized by the seller's intent to obtain monetary profit. That actual profit might not materialize is incidental. The situation calls to mind a notice hanging on an office wall, stating: "This is a nonprofit organization; it was not intended to be, but became so due to conditions beyond our control." Although clever, the remark is nevertheless definitionally inconsistent, for a nonprofit organization is one that does not intend to earn a profit on its transactions (it might profit, for example, from investments). On the other hand, an organization is considered profit making if such intent is evident, whether or not profit accrues or loss (negative profit) is suffered. This affords an entirely workable distinction to determine if a transaction is profit making. (But the profit/nonprofit dichotomy in exchange transactions can have different meanings in different situations, as Jagdish Sheth has pointed out: "For example, in many countries, the state owns and manages large corporations which are run like profit businesses although their mission is nonprofit. The obvious examples are foreign airlines and shipping companies" [1980].)

A Tangible-Abstract Product Dimension

The second dimension to be used in the model measures transactions along a tangible-abstract continuum. If a tangible good is involved, the exchange is concrete; if the product is an idea or a cause, the transaction is abstract. Both bicycles and birth-control information are products to be marketed; the former is a tangible good, while the latter is an abstract idea. This reasoning is not altered by the fact that birth-control information is usually associated with actual products, such as condoms, foams, and so on. Even among concrete products, some are more abstract than others. A home fire alarm system is a tangible product, but it is inextricably tied to the abstract idea of safety.

For the sake of the typology, the continuous tangible-abstract spectrum is categorized into four classes, standard practice in research methodology; one converts intervally scaled variables into ordinal or nominal classes to meet particular analytic needs. Here, the need is simply to create a manageably small number of categories.

The Matrix

Combination of the two-category profit dimension with the categorized tangible-abstract dimension yields the matrix shown in Table 2.1, in which several dozen illustrative exchanges are listed. The list is by no means exhaustive; nor are its entries proposed as the best examples. The reader will no doubt call to mind more creative choices; the selections are merely representative, and not all will be discussed in the text.

The top row lists exchanges for which no profit to the seller was intended to accrue; the bottom row lists exchanges in which profit was the principal motivation. The first column takes in tangible commodities, the second column considers services rendered, the third column covers ideas, and the fourth column lists causes or social issues.

Examples of ideas appropriate to cell 1, nonprofit tangibles, include purchases made at a consumer cooperative or in stores operated by charities such as the Salvation Army. Voluntary blood contributions are nonprofit tangibles too; however, if the donor is paid, the exchange is profit making and belongs in

TABLE 2.1

A Typology of Products

	Tangible Product	Service	Idea	Issue or Cause
	(1)	(2)	(3)	(4)
N	Consumer cooperatives	Library	Physical fitness	Child abuse
O	Girl Scout cookies	Post office	Seat-belt use	Malnutrition
N	Salvation Army store	Chamber of commerce	Value of education	Speeding
P	Blood donations	Public museum, zoo	Value of health	Smoking
R	Military base store	Red Cross	Military recruiting	Littering
O	Water	Public health care	Scouting	Pollution
F	Goods made by disabled	Higher education	Politics	Civil rights
I	Pets from ASPCA	Boys Town	Easter seals	Product safety
T	CARE packages	Underwriters Labs.	American Cancer Society	Metric system
		TVA	Marriage	Religion
		State park	Family planning	Voter registration
		Toll road	Two-dollar bill	Energy conservation
		Better Business Bureau	Peace Corps	Fair housing
		Public mass transit	Fund raising	Population control
		Consumer's Union		Forest fires
		YMCA-YWCA		
		Public broadcasting		

	(5)	(6)	(7)	(8)
P	All merchandise	Country club	Fashion designs	Fashion trends
R	Blood bank (paid)	Travel	Credit purchasing	Fluoridation
O	Investments in real estate,	Insurance	Legalized gambling	Smokenders[b]
F	securities, and com-	Performing arts	Franchising	Recycling wastes
I	modities	Private health care	Private brands	Free enterprise
T		Rental space	Patents	Tourism
		Health spa		Private religion ("Rev. Ike")
M		Fashion designing		Buy union label
A		Smokenders[a]		
K		Utilities		
I		Advertising agency		
N		Home improvements		
G		Spectator sports		

[a]Service—help clients stop smoking.
[b]Cause—alleviating smoke pollution.
Source: Constructed by the author.

29

cell 5. Public goods such as those disposed of by the General Services Administration could also have been listed in cell 1.

Cell 2 depicts nonprofit services rendered by such institutions as libraries, post offices, YMCAs, chambers of commerce, museums, the Red Cross, and so on. Offerings of nonprofit health-care organizations also fall into this category, as do those of universities and Boys Town.

Innovative ideas affecting personal lifestyles of individuals belong in cell 3, provided they originate without the profit motive. These include physical fitness, use of seat belts, boy and girl scouting, military recruiting, and the value of education. The furtherance of a political campaign (party or candidate) is an idea to be adopted and hence belongs in this cell. Fund raisers market the idea that a cash contribution should be made, the amount of cash being the price for adoption of the idea.

Cell 4, nonprofit social causes, includes campaigns designed to ameliorate child abuse, speeding, malnutrition, smoking, littering, forest fires, pollution; the list is long indeed. One may add the exchange of information on civil rights, product safety, the metric system, religion, voter registration, energy conservation, and so on.

Cell 5 designates profit-making exchanges of tangible products—food, clothing, automobiles, and so on—probably the largest proportion of commercial transactions. A share of stock representing part ownership in a corporation is included here, as are real estate and commodity investments.

Cell 6 lists profit-making services such as those offered by travel agencies, insurance companies, purveyors of the performing arts, and any items from cell 2 that bear the intent of profit: private nursing homes, day-care centers, and so forth. The service of providing space for which rent is paid is also listed there.

In cell 7 one example of an idea marketed by a profit-making organization may be seen in a new fashion design, say, by Christian Dior. While this firm markets a design service to the apparel industry (cell 6), at the same time it initiates styles sought by devotees of fashionable dress. These are matters that surely affect the lifestyles of these people, and being profit inspired, they have a place in cell 7. When adoption becomes widespread, producers of fashion apparel quickly capitalize on the popularization of such style trends (cell 8) for *their* own profit. Similar cycles are followed by patents and other creative commodities.

The idea sold by Smokenders, a profit-making firm, could belong in cell 6; however it deserves a place in cell 8 as well, when one considers the current feeling that smoking is harmful not only to the smoker but to those nearby and hence to society. Another cell 8 product is found among the various schemes for recycling waste materials. Such causes as free enterprise and tourism in America are profit motivated and also are classed as cell 8 exchanges. To find additional cell 8 illustrations one may peruse columns 1 and 2 for suggestions of institutions that, while marketing goods and services, might also promote societal welfare in the process. As an example, a chemical firm selling fluorides to the municipal water company market can be construed as a profit-making organization espousing the social cause of fluoridation. The same may be said for a marketer of pollution-control systems to industry.

Grey Areas in the Model

The assignment of most exchange types to the various cells is relatively straightforward, but some designations require stretching the imagination or indeed arbitrary placement. Thus mass transit is a service rendered, yet it is an idea in the private interest that sometimes erupts as a controversial issue. When an Indian family adopted Indira Gandhi's vasectomy program, did such submission constitute purchase of the tangible economic incentives offered by the government? Was it the adoption of the idea of fewer children? Or were people motivated by societal benefits of population control, a public issue? A donation of one's blood without monetary remuneration, say, to the Red Cross, presents an interesting type of exchange. Here the consumer adopts a cell 3 idea marketed by an agency: that it is a good thing to donate blood. In this case the blood itself is not the product; it is the price paid for the idea. If unpaid, a blood donation is a barter of blood in exchange for the idea. On the other hand, if the donor is paid in cash, the exchange falls into cell 5, the sale of a tangible product, blood.

A straightforward categorization is always difficult when one tries to classify human phenomena; apologias are always in order. Hunt (1976), for example, stated that his scheme does not "imply that reasonable people cannot disagree as to which cell (in his model) is most appropriate for each issue or particular piece of research" (p. 23). One may add that disagreement itself enhances appreciation of a concept. The inevitable presence of a typology's grey areas does not detract from its overall utility.

Implications

A Broadened View of Product Positioning

The typology highlights the reality that consumers make choices from an extremely large assortment. (See Chapter 4.) Marketing strategists delude themselves if they believe their mission is just to create preference for one brand over another. Ad designers must be aware of the great many alternative offerings vying for the consumer's time and attention, beyond just competing brands. To fabricate what may be a farfetched illustration, General Motors might have a stake in promoting the value of family life, because the man visiting his divorce lawyer is not able to concentrate on the question of whether to consider a Buick or a Ford. (But then some point out that divorces result in more auto sales!) In a more realistic vein, sellers of cigarettes (cell 5) are investing $5 million to combat the onslaught of the antismoking campaign (cell 4).

Thus marketers need not position products only against others in the same class; the broadened categorization scheme makes possible the positioning of products against an entire spectrum of offerings in an extended "evoked set" of the consumer, that is, against other transactions for which consumers exchange money, time, effort, psyche, and other scarce resources. Marketers should attempt to measure consumer attitudes not only toward their own products but also toward other offerings in the typology.

What Business Are We In?

The model can assist marketers in finding answers to what is sometimes an elusive yet crucial question: What business are we in? Does one sell cars or power, medical care or freedom from pain, social work or relationship, animal shelter or responsible pet ownership? Does the employment agency sell workers or productivity? Does the politician sell self-image or security for the voter? In terms of the typology, is the Better Business Bureau a cell 2 or a cell 4 organization, that is, does it render a service or does it promote a social issue or both? (Compare this with Townsend's well-known question asked of Avis: "Are we in the car rental business, or do we provide transportation? " For another example, the cosmetics producer Charles Revson is said to have remarked, "We don't sell lipstick, we sell hope.") If, as was pointed out above, Smokenders markets cell 8 as well as its cell 6 product, might this firm qualify for support from an anti-pollution agency?

New Markets for Ad Agencies

A number of offerings appearing in the top row, cells 1 through 4, are sometimes broadly classed as public services and fall within the aegis of the Advertising Council (see Chapter 7). What is interesting, however, is that these four cells show many exchanges whose campaigns are paid for and hence are outside the Ad Council's efforts. Thus, although they are marketed by nonprofit organizations, the measuring services such as Leading National Advertisers, Inc., count their ad billings in with commercial advertising. Examples include the Salvation Army, CARE, many fund raisers, public goods of the U.S. government, and labor unions.

The top row of the typology may thus suggest new areas for advertisers' interest in items for institutional ads, say, for image advertising, as well as concept advertising. By a conservative estimate, top-row exchanges presently account for less than 2 percent of the nearly $50 billion of total annual advertising billings in the United States. Does the broadened exchange typology suggest new markets for Madison Avenue? If, as was intimated in Chapter 1, the apparent trend is away from interest in material things and toward the ideational, should the marketing of advertising similarly be redirected? Will ideas and social issues be "encores," the new product types to be sought by the advertising industry?

This section has presented a categorization scheme for all "things" that are considered products in the marketing sense, that is, things that by their very nature, may serve to satisfy needs and desires of individuals. The products focused upon in this book occupy the right-hand half of the model presented in this chapter. Ideas and social issues represent the abstract concepts considered as items of exchange in this book.

EXCHANGE TRANSACTIONS IN SOCIAL MARKETING

Having put social products within an integrative framework of product offerings, the next task in developing the marketing approach to ideas is to examine methods by which concepts are marketed. What is the nature of the exchange transaction? It is called an exchange transaction because ordinarily something of approximately equal value to the product is given in return by the consumer to the supplier: An exchange of values takes place in the marketing transaction.

Where does social marketing occur? The traditional transaction takes place in the open marketplace. Goods and services are bought and sold through a bargaining process with each party trying to obtain what it perceives are the best terms available. By contrast, exchanges of social products occur in political, organizational, educational, leisure, health care, family, and a multitude of other settings. In its broadest meaning social marketing occurs virtually everywhere and all the time but under different labels—public service, organizational development, human interaction (for example, a marriage proposal), and so on.

> A transaction takes place, for example, when a person decides to watch a television program; he is exchanging his time for entertainment. A transaction takes place when a person votes for a particular candidate; he is exchanging his time and support for expectations of better government. A transaction takes place when a person gives money to a charity; he is exchanging money for a good conscience. (Kotler 1972, p. 48)

Marketing as Exchange and Exchange as Marketing

That the concept of exchange underlies marketing processes has been well developed and documented, notably by Richard Bagozzi (1974, 1975): "Exchange is a central concept in marketing and may well serve as the foundation for that elusive 'general theory of marketing'" (1975, p. 39). If marketing is exchange, what about the converse? Are not many exchanges also market transactions? It turns out that many forms of nonmercantile interaction among individuals and groups can be considered and studied as marketing phenomena. That is the theme of this book, and it is also the theme of a work by the cultural anthropologist Cyril Belshaw, who indeed maintains that "all enduring social relations involve transactions which have an exchange aspect" (1965, p. 4).

Bagozzi concurs: "Social marketing is the answer to a particular question: Why and how are exchanges created and resolved in social relationships? " (1975, p. 38). Carrying the argument yet further, Larry Isaacson and Steven Permut (1978) point out that

> The extension of marketing theory and practice from the private/ business arena to a host of other contexts in which exchange processes take place ... requires an appreciation for the very diverse nature of these exchanges, including understanding the different backgrounds, structures, goals and operating procedures of the institution and individual participants. We believe the insights gained by considering more diverse settings have not only a value in their own right, but add to our ability to comprehend and resolve problems in more traditional market settings. (p. 432)

The remainder of this section lists several methods of human interaction not usually seen as marketing, but presented here within a marketing orientation. This list of transactional types is by no means a serious review of exchange theory. Rather it is intended to serve as a convenient showcase to demonstrate some of the ways in which social products are marketed. Each of the types listed below is susceptible to analysis in terms of the six key marketing approach questions raised earlier in the chapter, and they constitute the methods employed by the distribution channels discussed in Chapter 7.

Information and Education Dissemination

In a broad sense, virtually all marketing activity consists of the dissemination of information and education. No matter what the product, the marketer must communicate information about benefits to the consumer to be derived from an exchange transaction. That point is emphasized throughout Chapter 8 where the product is information about government-sponsored manpower training, and strategic marketing planning is demonstrated from that viewpoint. Knowledge itself has been described by Gerald Zaltman (1979) in terms of "items" designed and transmitted to satisfy users (see Chapter 4).

The acquisition of information and education is a consumption process and includes, for example, participation in and attendance at lectures, as well as formal schooling. Roger Swagler (1979) studied what he called consumers' "information acquisition behavior" in which the price paid for the purchase is primarily in terms of time. He points out that the consumer's "stock of informational capital becomes a dominant factor in the consumer's decision whether or not to seek additional information." How similar this is to the situation of a food store buyer contemplating inventory replenishment. (It is interesting that both food and information might spoil with age!)

Interpersonal relationships offer many examples of educative exchanges in which the product is information, knowledge, recounted experience, or skills. Many youngsters can attest to parental efforts to promote some of the concepts shown in cells 3 and 4 of Table 2.1. And the price paid seems so high! Usually these products are packaged (couched) in "for-your-own-good" wrappings, and children become repeat customers to the extent that they find sense and validity in buying these ideas.

Gossipmongering

"Gossip is a valuable social commodity," writes Ralph Rosnow (1977): "There is in fact a close and very specific parallel between the functions and distribution of gossip and the patterns of marketing practices" (p. 159). He goes on to relate three varieties of gossip—information, influence, and entertainment—with the three patterns of trade identified by K. Polanyi, C. Arensberg, and H. Pearson (1957):

> *Redistributive trading* denotes that case in which resources are brought to a central operation and from there fairly dispersed, as when individuals make charitable contributions to some central collection agency which redistributes the donations to needy persons according to their requirements. *Exchange* is that case in which the value placed upon a commodity results from bargaining for economic advantage, as when goods or services are brought into the marketplace and sold to the highest bidder. *Reciprocative trading* refers to the establishment of an equitable ratio or balanced reciprocity in the giving and receiving of goods and services, as when farmers lend a helping hand to one another at harvest time.

Patterns of Trading Practices

	Redistributive	Exchange	Reciprocative
Information	*		
Influence		*	
Entertainment			*

> The rows in the table correspond to three primary functions or varieties of gossip—information, influence, and entertainment. Informative gossip exists for news trading and to provide participants with a "cognitive map" of their social environment. Gossip exploited for purposes of influence is a manipulative tool with which A attempts to gain an advantage over B, or over C by persuading B to revise his opinions of C. Gossiping for entertainment is engaged in primarily for mutual satisfaction and amusement rather than to convince someone of a moral position or to probe for news or confirmation of news. (p. 159)

In another treatment of the subject, Rosnow and G. A. Fine (1976) explored other parallels between gossiping and marketplace psychology:

> For example, it might be said that consumers of gossip, like consumers of any commodity in the marketplace, have their own brand of loyalties—columnists, tabloids, magazines. The consumption of gossip of all kinds may be analogous to the conspicuous consumption of goods and services in societies whose needs have been conditioned by competitive pressures; it also attests to the wide generality of a habit that ignores most sociological and demographic demarcations. Further, it can be observed that when news is scarce, the gossip-monger can exact a higher price for his tales. When the market for news expands, the amount of gossip in circulation will proliferate. If the transaction between A and B is mutually beneficial, whether equitable or not, it should result in some structural relationship in which future transactions can be more easily made. (1977, p. 162)

Rumormongering

Rumormongering is a form of exchange similar to gossipmongering, except that a rumor usually refers to some specific episode; gossip is more general. Trade in rumors dates back to ancient Roman emperors, who appointed public rumor wardens (called delatores), agent middlemen, to bring rumors from the populace to the palace and then to carry back other rumors to the people. "Psychological warfare is not new," comment Gordon Allport and Leo Postman (1947). They go on to ask:

> How much of history . . . can be regarded as the reactions of important groups of people to current rumor?
> A great deal, we suspect, for until very recent times the inhabitants of the world had little to rely on other than rumored information. Newspapers, the telegraph, the radio are late inventions. Before their advent the public had to rely upon some traveler to bring with him word-of-mouth reports, upon some Paul Revere to announce approaching danger, or upon the town crier to tell his own version of the day's news. Only a few statesmen and a few monarchs received written and sealed dispatches, and their sources was not necessarily rumor free. (p. 161)

For a rumor to exist two necessary conditions must be present: The tale must be important to both parties and the actual facts must be shrouded in some kind of ambiguity (Allport and Postman 1947, p. 33). Interestingly, both importance and ambiguity are key variables in the Howard-Sheth model of buyer behavior (1969), a cornerstone of marketing theory. A product's importance to a consumer motivates him or her to attend to advertising, while ambiguity in the promotion's message stimulates further search for information to clarify the ambiguity. There is a remarkable tendency to recall the message of rumor while forgetting its source or the channels through which it was transmitted. One reason is that rumor, true to a cardinal rule of the advertising profession, typically is heard more than once. Redundancy and repetition make the message clearer and tend to mediate "noise in the system."

Probably the highest price one pays for adoption of an idea in rumor form is the risk of using and conveying inaccurate information. (Mark Twain is said to have quipped, "The reports of my death are greatly exaggerated.") Another price is just the attention paid to the rumormonger who is in need of solicitude possibly to fill an otherwise humdrum existence. His inventory of rumors-for-sale renders his life more interesting. In return the rumor consumer obtains psychological benefits:

> In August 1945, a rumor spread to the effect that Russia declared war on Japan only because Russia received in exchange the secret of the atomic bomb. Those who believed and spread this tale were people who disliked the Russians and, perhaps to only a slightly less extent, disliked the Administration in Washington. Gnawing hatred motivated the rumor. But instead of saying candidly, "I hate Russia," or "I hate the Democrats," the rumor spreader seized upon a story that would *relieve, justify,* and *explain* his underlying emotional tension. (Allport and Postman 1947, p. 36)

Thus rumor helps one to reason and often provides a plausible explanation for confused and otherwise inexplainable ideas.

Public Relations or Publicity

Public relations or publicity is the marketing activity usually designed to promote, not a specific product offering, but rather the idea of a favorable image of an individual or an organization. Thus, while marketing's product is engineered to satisfy needs of potential consumers, publicity as a product must appeal to all individuals in society. The rationale for public relations stems from the realization that not only customers but many other publics influence the welfare of the organization. But there is another distinction between marketing and public relations: In marketing the sponsor is identified and makes payment to the medium for the service of message delivery. In the case of publicity, media space is usually not paid for, the notice appearing as editorial matter, and the sponsor's identity is not necessarily self-evident (Bernstein 1973).

Apart from such differences, public relations practitioners really play marketing roles as wholesalers of ideas:

They are powerful middlemen. Sometimes they mediate between their clients and the press, selling stories, overseeing interviews, putting out press releases. Sometimes they bring clients and government officials together, making introductions, explaining how the bureaucracy and its leaders operate. Sometimes they work with the client alone, revamping an image here, reshaping a position there. (Quindlen 1980, p. L21)

Many believe that public relations consists of correcting a false image that people have of some institution. If an institution suffers from a poor image, then the solution to that problem lies not in artificially changing that image through promotion techniques but rather in changing the causes of the negative image. The relationship between public relations and marketing lies in the very definition of marketing, namely, that marketers produce products designed to satisfy the needs and wants of its market (Kotler and Mindak 1978). The role of public relations in this scenario is first to find out just what is the image that people have and then to return to the institution with a program to modify the root causes creating that image, that is, to improve the institutional "product." Newspaper and other media publicity releases on behalf of the client are merely the mechanical aspects: they are not in and of themselves public relations. To be sure, publicity releases must be interestingly written, or they will not find readers. But a PR person who sets out to change people's perceptions without taking the necessary steps to correct whatever lies behind those perceptions cannot be said to be acting with integrity. A favorable image is not sold with mere words but with performance and action.

Public Opinion

Public opinion and public opinion polls (just another name for research in concept marketing) are well-known phenomena. To the extent that public opinion is marketed, the price paid in the exchange might very well be the surrender of the individual's freedom to choose a private opinion. Lacking the time, patience, and perseverance to inform oneself intelligently about social issues, one absorbs an opinion preselected by others as public and then degenerates to a state of unthinking conformism:

Stepan Arkadyevitch took in and read a liberal paper, not an extreme one, but one advocating the views held by the majority. And in spite of the fact that science, art, and politics had no special interest for him, he firmly held those views on all these subjects which were held by the majority and by his paper, and he only changed them when the majority changed them—or, more strictly speaking, he did not change them, but they imperceptibly changed of themselves within him. Stepan Arkadyevitch had not chosen his political opinions or his views, these political opinions and views had come to him of themselves, . . . liberalism had become a habit of Stepan Arkadye-vitch's and he liked his newspaper, as he did his cigar after dinner, for the slight fog it diffused in his brain. (Tolstoy, *Anna Karenina*, Modern Library Edition, pp. 10–11, in Carlson 1975, p. 43)

Unfortunately, most marketers of public opinion, principally the news media, select for distribution those views they consider to be most newsworthy and not necessarily those most beneficial to society. To that extent they are producer-oriented, in violation of the marketing concept. But public opinion is bought not only by individuals too lazy to think for themselves. It is also sought after, or should be, by politicians vitally concerned with the opinions of their constituencies (Zeisel 1980). Thus public opinion comes in at least two product forms, that which is sold, and that which is sought.

Propagandizing

Propagandizing is another form of human exchange amenable to a market-ing perspective. Propaganda is quite synonymous with mass communication, a one-to-many procedure for delivering messages. That the term suffers pejorative interpretation similar to "politics," stems from its use by governments to dissem-inate their own self-serving points of view on issues. Yet propaganda is not by definition a bad practice. Moreover, an evaluation of the use of propaganda depends on whose side the observer is on, as with Radio Free Europe, Voice of America, and Radio Liberty broadcasts, for example. Recently, en route to the university parking lot, a student remarked to the author that all advertising was "just plain propaganda." Upon arrival at her vehicle, a bumper sticker asked, "Did you hug your child today?" That of course was not propaganda.

Propaganda is a marketing transaction because it is a process in which a product is promoted, delivered, and paid for (with attention, support, risk, and such psychic factors as loss of freedom). But not every exchange is propaganda. For an exchange in the sense of social marketing to be considered propaganda, it must conform to three conditions set forth by Lazarsfeld and Merton (1949, in Schramm and Roberts 1971, pp. 459–80) for the effective use of mass media in what they call "propaganda for social objectives." These conditions are

1. Monopolization, or the absence of neutralizing counterpropaganda. If oppos-ing views tend to cancel each other out, then exchange has not been effected. In this sense, U.S. attempts to rally popular support for the Vietnam War can-not be called propaganda because of the presence of considerable antiwar publicity. But ideas spread by the Hitler regime and the Ku Klux Klan, vio-lently resisting opposition, surely fall under the propaganda heading. Interest-ingly, most commercial advertising must escape the propaganda rubric because

of competing and opposing messages inevitably counteracting ad effectiveness, for example, antismoking publicity versus cigarette promotion. (In the parking lot chat cited earlier, the student's perception would, according to Lazarsfeld and Merton, be inaccurate, for who would counter the hug-your-child theme?)

2. Canalization, or the channeling or redirecting of preexisting attitude and behavior rather than attempting to instill radical change. A nutrition campaign is propaganda because sound nutrition is entirely in harmony with human interest in good health: It asks only for a redirecting of dietary habits.

3. Supplementation of mass media campaigns with interpersonal word-of-mouth promotion. In the Soviet Union, "Red corners," "reading huts," and "listening stations" where groups can converse are encouraged in order to achieve a "clinching effect" of mass communicated messages. This phenomenon has also been studied as the "two-step-flow" theory of communication. It facilitates the exchange of concepts and justifies the appellation propaganda.

In the spirit of the zero-based approach promised in the Preface, the Lazarsfeld and Merton model tends to remove pejorative stigma from the propaganda concept.

These three conditions also further clarify the distinction made in Chapter 1 between ideas and issues. Virtually all societally beneficial ideas are promoted unopposed and thus enjoy monopoly in the marketplace; they are propaganda (an exception is the idea of conventional marriage which is opposed by the Sexual Freedom League). On the other hand, because issues are by definition two-sided, their sponsorship must be taken as less propagandist than ideas. Contrary to accepted usage, including that given in most dictionaries, commercial advertising and issue advocacy are less deserving of the propaganda label than the promotion of the most societally beneficial ideas.

Lobbying

Lobbying is a form of marketing conducted by an estimated 15,000 professionals who canvas legislators in the U.S. Capitol's corridors and lobbies (hence their title) on behalf of their clients. They are middlemen of social and political issues serving between special-interest groups and lawmakers. The product offering is usually a strong position on an issue, in exchange for favors, political contributions, and the services of election or campaign workers. The lawmaking consumers of this product pay for their purchases with time spent attending to lobbyists, but more significantly they must sometimes trade off their own convictions as well as those of constituents who hold opposing views. Lobbyists include representatives of the National Association of Manufacturers, the U.S. Chamber of Commerce, trade and professional organizations, such as the American Medical Association, National Rifle Association, and American Petroleum

Institute, and labor unions. Billed as the most powerful lobbying group of all is the Business Round Table, a consortium of the heads of nearly 200 leading corporations whose aim is to place a "business imprint" on major legislation.

The lobbying process provides a valuable forum in the marketplace for ideas. To a great extent legislators rely on lobbyists as sources of information from their constituencies. Yet lobbying, like propaganda, frequently is discussed in a pejorative tone, a perception that is mediated when lobbying is seen as a two-way need-satisfying exchange, with each side obtaining benefits from the procedure.

Advocacy

Advocacy is an exchange transaction in which a highly credible source popularizes a concept and thereby generates widespread demand for it. It is a marketing process in every way. For example, Sinclair Lewis's book *The Jungle* called attention to shoddy practices in the meat-packing industry; when the book joined the best-seller list, it became a mass medium. Its ideas quickly matured into a social issue with resulting passage of the Meat Act of 1906. Purchasers of that issue paid the cash price for the book and a price of time spent in reading and discussing it. In turn, they promoted the issue in the form of public outcry to lawmakers, the ultimate customers who bought the idea in exchange for promise of reelection. A marketing view of the process is thus simply that of a distribution channel, discussed in that light in Chapter 7, where advocates are described as channel elements.

Fund Raising

Fund raising is another transaction readily viewed here from a marketing orientation. A solicitor of funds is a marketer of the concept that it would be a good idea to contribute to a charity and the buyer of that idea pays for it with the amount given, the price. Delivery of the product is usually made in the form of a document of acknowledgment, which the donor receives with much delight and ego enhancement.

A classic case study of marketing's successful application to fund raising is given by W. Mindak and H. M. Bybee (1971). The authors describe their use of consumer research, segmentation strategy, product positioning, and promotion campaigning in a competitive "charity market." Of the two main promotion methods, mass and interpersonal, Stephen Long found the latter to be more effective in fund raising (1976). Various fund-raising techniques were tested in a marketing research experiment by Peter Reingen (1978). That study highlighted the value of the foot-in-the-door technique for achieving compliance with respect to donations to the Heart Association. The foot-in-the-door theory suggests that compliance is more likely to a second request if a small request is first made, just to get the "foot in the door." The notion is based on self-perception theory, which in turn asserts that attitudes and beliefs are inferred from self-observation of one's behavior.

Economists provide cogent arguments pointing to social pressure as the principal force motivating consumers to adopt the idea of philanthropy. In a strong statement to that effect, Bruce Bolnick maintains that at the root of philanthropic behavior lies a social interdependence among people and that charitable contributions are made only to ward off the accusation by others of the donor's selfishness (in Philps 1975, p. 198 passim). The opportunity to give visibly to charity is a product that should be designed in such a manner as to satisfy the donor's need for approval, belongingness, status, self-esteem, and last if indeed not least, tax shelter. Because people have these felt needs, professional fund raisers serve as problem solvers in the true marketing sense.

The entire idea of giving, not only of funds but also the giving of objects as gifts, has long attracted the attention of sociologists and cultural anthropologists. For scholarly yet highly readable treatments, one should see the works of Sahlins, Mauss, Titmus, Homans, or Levi-Strauss, for example, and an interesting marketing statement on gift giving is Belk (1976). Because gift-giving phenomena ordinarily deal with the exchange of tangibles, for example, the potlatch, and the kula (Mauss 1967), they are not included in the present study. It should be mentioned however, that in some societies the gift is not the real product in the exchange, but rather the price paid. As Marcel Mauss pointed out, gifts aim to buy "peace; to express affection, regard or loyalty; to unify the group; to bind the generations; to fulfill a contractual set of obligations and rights; to function as acts of penitence, shame or degradation, and to symbolize many other human sentiments" (1967, p. 45).

Philanthropy has undergone changes parallel to those of other mercantile activities. In preindustrial societies, assisting one's neighbor was a person-to-person process analogous to barter or purchase of handcrafted wares. Present-day charity is a matter of public administration, or redistributive trading, according to the Rosnow model cited earlier in this section.

Nonmarketing Exchanges

It would be somewhat specious to argue that all social interchange is precisely and entirely marketing (although one could, without great effort, identify some aspects of negotiation or bargaining in any occurrence of human interaction). Thus this section does not include as exchange transactions ordinary conversation, group discussion, or social letter writing. For while these are, to be sure, exchanges, they are not necessarily transactional in nature. All exchanges involve give-and-take, but for them to be transactions in a marketing sense, there also must be present a deliberately introduced product offering with the buy-and-sell intention.

Debate is also excluded. A debate is a contest whose purpose is more to determine the relative quality of discourse of the protagonists than to convey the focus ideas. That in the process issues are exchanged and even diffused among members of the audience is secondary to the choice of the winner. A debate is thus like a sporting event at which, although the fans have interest in, and enthusiasm for the theme (the sport, the issue), they cheer primarily the team that bests its opponent. A debate is a service designed to satisfy people's need to observe others "doing battle" or performing in one way or another. In short, participants in a debate, like players in the performing sports and arts, while they impart to their clients much that is ideational, their exchanges are primarily entertaining; they render entertainment, a service; "the play's the thing."

This last section has discussed some of the methods by which ideas and other concepts are infused and disseminated. An attempt was made to demonstrate that these exchanges are to a large extent marketing activities.

SUMMARY

By discussing several aspects of the marketing approach to ideas, this chapter has set the stage for the scenario that unfolds in the remainder of the book, where marketing principles are actually applied to concept dissemination. Several basic marketing expressions, including social marketing (idea marketing, concept marketing), were defined and marketing was presented as a problem-solving process. Ideas have now been contextualized in three different ways. In Chapter 1 they were shown to occupy positions within a reasoning process, in a hierarchy beginning with the existence of a problem and culminating in social change, and, in this chapter, in a quasi-typology where ideas were placed within a gamut of all types of product offerings.

Several selected forms of human exchange were portrayed as marketing types— information acquisition, gossip, rumor, public relations, public opinion, propaganda, lobbying, advocacy, and fund raising.

Having argued that ideas are products of human exchange, and that exchange phenomena are marketing transactions, it must follow that ideas can be studied as any other product, that they are bought and sold, priced and advertised, packaged and distributed.

3

IDEA PRODUCERS

A great society is a society in which its men of business think greatly of their functions.

— Alfred North Whitehead

THE EMERGING CONCEPT SECTOR

This chapter explores a sector of the economy believed to be at the threshold of a fascinating emergence. The sector constitutes those institutions sponsoring ideas and social issues—concepts—in contrast to organizations purveying goods and services. As yet unnamed, one could assign to it an appellation such as the area industry or, more eloquently, the concept sector. The concept sector cuts across traditional boundaries of sector distinction because its members include profit-making, nonprofit, and public organizations as well as the hybrid "quasi's." It is characterized by the criterion that its product mix consists of abstract concepts unrelated to conventional products.

Managers in the concept sector design (social) products and perform the entire gamut of marketing functions. Whether they realize it or not, they are businesspeople; they are merchants. But to delimit the scope of this chapter, only originators—producers of concepts—will be discussed. (They shall also be referred to as "sponsors" or "initiators" of ideas.) Middlemen operating between the producer and consumer are discussed in Chapter 7. They include the mass media, opinion leaders, and pressure groups of various types.

Concept producers seem close to the realization that marketing philosophies and methodologies are applicable to the social products they sponsor. Some have known it for years. But to most others, it is a revelation, and one may expect that those newly initiated will embark upon exciting ventures.

In reality, the concept sector is ancient. What is new is its formulation as a businesslike activity through the application of marketing thought. Ideas are nonmaterial products that have been bought and sold in both open and closed marketplaces since time immemorial. From Plato's notions about the nature of a perfect republic to Marx's thoughts about an ultimate classless society, the merchandising of concepts has been ever present.

Government, A Special Case

In fact, politics is a special but important case of idea marketing, with the politician marketing the idea, "Vote for me! " Perhaps one of the oldest members of the idea sector, only recently has the politician been studied formally from a marketing viewpoint (Rothschild 1978; Palda 1980). The candidate's name is a brand name for ideas (products) that are promoted in elaborate campaigns and bought by consumers who make up the electorate. Sometimes a high price is paid for the purchase! Once they have successfully sold the "vote for me" idea, politicians produce and market a host of other concepts, in aspiration of yet additional objectives: "More news emanates from officials than from any other source. ... Bureaucratic need accounts for the volume of details on the inner workings of government published in the American press. Officials engaging in intragovernmental politicking to achieve the policy outcomes they desire exploit the press tactically" (Sigal 1973, p. 336).

Legislative and regulative agencies themselves make an important contribution to the concept sector. For example, advocacy of one side in an issue is given tremendous impetus when it attains legal status. A current case in point in the United States is the issue of mainstreaming disabled youngsters in public schools—including them in regular classes—in contrast to educating them in special facilities. Public Law 504, against discrimination, and specifically, Public Law 94142, give parents the legal right to insist that public schools mainstream all children having such disabilities as muscular distrophy, retardation, hearing impairment, and so on, in the belief that mainstreaming provides the least restrictive environment. In many cases compliance has necessitated large expenditures by school systems for equipment, structural modifications in buildings, and special staff. Most people would not concern themselves with the idea that handicapped children should be schooled in the same classes as normal children. But after enactment of mainstreaming laws, society was confronted with the reality of the idea, and people soon caught on to its democratic implications.

Because politics is a discipline in its own right and discussed in a huge literature, this book only touches upon the subject peripherally. For example, the roles of lobbyists and other special-interest groups are mentioned in Chapter 7. Let it suffice here to merely give some idea of the magnitude of promotion of ideas by government.

The U.S. government will spend $475 million on advertising in the year 2000 as compared to the 1976 figure of $115 million, according to Gene Secunda, senior vice-president, J. Walter Thompson. "Government has learned from the advertising profession," he said, that frequency of exposure in media is vital to getting your given message across and remembered. Federal and local governments are using paid advertising more than ever to sell products (the postage stamp campaign for the U.S. Postal Service), to sell services (Amtrak's train travel), to recruit personnel (armed forces recruitment advertising), and to promote ideas (the Energy Research and Development Administration's Energy conservation program). (*Marketing News*, May 19, 1978)

In all, public and nonprofit expenditures on advertising in the United States are approximated at $2 billion annually (Rosenberg 1977, p. 80). Only 23 organizations, corporate and otherwise, had larger ad budgets in 1979 than the U.S. government. This poses a question about government domination of the concept sector:

> ... the growing advertising budgets of federal government agencies do indicate the increasing need to promote ideas and services. But this growth may represent social harm, in terms of government monopolizing the marketing of ideas ... (which) could have a very dangerous, dampening effect on the free marketplace of ideas and concepts. (Novelli 1980b)

The author believes that the concept sector is sufficiently broad to mediate that possibility. In a democracy, ideas are infused and spread by so many sponsors, one hopes that, although government might be the most prominent, it is not the most controlling or overruling advocate influencing the concept market.

Nor can the idea marketer afford to underestimate the importance of involving bureaucrats in the planning of programs. Calling government a "neglected cluster of professionals," Clifford Wharton (1977) raises the question: "The politicians are the persons who must adopt, finance, advocate, and defend the policies, programs, and projects recommended by scientific and technical professionals. Have we neglected the politicians' critical role?" (p. 17).

Most governments engage in the marketing of social products. For example, it is commonplace to see huge posters in (primarily) socialist countries portraying political leaders in the effort to enhance the nationalist image. There, too, are posted photos of outstanding conscientious factory workers in campaigns designed to stress productivity in industry for the good of the state. These programs also disseminate the state's economic achievements, emphasizing levels of production of critical materials, such as uranium. For another noteworthy example, the Chinese government, with the flip of a switch, broadcasts to a billion people the admonition that family size should be limited to one child. In fact, in many parts of the world one almost perceives more evidence of the marketing of social, economic, and cultural items than tangibles.

Commercial Firms

Although the majority of idea initiators are public and nonprofit institutions, a study described later in this chapter indicates that about 25 percent are commercial firms sponsoring ideas quite apart from ideas that underlie their conventional goods or services. The present work considers beyond its scope those ideas about products, per se (the "sizzle behind the steak"), and instead focuses only on intangibles when they are themselves taken as products. Some commercial establishments do espouse ideas that, although profit-inspired, are product-independent and thus qualify for inclusion here. If Christian Dior designs a princess style knee-length gown, a new product is launched, but in the process the general idea of knee-length dresses is advanced. Similarly, Resorts International, Inc., could promote either its casino (a service) in Atlantic City or the idea of legalized gambling. Oil companies, in what appeared as a strategy of the demarketing of their tangible product, sought to attain image enhancement by advertising the idea of fuel conservation. Indeed all such "institutional" ads fall within the idea rubric, as by definition they directly promote no products or services but only the good name of the firm—an idea (Sethi 1979).

Until recently business firms in the United States were constrained from voicing their opinions on issues. For decades, "commercial speech" was not entitled to the same First Amendment protection as "political" speech. But these restrictions are undergoing liberalization:

> From the marketplace of goods and services, corporations of late have begun to push into the marketplace of ideas and are demanding the same rights as everyone else.
>
> Last year they scored a major victory when the United States Supreme Court ruled that companies could campaign for or against state referendums. (Graham 1979, p. A8)

Trade associations as spokesmen for individual firms within any given industry constitute a significant portion of the concept sector. To the (large) extent that they promote use of the tangible products merchandised by their constituent member firms, they are beyond the scope of this book. But some trade associations are sources of ideas only indirectly related to product promotion. Many have community affairs and/or public affairs departments. Thus the United States Brewers Association maintains an Alcohol Programs Division fostering responsible use of alcoholic beverages.

What about the employees of an organization supplying ideas and issues? Should they be possessed of a higher level of altruism than their counterparts in commercial enterprises? Because these institutions market ideologically and sociologically oriented products, does it follow that they would require of their personnel a value system differing from that of employees in firms purveying goods and services? Is it safe to assume that by the very nature of the work, one is likely to observe a greater degree of charity on the part of individuals engaged in the concept sector? It would seem these questions demand positive answers yet there does not appear to be much evidence one way or the other.

HOW DO THEY MARKET?

One may expect that business organizations apply their experience in commercial marketing to the sponsorship of ideas and issues as well. But what about public and nonprofit institutions? In general, how much do idea merchants know about their craft? How, in the first place, do they feel about marketing? How do they *do* marketing? In order to learn about the nature of marketing as practiced by concept sector institutions, the author conducted a study to ferret out answers to such questions. The project took the form of an exploratory survey of a variety of organizations whose principal commonality is their mission to sponsor an intangible or social product (Fine 1981b).

Study Design

A compendium of social products (see Table 1.1) evolved out of several focus group discussions attended by a team of market research students. From this list, items were then allocated to team members who were charged with the task of seeking out institutions sponsoring the specified concepts. The product was carefully identified by writing it at four designated points in the questionnaire, once on each page (see Appendix B).

The sample was a "convenience" sample of such organizations. They were selected informally; no systematic methods or randomization were employed to select respondents, except that team members attempted to include both local and national institutions in the study. Every effort was made to administer the questionnaires by personal interview. In cases where they were mailed, follow-up phone calls were made to those institutions not responding within a few weeks. Out of 475 institutions contacted, 222 questionnaires were returned, of which 197 were suitable for analysis—a usable return rate of 41.5 percent. Others were either returned by post offices as undeliverable or improperly or incompletely filled out. A few institutions were excluded when it became clear from the responses that they promoted not ideas but goods or services.

Survey instrument design was guided generally by the knowledge, attitude, practice (KAP) model familiar to social marketers. One seeks information about what respondents know, feel, and are doing about a particular topic. That model has been applied widely in nutrition and birth control studies and is a useful research guide for many social cause projects. In addition to questions asking for descriptive characteristics about the institution, respondents were asked if they had "considered their sponsored idea as a 'product' to be marketed" (never, rarely, sometimes, frequently, or constantly). Another question asked whether the institution has "a marketing department or equivalent." Respondents' perceptions were sought relating to organizational goals, terms associated with marketing, familiarity with and use of marketing concepts, and experience with various promotional methods and media. The instrument is reproduced in Appendix B.

Results of the Study

Frequency analysis results are given in Table 3.1 in separate columns for 49 business firms (25 percent of the sample), 89 private nonprofits (45 percent), and 59 government agencies (30 percent). More than half (112) of the institutions surveyed had been established over 20 years and had budgets in excess of $1 million. Most of the institutions (84 percent) in the study were main facilities; only 31 out of 197 were branch offices. They served a fairly evenly distributed representation of national, regional, state, and local jurisdictions. The business firms and public agencies in the sample were generally larger than the private nonprofits in terms of number of employees.

In all of the three classes of institutions a majority reported they "constantly" considered their designated concepts as products to be marketed. On the other hand, responses to the "marketing department or equivalent" question varied significantly according to type of institution, with the private sector predominantly positive and the others negative. Related to that result, and to no one's surprise, was the finding that business firms had larger marketing staffs, and indicated more knowledge of marketing concepts, than their public and nonprofit counterparts. Yet, in actual utilization and effectiveness of promotional methods, very little difference seemed apparent between the institutional types.

Questions 15 and 16 were intended to capture respondents' perceptions about the primary goal of the organization. Aware that an individual could have personal impressions about the organization's goals differing from official policy, each was first asked about his or her own feelings on the matter, just to "clear the air." Yet, in the final analysis, little difference was found between personal feelings and organizational policy with respect to goals. The nine categories of objectives were collapsed into four: acquisition of and return on resources, survival, increase and satisfaction of clientele, and educating the public with existing and new concepts (products). Not surprisingly, goals of private sector firms emphasize resources. However a majority of nonprofits (54 percent) see their principal objective as public education, something true of only 8 percent of the private firms. With public agencies, on the other hand, a large number (42 percent) mirror business firms' concern with resources, as against the goal of education (22 percent).

If stated objectives are indicative of organizational policy, it appears that

TABLE 3.1

Frequencies on Selected Variables in the Institutional Study

Characteristic	Business Firms (n = 49)	Nonprofit Organizations (n = 89)	Public Agencies (n = 59)
Age of the institution			
Less than 6 years	15	15	6
6–20 years	6	22	21
Over 20 years	28	52	32
Annual budget (000s)			
Less than 100	6	26	8
100 to 1000	11	28	15
Over 1000	32	35	36
Number of employees			
Less than 20	15	43	17
20 to 100	7	29	12
Over 100	27	17	30
Considered idea as a product			
Rarely, never	6	13	9
Sometimes, frequently	9	27	17
Constantly	34	49	33
Marketing department or equivalent			
Yes	40	57	35
No	9	32	24
Organizational goals			
Resources	21	18	25
Survival	7	9	2
Clients	17	14	11
Education	4	48	20
Knowledge of marketing, average	7.08	5.88	6.03
Attitude toward marketing			
Advertising	21	3	5
Propaganda	0	0	0
Public opinion	4	6	2
Persuasion	8	10	8
Public interest	2	15	16
Puffery	0	1	0
Education	8	47	25
Public relations	1	2	2
Other	5	5	1

(continued)

TABLE 3.1 (continued)

Characteristic	Business Firms (n = 49)	Nonprofit Organizations (n = 89)	Public Agencies (n = 59)
Marketing practice, average			
Television	3.14	3.68	3.48
Radio	3.27	3.70	3.75
Magazines	3.27	3.54	3.42
Newspapers	4.20	3.98	3.95
Direct mail	3.50	3.78	3.71
Billboards	2.58	2.48	3.02
Word of mouth	4.33	4.25	3.90
Sales representatives	3.41	2.83	2.85
Marketing consultant	2.61	2.30	2.73
Yellow Pages	2.94	2.27	2.19
Ad agency	3.22	2.30	2.88
Phone canvassing	2.45	2.58	2.46
Consumer surveys	2.92	2.42	2.78
Other (brochures, conferences, hot lines, posters)	0.53	0.65	0.46

Source: Constructed by the author.

public and nonprofit institutions share a pattern of disdain for their clients. In fact, even business firms place client satisfaction second to resource conservation as a main objective. That less than 20 percent of public and nonprofit institutions and only 33 percent of the firms consider their principal goal to be satisfying customers is one of the sadder findings of this study. It highlights the need for a marketing approach to concept dissemination. But the objective of survival fared worst of all, making the poorest showing with public and nonprofit organizations and ranking second to last with private firms as well. It appears that *the concept sector is a society of the here and now!* (See the discussion in Chapter 4 relating to "encore" products.)

Items 17 and 18 of the survey instrument listed a series of "terms one might associate with marketing" and asked respondents to select the one believed "to be most descriptive of your marketing process." As with the goal question, an attempt was made to divorce personal feelings from organizational policy. Given popular myths about marketers forcing unwanted goods down the throats of unsuspecting consumers, it is astonishing that not one organization selected propaganda as a term associated with marketing, and only one in the entire sample of 197 selected puffery. (Yet it would be naive to overlook a social-desirability bias in these responses.) Education again ranked first among public and nonprofit institutions but only moderately with business firms. Conversely, advertising was significantly first choice with the private sector but unpopular with publics and nonprofits as "terms associated with marketing." The latter group also associates "public interest" with the marketing connotation, and all institutions seem aware that marketing is a form of persuasion.

Knowledge about formal marketing concepts was measured by listing nine concepts including consumer orientation, segmentation, positioning, and so on, with provision for "other," and asking whether each is familiar to and used by the organization. For each case, a composite score was calculated as the number of familiar concepts, so that each could receive a score from 1 to 10. Private sector firms with an average score of 7.08 proved to be most knowledgable about marketing, followed by government agencies (6.03) and finally the nonprofits (5.88).

The most unfamiliar concept of all is the key marketing model, the four Ps—product, price, promotion, and place. To be sure, many individuals might be quite familiar with these marketing-mix elements without being aware of the four Ps appellation. Nonetheless, the fact that ignorance of that expression pervaded all three sectors is an indictment against marketers themselves. *One may suggest that marketing needs marketing!* Significantly, all sectors also agree in reporting they "always use" consumer orientation, a finding in direct contradiction to the poor showing earlier of client satisfaction as an organizational goal. This raises some question as to the candor with which attitudinal and opinion-based information was obtained, what social researchers call response bias.

Some Observations About the Survey

The survey drew written comments from approximately one respondent in four. Many expressed acceptance, delight, and surprise at the prospect of a systematic study of idea sponsors. What came through in these comments was genuine interest in, and a need and desire to learn more about concept marketing:

> Completing this form was very useful to me—the process, it helped me to focus on actually what we're seeing, promoting. That is something I've had little time to consider (a local chapter of Parents Anonymous).

> This is a very interesting concept (social marketing). I would be interested in results of the study, as well as knowing whether the project will be extended to include the developing of a marketing plan for an agency such as ours (a state division of civil rights).

A score or more respondents said that they had retained photocopies of their questionnaires for the purpose of discussing the project with team members after mailing back their originals.

A most significant finding to emerge from the study is that institutions sponsoring ideas and social issues certainly do engage in marketing practices, but for the most part, in an ad hoc manner. Many seem unaware of, or are reluctant to admit the fact that they are promoting a "product." This was clear from some of the reasons (question 10) given for a response of "No" to the question, "Do you have a marketing department or equivalent?" In each of the cases cited below, after denying the presence of a marketing department or equivalent, respondents indicated effective use of advertising media, and some also admitted that several staffers were involved with marketing. The inconsistencies in these responses reveal some confusion about marketing:

> PR is handled by our executive director (an organization sponsoring prevention of wife abuse).

> Congress does not provide funds for marketing in its VD control appropriations (education specialist of a federal public health agency who then reported engaging in extensive media activity).

> Would publicity qualify for equivalent of marketing? (director of public relations of an institution promoting the idea of responsible pet ownership).

> We have never thought of ourselves as marketing a product. We have people who are assigned ERA as their "item" (an administrator of a regional League of Women Voters).

> Don't understand the term (marketing); we do lobbying, letter writing to appropriate government and commercial concerns (a group crusading for the rights of the left-handed).

> We do not promote literacy; it is a fact of life. If people want to be helped they come in. Word of mouth and referrals are our best means of promotion (a reading improvement association).

> Not applicable (a National Guard recruiting officer!)

> Marketing fluoridation is not a function of government—promotion and public awareness is (an official of a public health service).

> We disseminate information without the marketing connotation. Besides, demand is too great to justify marketing (a national center for the prevention of child abuse).

> We are a weekly newspaper; we do sell ads but not ideas (a gay rights organization).

A prominent institution promoting the United Nations asserts it "constantly" considers arms control as a "product to be marketed" and engages in multimedia campaigns, yet it emphatically denies it has a marketing department or equivalent because "each program develops its own strategy for its own audience." And the same situation apparently prevails with a national retail organization fighting shoplifting, a dental association espousing fluoridation, and the national headquarters of a major political party in its campaign to stimulate voter registration. After 75 years in existence a national group "never thought of suicide prevention as a marketable product." "Promoting (motorcycle) helmet use is everyone's job," states a national commission on highway safety as a reason for its diffidence to marketing.

Beyond the questionnaires, a number of mail and phone communications between respondents and team members revealed the same tenor of narrow and confused perceptions about marketing. Typical was the following remark in a letter from the public information officer of a federal agency: "We do not market anything. We do advocate firearms security, good citizenship, and responsible ownership of guns, and we have sponsored programs endorsing these concepts." Unbelievably, some private sector firms suffer from similar confusion. A multibranch savings and loan association widely advertises the idea of interest-bearing checking accounts but "does no marketing because we have no person with that expertise."

A line in the *Arabian Nights* admonishes: "He who knows and knows not he knows, he is asleep; awake him." A sizable segment of institutions espousing social causes admit to their marketing role only after being awakened to that reality. It is ironic that although they themselves are promoters of concepts, they have been slow to adopt the marketing concept. On the other hand there is ample evidence that members of the idea sector are increasingly assuming consumer orientation and engaging in strategic marketing planning both for their own benefit as well as that of society.

Shortcomings of the Study

Recognizing one's blind spots is an integral part of research evaluation. For one thing, the concept of social marketing should have been explained more thoroughly at the beginning. Furthermore, if the questions relating to the various media had preceded the "marketing department or equivalent" item, the concept of idea marketing might have been clearer. Perhaps the most serious blind spot was the researchers' inability to anticipate the large number of de facto marketing activities in which institutions engage but under names other than marketing. These include education, publicity, arranging for guest speakers, publishing brochures, and so on. An executive of an organization concerned with child abuse wrote, "When you change 'marketing' to public education, the questionnaire becomes applicable."

The presence of technical marketing terms bothered a few respondents: "Dear Seymour, You were doing fine until question 19 and then your academic prejudice took over," commented an advocate of mainstreaming children.

THE CHANGE AGENT AS IDEA PRODUCER

Having dealt with organizational sponsors of ideas, this chapter would be incomplete without mention of the individual advocate of ideas and issues: the change agent. Although the subject of social change has been excluded from this study, it is relevant to note that advocates of change are surely producers of concepts within the meaning of this chapter. The author is grateful to Harold Demone, dean of the Rutgers Graduate School of Social Work, for communicating the following cogent passage about leading "role innovators," as he refers to them:

> Ralph Nader, attorney role innovator, is described by *Time Magazine* (Dec. 12, 1969) as, "The U.S.'s Toughest Customer" and "an almost legendary crusader." He sees the law as a powerful instrument for positive social change. All consumers are his clients even though few have requested his assistance. To Nader, legal services are a right not a privilege. He has been principally responsible for the enactment of six major Federal laws—the National Traffic and Motor Vehicle Act of 1966, the Wholesome Meat Act of 1967, the Natural Gas Pipeline Safety Act, the Radiation Control for Health and Safety Act, and the Wholesome Poultry Act, all enacted in 1968, and in 1969 the Federal Coal Mine Health and Safety Act. His other targets have been equally varied: monosodium glutamate in baby food, fatty hot dogs, unclean fish, tractors, medical X-rays, color television radiation, and many Federal agencies.
>
> Another change agent of note was Saul Alinsky who spent more than 30 years organizing the poor, only to move to organizing the middle class late in his life. His premise was that all people had power if they developed political and organizational skills. *Time Magazine*, in a 1970 essay devoted to Alinsky, suggested that he "has possibly antagonized more people—regardless of race, color, or creed—than any other living American" (March 2, 1970, p. 56).
>
> To Alinsky, conflict was the road to progress, sharing of power the essence of democracy. His targets were most often city officials, corporations, and slum landlords. His tactics included boycotts, pickets, rent strikes, and a variety of imaginative stunts. . . . An important example of a contemporary change agent with national influence is Harvard psychiatrist Robert Coles. Through his 13 books and more than 350 articles he has worked to communicate the message that most poor whites and blacks and working-class whites are healthy in mind and courageous of spirit. According to Coles, they are possessed of untapped strengths that if utilized and understood, could be most important for America (*Time Magazine*, 1972). . . .
>
> Change agents need not be professionally committed to social change over time. The 1950's and 1960's saw many fluoridation battles across the United States, and dentists led the way. Since dentists are not known as a group for their role innovating behavior,

this was a most important example of an issue finding advocates. Irwin Sanders (1969) says, "Many dentists have been thought of and many thought of themselves as repairmen rather than medical men. ... They were said to be more interested in techniques of filling teeth than of viewing caries as a disease." Yet, they assumed a public/ political role having the customary successes and suffering the usual failures common to the political arena. Given the right issue and the right time, individuals (and professionals) ordinarily removed from the public arena will risk their image and participate in political processes. (Demone 1978, pp. 11-12)

What emerges is a picture of a charismatic agent as a source of concepts. Either a powerful personal magnetism (ethos) and/or a contagious personal zeal (pathos) gives credibility to the ideas he or she espouses. Lobbyists, propagandists, public relations firms, advocates, fund raisers, and rumormongers are also involved in the origination and/or dissemination of ideas and issues. Their roles in the concept marketing scenario were discussed in Chapter 2.

Source Credibility

The concept initiator, as the source of the message to be communicated, has a special responsibility in concept marketing. A concept makes more sense to the audience when it is promulgated by a reliable and dependable person or organization. But credibility is diminished if an idea is first espoused and later repudiated. One is not sure about the temperature of a compress to be applied to an ankle sprain, because medical practice seems to vacillate between hot and cold. Again, whether the protein content of eggs is beneficial or their cholesterol content harmful remains a debate among nutritionists. What results is a diminution in tolerance for all sorts of health information. Idea initiators must take great pains to be certain that they present accurate and complete information before setting out on their sales territories.

Two concepts from social psychology are germane to a discussion of communication sources. The first holds that an important criterion by which an audience evaluates a source is the *reference group* to which that source belongs. This is particularly true in considering persuasive communication across cultures. The second is *congruity theory*, according to which interaction is present between the source and the message such that negative (or positive) aspects of source are mediated by opposite aspects of the message: "For example, if a negative source (an habitual drunk) says something favorable about a positive concept (fine wines), the attitude toward fine wines would become less favorable while the drunk would rise in the individual's estimation" (Lorimer and Dunn 1968, p. 356).

SUMMARY

This chapter has postulated the existence and potential importance of a concept sector in the economy. Its members are individuals and institutions initiating ideas and social issues. They were examined in a survey whose results attest to the need for formalization of the sector's structure as well as a need to market marketing to its members.

Admonishing concept sponsors to employ solid social science research in planning for concept dissemination, Harold Mendelsohn (1973) argues that "Most evidence on the failures of information campaigns actually tells us more about flaws in the communicator—the originator of messages—than it does about shortcomings either in the content or in the audience" (p. 51). This chapter has responded to that mandate.

The major issue in the emergence of a concept sector is what sociologist Max Weber described as the routinization of charisma—the exercise of influence. It has been a part of human character as far back in time from which written records are available and presumably before that. The principal purpose in this book is to convince readers involved with social marketing that it is a viable discipline. Attempts to structure and systemize that discipline should mediate the creeping, ad hoc, anecdotal nature of concept dissemination and give structure and course to the process.

PART II

4

PRODUCT STRATEGIES IN SOCIAL MARKETING

The public buys its opinions as it buys its meat, or takes its milk,
on the principle that it is cheaper to do so than to keep a cow.
So it is, but the milk is more likely to be watered.

—Samuel Butler

PRODUCT MANAGEMENT

Product management is the planning and control of activities related to
the things an organization offers to its constituents. It includes branding and
packaging decisions, product positioning, study of the product life cycle, the
product mix, product forms, product differentiation, and new product development. Although they are standard fare in any marketing treatment of ordinary
goods and services, these topics are usually considered irrelevant in the promotion of concepts. The goal in this chapter is to demonstrate their application to
the dissemination of ideas and social issues. This chapter also introduces the
theory of market segmentation because it is closely linked to several facets of
product management.

What Is a Product?

To define a product it is useful first to review the definition of a
market. A market is people, having certain needs and wants, as well as a supply
of some resource, for example, money, and the willingness to expend that resource
in order to satisfy their needs and wants. For something to be considered a
product in the marketing sense, the prerequisite is that it be capable of being
exchanged for some scarce resource (the price), an exchange that satisfies. The
product is offered by a provider or supplier who obviously places more value on

the resource than on the product, while the consumer believes there is more satisfaction or utility in owning the product than in owning the resource. So an exchange takes place.

A product, then, is anything having the ability to satisfy human needs or wants. The test for whether the thing is or is not a product lies in its exchangeability—its capability of being traded for some other commodity—for a price. Ben Enis pointed out that "exchange is differentiated from other methods of want satisfaction: origination—the creation of form utility (by discovering, harvesting, mining, manufacturing, etc.); force-taking of utility without offering a payment (for example, by burglary, war, extortion, or conquest); or gift-conferring utility without the expectation of payment" (1973, p. 58).

Other Names for Products

This broader meaning of product permits inclusion of concepts that have been referred to by various other appellations. *Public goods* are involved in those exchange transactions in which the marketer typically is a governmental agency and all individuals in the community are direct consumers because they are affected by "consumption" of these goods, which include flood control, unemployment insurance, and energy conservation programs. They are purchased in exchange for the price of taxation. Society, through its institutions, determines that certain public goods (education, rapid transit, health care) are so meritorious that such *merit goods* "are produced at considerable cost, but offered at zero (or low) price" (Wish and Gamble 1971, p. 80, passim). Respect, love, and status have been called *impalpable goods* (Phelps 1975, p. 14) and are sometimes paid for with cash, but more often with such social or intrinsic prices as time, effort, psyche, and change in lifestyle (see Chapter 5). John Dewey referred to "ready made *intellectual goods*" as information provided by mass media (1939, pp. 45-46) in quite the same spirit as the present work considers ideas. Ideas and issues are called *planks* when they are placed on sale as part of a political platform. Finally, S. Levy and G. Zaltman (1975) wrote about:

> The providing or getting that goes on between people in their private lives, where the content of the exchanges that occur are such as parental attention, filial devotion, sexual gratification, reprimanding, and teasing, may be termed intimate marketing. This category is a matter of analytic perspective. Analyzed by a religious person, marriage is a sacrament; by a political scientist, it may be viewed as a power struggle or a unit with a particular sort of voting pattern; and a lawyer may note if the marriage is legally contracted. A marketing analyst would ask what each member of the marriage offers, provides, gives—in traditional parlance, "sells"—and what each member wants in return, whether interpreted as a price or as that which he "buys." (p. 42)

Whatever its name, then, the product is the "thing" that is to satisfy needs and wants of the market. Just as it was necessary to define market before discussing product, the concept of market segmentation is introduced next because it will be relevant to some of the product strategies taken up in the remainder of this chapter.

MARKET SEGMENTATION

Market segmentation is the partitioning of a market of consumers according to some criterion in order that marketing planning may be custom-tailored to suit the unique needs of each segment. By catering to differing characteristics possessed by several submarkets, it is hoped that deeper overall penetration of the target population will be accomplished. A prerequisite for a segmentation study is the selection of a criterion most likely to account for differential response to the four controllable marketing factors, and on the basis of that criterion, partitioning the market, that is, forming submarkets such that each submarket is different in some way from the others. Ideally the differences between these groups should be indicative of the unique manner by which each group responds to differences in product offerings and/or to differences in the promotion strategy planned by the marketer.

Segmentation research is typically carried out by consumer survey. The survey instrument contains questions designed to take measurements not only on the segmentation criterion, usually selected in advance, but also questions to measure other characteristics (variables) about the consumer. Together the discriminating criterion as well as the other characteristics make up the total set of variables in the study. It is the average values on all these measurements that yield a profile of characteristics for each segment, profiles providing some idea as to how the segments differ. They offer clues as to how product design and promotional campaigns may be differentiated for each segment.

How Many Segments?

The chief objective of segmentation is not merely to increase product acceptance, but to do so efficiently. At the extremes, either only one segment exists, that is, the market is presumed completely homogeneous, or there are as many segments as individuals (competely heterogeneous). How many should be specified? With fewer segments, the marketing task is simplified; appealing to too many segments can become expensive and unwieldy. (In a Department of Transportation campaign, no less than 23 target audiences were identified for promoting the 55-mile-per-hour speed limit. They are listed in Table 4.1.) Yet one wishes not to overlook significant differences between target subgroups.

Ideally, a segment should be sufficiently large such that it is worthwhile

TABLE 4.1

Audiences for Promotion of the 55-Mile-per-Hour Speed Limit

Young drivers
Older drivers
Commuters
High-mileage drivers
Truck drivers
Vacationers
Drivers observing 55
CB radio users
Bus drivers
State employees
Police
Judges
Legislators
Media personnel
Medical profession
Lawyers
Trucking companies
Bus companies
Teamsters Union
Corporations
Insurance companies
Automobile clubs
Service organizations

Source: Department of Transportation 1978, p. 33.

cultivating with a custom-made marketing mix. If too few customers make up a submarket, it usually will not pay to modify the product, price, promotion, or distribution to suit those individuals. The optimum number of segments, then, is a compromise between the largest number accounting for actual group differences and the smallest number containing a worthwhile number of target individuals. Usually, clusters of segments can be combined to form a smaller total number of segments.

Criteria for Segmentation

The crucial aspect of this process is the selection of the criterion upon which the segmentation scheme is to be based. There is a large body of literature dealing with the choice of segmenting criteria (see, for example, Frank, Massy, and Wind 1972). Of all the criteria upon which consumers differ, which should be selected for a particular segmentation strategy? Virtually every product suggests one or more criteria, and one selects the criterion believed to be most relevant to the focus product/situation. For example, to promote "Buy union label" one might segment on the basis of preference for American goods versus imports; the marketer of legalized gambling could use some attitudinal measure as a relevant criterion; a fair housing study might segment on frequency of job relocation.

In an empirical study of the social product, mass transit, Christopher Lovelock (Lovelock and Weinberg 1978) segmented a market based upon various travel characteristics. Church nonmembers have been segmented into three classes called resisters, disinterested, and uninformed (Kotler 1980). A study in India showed that interest in birth control devices could be determined by examining external features of the dwelling occupied by the family, and Senator George McGovern's 1972 presidential strategists found that Volvo owners were a fruitful source of campaign contributions (Dionne 1980). Finally, physical features such as terrain and rivers, could play a role in segmenting for what has been called spatial diffusion of innovation:

> First, anything that moves must be carried in some way. Secondly, the rate at which some things move over geographic space will be influenced by other things that get in the way. Thus we must consider initially the carriers and the barriers that can influence particular movements . . . of ideas spreading through a group of people. (Abler, Adams, and Gould 1971, p. 389)

Sometimes a total market of consumers is segmented not on one criterion, but by a general descriptive category described by several criteria. The aim is to find different groups to address and then to plan different means of approaching each.

In summary, an effective segmentation program must ensure that:

1. The segmentation criterion selected is appropriate for the particular product.
2. Individuals belonging to different segments are likely to react differently to one or more marketing policy instruments.
3. Those within a given segment demonstrate relatively homogeneous behavior.
4. The number of segments formed is such that it is economically feasible to reach the most important target groups.
5. Segments be sufficiently large and reachable so as to warrant individualized cultivation.
6. The program will lead to modification or manipulation of one or more marketing mix components. In other words, should the newly identified segments be addressed by modifying the product (next section), the price (Chapter 5), promotion (Chapter 6), or distribution (Chapter 7) strategies?

PRODUCT STRATEGIES

Branding

A few years ago, a man named John Adams won the Republican nomination in New Hampshire's First Congressional District. Adams was an unemployed taxi driver who did almost no campaigning. He made no speeches, issued no press releases, spent no money. He figured that with a name like his he didn't need to. People choose products, including political candidates, based on the familiarity of the name (*Newsweek*, September 27, 1976, p. 36).

The motivating objective in branding strategy is the creation of habitual purchase of the product by consumers. A brand name, once remembered, vastly facilitates repeat purchase because the product and its name become closely associated with each other. In fact, successful branding strategy results in a name that becomes virtually synonymous with the product and often carries more status than the product itself. Thus one is more likely to contribute to campaigns of the United Way than to just any program of combined charities. People quickly develop confidence in a brand product and enjoy peace of mind from the perceived assurance that a "good buy" was made. They also perceive higher degrees of quality and reliability in a brand, all of which increases familiarity and automatic and loyal devotion to the brand. While many Americans abide by the 55-mile-per-hour speed limit, the state of Connecticut developed a particular reputation for diligence in policing speed laws. Its campaign assumed the status of a respected brand, the Connecticut speed laws, which stood out among those of neighboring areas. Upon entering Connecticut's highways, drivers became especially aware of their speedometers.

A brand name should be promoted with the goal of making it well known, respected, and even generic. At the same time the assignment of a brand to a concept serves as an incentive to the sponsoring organization to create and maintain high standards. For long-term welfare of the firm, the producer of a brand item tolerates nothing but high-quality output.

The very name of the sponsoring organization or movement serves as an appropriate brand for an idea. Examples are Boy Scouts, Christian Dior, Goodwill Industries, ERA, Gay Rights, NORMAL (National Organization for Repeal of Marijuana Laws), I Love New York, WIN (Whip Inflation Now), Boys Town, Red Cross, New Deal, and CIA. The appropriateness of the brand name cannot be overemphasized. Thus an organization promoting education for Hispanics is called Aspira, Spanish for "aspire," and a museum in San Francisco calls itself the Exploratorium.

Criticizing institutions for neglecting the sociolinguistics of innovations, Everett Rogers and Dorothy Leonard-Barton (1978) pointed out that "what an innovation is called often is an important factor in its acceptability" (p. 490). They offered as an example government family planning programs in India, where contraceptives are taboo because they are believed to be associated with prostitution. Marketers applied a theory from the field of anthropological linguistics to the problem and changed the name of condoms from "F.L.," or "French Letters," to "Nirodh," a Sanskrit word for "protection." As a result of the name change, audience perceptions were altered and acceptance improved appreciably, according to postpromotion research.

Packaging

How are ideas packaged? In the context of the promotion of nutrition information, the question was put to a public health official of a third world country. He replied, "You can't sell sound nutrition practice in a vacuum; you must package it together with such ideas as clean water, sanitation, and preventive medical care." The implication is one that is common in conventional marketing, for example, the idea of "accessorizing" in the sale of clothing. The salesperson suggests a handbag and gloves while completing the sale of a pair of shoes.

Yet one rarely sees joint campaigns for such related causes as gun control and support the police, responsible pet ownership and antivivisection, or scouting and forest fire prevention. One might propose to the "I Love New York" promoters a package of traffic amelioration through car pooling or mass transit for visiting several points of interest, centers of performing arts, museums, and so on—the possibilities are endless. Energy conservation can be wrapped up in the same "box" as pollution control, shop by bicycle, and physical fitness (Fine 1980b). A good deal of synergy derives from combining the efforts of organizations espousing innovations that can be linked together in some manner.

The words of a great poem are no more beautiful when set in fancy type and printed in a handsomely bound volume than when the poet first scrawled them on scratch paper. Yet, until the poem was attractively packaged, few could appreciate it. A scholar presents a new theory by packaging carefully written sentences into an article, which is delivered to a consumer audience. Indeed, the term vehicle is used to mean a journal said to "carry" the article. Abstract products need the application of correspondingly intangible packaging principles.

Product Positioning

The strategy by which the marketer attempts to carve a unique niche for a product within a marketplace of competing projects is called "product positioning." It is employed with the objective of finding differential advantage for the product. Comparison is made on the basis of those characteristics or attributes (taste, color, texture, durability) deemed most relevant. The use of product attributes as a basis is rooted in the mathematical concept of a space such as the two-dimensional space depicted by an x-y plane. The point $(3,2)$, for example, is positioned by counting off three units along the x axis (dimension) and two units along the *y*. If the variables *x* and *y* are specified to represent, respectively, power and fuel economy, then an automobile may similarly be positioned in that "product space." Of course, automobiles, like all other products, possess more than just two attributes, but only two may be drawn on a two-dimensional sheet of paper.

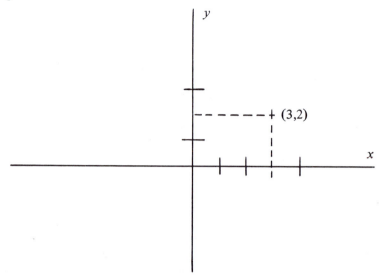

One could draw a three-dimensional product space and include another attribute, say, length, legroom, or some other pertinent attribute. More attributes yield a more thorough positioning process. Marketing researchers have a procedure called multidimensional scaling for statistically exploring virtually any number of attributes. This analytic technique makes it possible to compare simultaneously competing products on the basis of many dimensions.

To translate the idea of product positioning from the realm of tangibles to that of concepts, one need consider the set of attributes appropriate to ideas and social issues—relative advantage, compatibility, complexity, trialability, and observability—defined in Chapter 1. In addition to these universal attributes, specific products may be identified by some unique attributes. Thus the idea of using motorcycle helmets ranks high on the attribute of trialability, because one is not forced to buy "all or nothing," as with the adoption of vasectomy. Trialability is a universal attribute, that is, virtually all concepts can be measured along a trialability dimension. But helmet use advocacy can also be rated, for example, on a convenience continuum, which is applicable to only some concepts. A comprehensive program of product positioning takes into account both the universal and the product-specific attributes. But it is not an easy task to operationalize attributes of concepts:

In the marketing context, it is very difficult to define the attributes of brands that give rise to differences in the worth of those brands. Describing the value-generating attributes of social alternatives is even more difficult. ... (However), failure (to give the matter serious attention) would be an admission that improved social alternatives and individual social choice behavior are the products of painful trial and error. (Pessemier 1972, p. 5)

While attributes are objective descriptors inherent in the design of the product, they may or may not constitute the precise criteria on which consumers make the purchase decision. Individuals make subjective perceptions or interpretations about attributes. These are called choice criteria: "It is essential to distinguish between the attributes *per se* and consumers' perceptions of these attributes, because consumers differ in their perceptions. It is the perception that affects behavior, not the attribute itself" (Howard 1977, p. 28).

It is tempting for a marketer to specify attributes and to construct a product space containing those attributes as dimensions. But that is a producer-oriented view. More meaningful, although more difficult to conceive, is a preference map, the dimensions of which are not attributes but choice criteria. Ideally, positioning should be based on consumer perceptions.

Positioning and Segmentation

The real problem here is that the theory of product positioning refers to characteristics that are product-specific and hence involve attributes. As soon as one introduces factors differentially preferred by individual consumers, strategy shifts from product position to market segmentation theory. A product is positioned on the basis of characteristics inherent in the product but markets are segmented based on characteristics of the consumer, as will be demonstrated in Chapters 8 and 10. The concept of the 911 emergency number can be positioned low along a complexity axis. On the other hand, its adoption also depends on the user's trust in the police, a choice criterion peculiar to the person and not to the product. If a very large majority of people score high on trust in the police, the market can be considered homogeneous, a single segment. But if two or more submarkets exist, for example, low scorers and high scorers on trust in the police, then positioning on complexity is confounded by the heterogeneous nature of the population.

"Don't Drink and Drive" is another case in point. This is a very trialable product, but is also one whose promotion typically evokes fear—fear of accident, or fear of the police. Product management could dictate, then, positioning this concept on trialability and then segmenting the market on the basis of fear appeals. (Some British "Think Before You Drink Before You Drive" commercials pull no punches, employing gory illustrations of people flying through windshields.)

When utilizing product positioning to examine market needs vis-a-vis product offerings, the institution's strengths and weaknesses must be kept in mind. If the supplier's existing resources and capabilities permit a particular type of offering that differs from that which the consumer seems to be demanding, then something needs to be done to correct the mismatch. This calls for either internal changes at the supply side or a communication strategy designed to modify market preferences. Government programs for vocational training of the hard-to-employ have recently faced this sort of dilemma. Most programs under the Comprehensive Employment and Training Act (CETA) prepared recruits for entry-level jobs and paid very little attention to their capacity to remain on the job beyond a minimum initial period. But employers were more concerned with benefits accruing to themselves from long-term relationships with employees than with just satisfying their temporary needs. The basic idea of federally supported vocational training had to be repositioned. The product was not "employ the hard-to-employ," but rather, "we'll help make the hard-to-employ easier to employ." The product was shifted to a more positive position on an employability dimension by modifying the program to include a psychosocial component (detailed in Chapter 8).

To summarize, product positioning involves the following: (1) Determining just what the competing brands are. They could be other brands of the same class, or they might be substitute or alternative things vying for the consumer's attention. A high school graduate in quest of career formation strategy can choose between two universities, or decide to postpone higher education in favor of a job. (2) Determining the most important criteria by which consumers choose the products under study. Graphically, the researcher is limited to sketching two or at most three criteria on a sheet of paper. (3) Determining where on these dimensions the product and its competing products are situated. (4) Plotting the position deemed by consumers to represent their most desirable choice, the ideal point. (5) Examining the relative positions of the focus product, competing offerings, and consumers' ideal and from the resulting picture framing strategic plans for product design and the other marketing factors (promotion, pricing, and distribution).

Product Differentiation

Product differentiation is the practice of rendering one product different from another. The difference might be real, for example, in design, color, or package, or it could be a difference perceived by the consumer, as when high quality is attributed to something because a high price was paid for it, or because it was purchased from a prestigious merchant. A strategy of product differentiation may enable the marketer to position a new product (or reposition an existing one) as distinctly different from other products already on the market.

This strategy may have two underlying objectives: to justify a difference in pricing or method of promotion and to cater to unique needs of some particular market segment.

Clearly, product differentiation strategy follows logically from that of market segmentation. If segmentation research reveals the existence of sub-markets having unique needs or tastes, and if those markets are large enough so as to be worthwhile to cultivate, then it makes sense to offer a product to match the unique needs of each group. Writing about knowledge considered as an innovation, Gerald Zaltman (1979) states: "An innovation-related guideline is: If discernibly different user groups exist, consideration should be given to the need for correspondingly differentiated knowledge. It may be necessary to design different versions of an item of knowledge to maximally satisfy different user characteristics" (p. 90).

The strategy of product differentiation, or what might in this book be called "concept differentiation," is implemented by adding a unique twist to the product offering. For example, proponents of minimum wage laws might think of a codicil ensuring some level of productivity to employers. The school prayer issue might have been presented with a provision permitting individual prayers. The "Save Chrysler" campaign planners, aware of differences in various audiences, beamed different messages to labor, to business interests, and to government officialdom.

Sometimes a product is differentiated to so large a degree that it assumes an entirely new form—the subject of the next section.

Product Form

A social product is available in various forms just as, for example, an automobile may be had in the form of a sedan, compact, and so forth, and health services might be obtained in preventive or ambulatory form or by recorded phone call (Tel-Med). Summer school is one form of the class of products called education. The form in which a product is to be marketed depends upon the nature of the need to be satisfied by the particular offering. An example is seen in the concept of nutrition. The form taken by a nutrition program depends on the type of malnutrition it is to relieve. Nutrition researchers at an eastern medical college have found that certain maladies of the elderly are vitamin-based and have developed a malnourishment preventive package for the aged. Where the problem is inefficient overconsumption of meat (3 to 6 pounds of grain are needed to yield 1 pound of most meats), the idea is to espouse mitigation of such waste. This is the situation in many postindustrial societies such as the United States. Other types of overnourishment similarly call for demarketing. The lifestyle of the sit-down family dinner is giving way in America to rushed overstuffing:

"And no sooner is the table cleared and dishes washed, then the eating starts again. Someone makes a sandwich. Older kids go out for a while, come back with friends, fix food and do homework together, or sit in front of the TV and snack." A bedtime snack is the rule, not the exception, says Dr. Fine, and even then it doesn't end—"People can't sleep, they are restless, they are hungry. They get up and raid the 'fridge,' the pantry for cereal, eat apples and cheese, raid the leftovers they would not eat at dinner." (Star 1973, p. 36)

Allen Griff suggests replacing the "good for you and good tasting concept" of marketing themes with the idea of "pleasure in moderation," an idea already provided by the alcoholic beverage industry (Griff and Mead 1978, p. 39).

In most other parts of the world, of course, the problem is undernourishment. There programs must assume the form of a scheme to assist the household in operating within the limits of its nutritional resources in order to maximize for all members the benefits to be obtained from these resources. The actual formulation of each particular malnourishment prescription in a given locale will depend on which foods are most readily available, which are most compatible with current tastes and preferences, and to some extent, physiological tolerance to certain foods. For example, milk is an excellent source of calories for all people but has differing tolerance response across racial types: About 60 percent of Ashkenazi Jews have low tolerance for milk, while for Anglo-Saxons that figure is 10 percent. The U.S. recommended daily allowance (RDA) of calcium for a pregnant or lactating mother is 1.3 grams, but whether this amount is obtained from milk, leafy vegetables, or citrus fruits will depend on ethnic factors, among other things. One prominent nutritionist, David Call, attests to the "complete lack of scientific consensus (on the particular prescription) among nutritionists in many countries" (in Berg, Scrimshaw, and Call 1973, p. 204).

The concept of product form suggests a strategy enabling the consumer to distinguish among several types of product offerings. The aim is to make a unique type available to suit distinct needs of each market segment.

The Product Life Cycle (PLC)

As with living organisms, most products follow a cycle from their inception, through periods of growth, and to eventual demise. Marketers are interested in knowing just where along the product life cycle (PLC) a given offering resides at a given point in time. Each stage could require a specific marketing mix with different combinations of promotion, pricing (not necessarily dollar pricing—see Chapter 5), and distribution components. Social products similarly follow stages analogous to the pattern hypothetically assumed for ordinary products, and in fact insights into the life cycle of social movements are covered in sociological writings. Calling these "stages in the life cycle of a cause," Philip Kotler (1971a) presented a scheme reproduced in Figure 4.1.

FIGURE 4.1

The Product Life Cycle of a Concept

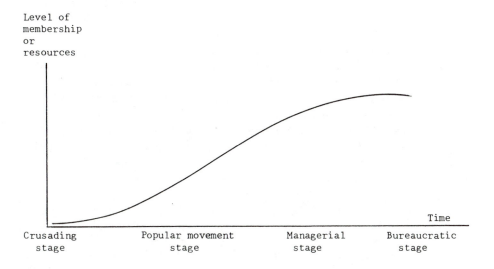

Level of
membership
or
resources

Time

| Crusading | Popular movement | Managerial | Bureaucratic |
| stage | stage | stage | stage |

Source: Kotler 1971a, p. 697.

In the crusading stage, a primary goal is to enlist followers. A large number of supporters is crucial because early adopters are known to comprise an important word-of-mouth channel. Furthermore, idea marketers need a large following if only so that later promotion messages can boast of having many advocates. For example, the idea of car pooling is being touted by mass transit organizations and various interstate transportation authorities. That idea is likely to become more popular, as will the use of solar energy, with continued increases in fuel costs. On the other hand, nudism seems destined to remain within an early stage for a variety of reasons, including societal reactions to nudism and nudists' feelings about those reactions. Similarly, adoption of the metric system must overcome deeply rooted habits. The crusade by utilities of the idea of nuclear power is also meeting with popular resistance. Such ideas remain in the crusading stage for a long time.

Interest in an idea enjoys its most rapid growth during the popular movement stage when the zeal of the original crusaders is augmented by new supporters. The issue of illiteracy amelioration, for example, has been formally adopted by the advertising profession concerned with increasing the size of audiences for print messages. Universities will be stepping up the promotion of continuing education in the effort to compensate for expected declines in new enrollment.

Interestingly, the early crusaders for that product were not marketers but consumers, the turn-of-the-century immigrants.

The managerial stage is characterized by a shift in emphasis from the issue itself to the individuals who manage the sponsoring institutions: "As the ranks of this movement swell, new problems must be coped with, such as developing clearer definitions of roles and responsibilities, and attracting adequate resources to keep the organization going. New types of leaders start being favored—those who have organizational skills" (Kotler 1971a, p. 698).

The recycling of waste materials, a popular issue for some time, is gradually being absorbed by private sector firms, which find new avenues for profit in the movement. In the bureaucratic state, the shift in focus is more confirmed. The goal of organizational survival is considered above that of advocacy of the cause: "The cause is run like any other business with a product to sell, with a rigid hierarchy, established policies, much functional specialization, and so on. Even the job of maintaining a following and support is handled as a specialist function" (Kotler 1971a, p. 698). Examples include consumer cooperatives, housing authorities, and many fraternal organizations. Interest in politics as an idea, has, in the last 40 years, followed a life cycle somewhat resembling the Kotler model. One may assign names to four arbitrary stages in the PLC of politics, as suggested in Figure 4.2.

The life cycle of one social issue, reforestation of denuded areas, may be predetermined mathematically. The cause is vigorously taken up at times when timber liquidation exceeds replanting rates and abates when stands are permitted to grow to maturity. But the optimum rate of tree harvest is determinable by formula as a function of timber acreage and life span of the species. Cries for reforestation can be predicted to follow large-scale premature harvesting (although to be sure, "preserve nature" campaigns arise at other times as well). It is sometimes possible to link the marketing PLC to factors inherent in particular situations, in this case botanical stages.

A great many concepts are of such a nature that the more rapidly they move along the PLC, the sooner they decline. That is, the more widely they are adopted, the sooner does the need for them come to an end. These are called single-purchase items and include population control, shoplifting prevention, foreign aid, cancer research, and literacy, to mention a few. They may be labeled self-terminating because their PLCs share the common characteristic that rates of decline are directly proportional to rates of adoption. Hence their very adoption leads to their demise, an automatic or self-terminating process.

Organizations sponsoring self-terminating ideas have a special need for "encores" waiting in the wings. Social marketers must ask themselves the same hard-nosed question so often raised by forward thinking product managers: "What will we offer for an encore?" What is more, that question must be asked early in the life cycle of a product, long before the product approaches its decline. When the need for military recruitment draws to a close, one wonders why the elaborate apparatus that has been established—the kiosks, the personnel, the

FIGURE 4.2

The Product Life Cycle of a Concept, 1948–76

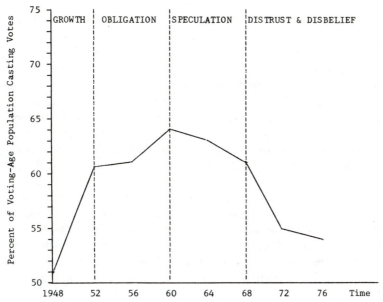

Source: Adapted from Manuel D. Plotkin, *Statistical Abstract of the United States* (Washington, D.C.: Bureau of the Census, 1978), p. 520.

advertising programs, and so on—are dismantled. These facilities could, with little effort, be converted for use in promoting any of a large number of new causes. This issue is revisited in the next section.

Even if the offering does not die, it might become fatigued and wear out from decline in interest, as William Novelli reported in the case of a hypertension control program; he suggested: "This brings us to a need for product restaging (revitalization) a la package goods marketers (the 'New and Improved' syndrome)" (1980b).

Stages of a PLC are by no means discrete as described. The process is continuous and its pattern often erratic and difficult to forecast. The theory cannot serve as a universal guide to planning but rather as an instrument to measure the effect of planning.

The Concept of Product Mix: New Product Development

What about the entire mix of products offered by an institution to its consumers? Is the assortment too wide, too narrow, or just right? What is "just right?" Often these are difficult questions to answer, but generally it does not make good business sense to be a "one-product house." Sometimes very little additional investment of resources is required to broaden the product mix to include one or two ancillary products. If the product mix is too broad, it can become unwieldy and difficult to manage. If it contains too few items, the organization could become overly dependent on the success of any one of them.

A sound strategy of product (or idea) management calls for a succession of new products along a gamut of readiness ranging from those approved and ready for launching, all the way back to those still on the drawing board, or just germs of ideas. These are the "encores" awaiting introduction as soon as the present star performers begin to lose ground. Reiterating an earlier point, no sooner is a new product launched than a newer product must be developed to follow its predecessor, to generate sales volume when the first item begins to decline. The March of Dimes nearly had to close its doors because it waited until the polio scourge was resolved before deciding to adopt birth defects as a cause (Gaedeke 1977, p. 348). It is not inconceivable that child adoption and foster parenthood agencies will turn to related causes, such as child abuse prevention, because the success of the abortion movement has radically reduced the supply of babies available for adoption. The idea of product continuity is most relevant in multiple issue organizations, such as the Urban Coalition and the American Civil Liberties Union. These groups have no less a need for research and development than does General Motors.

One may argue that when the mission is accomplished, it is appropriate that the institution close its doors, especially if it has become bureaucratized. Is it artifactual to search for problems only because established problem-solving apparatus is at hand? Under certain circumstances, a goal of survival of the organization might be highly justified, as with fund raising, advocacy, and many social causes. The bureaucratic instinct for self-preservation is very real. In other instances, it seems reasonable that objective attainment should spell demise. For an extreme example, an army is better equipped and better trained at the end of the war than at any other time, yet it does not, these days, look for other wars to fight. Whether social technology should or should not be institutionalized only to preserve resources remains a debatable question.

Translated into business language, that question asks whether concept producers rank survival as a high priority goal. According to the study described in Chapter 3, survival was listed as a main objective by the smallest number of sponsoring institutions; most indicated their main objective was to educate. But these were self-reported responses and must be seen in that light. Preservation of jobs and maximization of organizational size and complexity (in the Weberian spirit) are latent and entirely understandable goals of all or most institutions.

The foregoing discussion about perpetuity of the product mix raises still another matter. Some social products seem to warrant a place in an ongoing institution; others are best handled in venture format. In the former category one sees those ideas and issues pertaining to such ever-present needs as health, crime prevention, world peace, and ecology. But concepts arising from traumatic or short-lived circumstances are usually marketed more dramatically and with greater impact by a single venture, or task-force approach. Examples include "Save Chrysler," "Free the Hostages," the two-dollar bill, and voter registration.

Positioned between the organizational format and the one-time venture are the self-terminating causes whose sponsors, although institutional, should disband when their purposes have been achieved. Clearly, the nature of the product or mission determines the organizational form.

Research and development strategies for expanding the product mix typically begin with suggestions for ideas through such techniques as brainstorming, defined as a process of generating creativity in group discussion relative to a problem. Ideas from a brainstorming session are just the possible solutions to the problem, the unique marketing method for attacking problems as described in Chapter 2. In conventional product management, idea generation is only the first of a sequence of R&D steps—concept screening, concept testing, technical and financial feasibility study, physical development, product use testing, and test marketing. But with an institution mandated to disseminate a social product, idea generation is itself the entire R&D process, because the idea *is* the product.

It is interesting in this connection to note the method employed by membership-oriented groups to select the product mix of social issues they are to promulgate. These are groups, such as the League of Women Voters and Common Cause, that purport to support and promote important current issues but are at the same time vitally concerned with growth in membership. As such, the search for issues is often performed among members rather than the public at large. In June 1971, Common Cause (Gardner 1972) conducted a referendum within its membership, producing the "issue mix" listed below, in order of importance:

1. Withdrawal of all American forces from Vietnam
2. Environmental protection
3. Revitalization of government
4. Equal opportunity in every aspect of American life
5. Overhaul of the criminal justice system
6. The elimination of poverty
7. Health-care delivery
8. Improved education
9. Decent housing for every American family
10. Programs to foster family planning
11. Improved urban transportation
12. Rural economic development
13. Employment programs
14. Consumer protection
15. Sustained economic growth

(At the present writing, Common Cause's primary concern is with energy conservation.)

A similar R&D procedure was followed by the National Council of Jewish Women (NCJW), combining general members' opinions with those of selected individuals invited to participate in a Delphi panel. (A Delphi panel is a technique of surveying experts in one round of interviews, which is then followed by additional rounds until consensual results can be drawn.) The organization recognized its need for strategic product planning: "Social issues constitute potential products for the NCJW in its role as a private, nonprofit service organization. The planning committee was, therefore, confronted with the task of preparing a market opportunity analysis within the context of social marketing" (Parameswaran, Goldstucker, and Greenberg 1978, p. 355).

The study produced the following list of issues, sequenced, as before, in order of importance to members:

1. Need for reform in public education
2. Multitude of problems relating to breakdown of family
3. Needs of senior citizens
4. Disregard for rights of children
5. Need for energy conservation
6. The high cost of medical and health care
7. Unemployment
8. Problems of the disadvantaged
9. Need for reform of juvenile justice system
10. Declining importance attached to present Jewish heritage
11. Inefficient criminal justice system
12. Women's issues
13. Environmental pollution
14. Privacy and constitutional rights
15. Problems related to mental health
16. Administration of national organization

Finally, another area of new product development in concept marketing is the process of constructing political platforms. Here again a candidate often faces conflict between taking positions believed to be in the best interest of the nation and "offering for sale" those concepts desired by local constituents, the voters. Deploring the latter, the marketing approach, J. William Fulbright (1979) criticized: "The new breed of Congressperson seems more inclined to test the market first, to ascertain what is in current demand, and then to design a program to fit the market" (p. 19).

Expansion of product mix sometimes crosses lines that separate ideas, goods and services. Roger Ricklefs (in Gaedeke 1977) describes how museums run gift shops and conduct festivals celebrating the cultural heritage of ethnic groups and foreign peoples. The Oakland Museum in California reportedly attracts thousands of visitors to such festivals. The Metropolitan Museum of Art in New York City has even conducted industrial nonprofit marketing of an idea as it "licenses Springs Mills Inc. to adapt sheet designs from the Met's 18th and 19th Century textile collections. In exchange, the sheet maker pays the Met royalties of more than $200,000 a year" (p. 171).

Libraries similarly have broken out of their traditional role as book lenders:

> In the Salinas, Calif., library, teen-agers have brightly painted a young-adult room where they hold guitar "jams." In the current-events room of Pittsburgh's Carnegie Library, a United Press International news-printer clatters away 12 hours a day. In Erie, Pa., a child can borrow a guinea pig from the library for a week; its juvenile department also boards mice, rats, gerbils and a 42-inch boa constrictor for children to play with. (Ryan in Gaedeke 1977, p. 173)

PROBLEMS IN STRATEGIC PLANNING FOR SOCIAL PRODUCTS

The social product strategist encounters essentially the same marketing dilemmas as does the conventional marketer, plus a few others that are born out of the very newness and abstract nature of the concept of ideas as products. Paul Bloom and William Novelli (1979) cite two particular product strategy problems confronting social marketers. The first is a loss of flexibility in product design due to governmental restrictions associated with many ideas. As examples, they note that "social marketers may be able to market only one way to get a home insured against floods or one way to get a child immunized" (p. 7). One may add that the 200-mile fishing limit, tax shelters, prayers in school, and draft registration can only be promoted within frameworks provided by statute. Second, they point to the difficulty in formulating product concepts:

> They frequently find that the "product" they are selling is a complex behavior which may, in some cases, have to be repeated over a considerable period of time. It therefore becomes difficult to formulate a simple, meaningful product concept around which a marketing and communications program can be built. Effective concepts like a "squeezably soft toilet paper" and an "extra thick and zesty spaghetti sauce" do not come readily to mind when thinking about selling behaviors such as drug-therapy maintenance or the use of an in-home colon-rectal cancer detection test (i.e., the hemocult test). (p. 7)

SUMMARY

This chapter has attempted to demonstrate the application of product policy and strategy familiar to marketing practitioners to their counterparts in the concept sector. Briefly, sound product management is achieved if acceptable answers have been found to four fundamental questions:

1. Who is our market? The marketer wishes to identify a potential audience in terms of its size, needs, wants, and readiness to relinquish scarce resources in exchange for the product offered.
2. What is the best way to partition or segment that market?
3. What is our product? Exactly what, in the first place, is the thing to be offered to this audience?
4. What are the opposing forces competing with us and what is our comparative advantage? An assessment must be made of the institution's ability to provide the product more effectively than any other in the industry in the face of countervailing influences.

Answers to these questions lie in the systematic formulation of product strategy. Ideas and social issues should be branded, packaged, positioned, and examined in terms of the same strategic factors with which conventional offerings are merchandised. Products rarely exist in isolation but rather are marketed as part of an assortment or "mix" containing other items or other forms of the same item to suit varying tastes of target market segments.

5

BEYOND MONEY: THE CONCEPT OF SOCIAL PRICE

He is well paid that is well satisfied
—Shakespeare, *Merchant of Venice*

Although ideas and issues are often spoken of as being great or weighty, they have no mass, cannot be physically delivered, and are not ordinarily exchanged for cash. Yet, for a marketing transaction to take place, something must be paid out by the purchaser. This chapter delves into price as a marketing factor and calls attention to a reality of pricing sometimes overlooked by marketing planners. That reality is the concept of the price—beyond the monetary price—paid by an individual in purchasing a good or a service, but especially in adopting an idea or taking a side on an issue.

Many characteristics associated with a particular product offering are studied by marketers as product attributes, while the possibility that these very characteristics may be perceived by consumers as integral parts of the price paid in purchasing that product is overlooked. Thus the amount of time spent waiting for attention at the doctor's office may in one context be construed as an attribute of that form of health-care service. However, viewed in another light, the time expended might be seen as a nonmonetary price paid in addition to the cash fee. Other nonmonetary prices include the effort expected of the habitual driver who turns to mass transit, and the shame endured by the adopter of the idea of a radically unusual hairstyle.

In any given situation, whether a characteristic is likely to be perceived as a product attribute or as part of price will not always be obvious. The important

―――――――――――

A version of this chapter was presented at the American Marketing Association Conference on the Marketing of Services, Orlando, Florida, February 9, 1981.

concern to marketers is the determination of which viewpoint suggests more effective strategies for marketing planning. That is, if consumers do indeed perceive themselves as expending resources beyond money when they make purchases, it becomes important for purveyors to take into account these "things" given up in exchange for the product offerings.

The price vs. product attribute distinction may be restated in terms of what has been called the "approach-avoidance" concept. Product attributes comprise an approach vector because they attract the consumer whereas price factors repel him or her. The latter are components of an avoidance vector. The model thus has an element of pleasure/pain theory built into it (Sheth 1980). These considerations have their most obvious usefulness in the planning of promotional strategy, but they may also be important in the design of the product itself.

PRICE

Price is the most quantifiable, tractable, and readily analyzed element in the marketing mix. It is virtually the only marketing factor addressed by economists. Price is generally defined as "the amount of goods, services, money value of the same, (that is) set as the required payment given by the buyer for some amount of goods or services offered by the seller" (Alpert 1971, p. 4). This definition applies whether the price is called admission, assessment, charge, collection, compensation, contribution, dues, fare, fine, fee, honorarium, levy, interest, penalty, premium, rent, reward, tariff, tax, toll, or tuition.

The Monetary and Social Components of Price

The price construct has two components. One is that which is most generally associated with price, the price paid in cash by the buyer to the seller. The other is a nonmonetary or intrinsic component extending *beyond* money, which is "paid" by the buyer in every type of exchange:

> ... the price can also be nonmonetary. Thus it can include many things more personal than money, such as time, effort, love, power, prestige, pride, friendship, and the like. Alcoholics Anonymous, for example, charges a very high price—commitment not to drink and public admission of one's problem. The Third Nail, a drug rehabilitation center, expects its clients to abstain from drugs and to contribute time and effort toward the maintenance of the center. (Shapiro 1973, p. 130)

It is suggested that nonfinancial prices be formally distinguished from money prices and the appellation social price be assigned to the former. Other terms could be used: ancillary price, supplemental price, collateral price, intangible price, intrinsic price, symbolic price, psychic price, and so forth. But the term social price seems most appropriate, particularly because it resonates well within the social marketing rubric. The notion of social price is exemplified in such everyday remarks as "We paid dearly for . . ." or "Freedom at any price"; one is said to "spend" time and "pay" respect, compliments, and attention.

A Compensatory Formulation

The total price one pays in an exchange is made up of the financial amount and the sum of various social prices, that is,

$$P = p_m + \sum_{i=1}^{n} P_i \tag{1}$$

where P is the total price, p_m is the monetary or financial component, and P_i represents the set of social prices associated with the transaction. According to this model, a marketer can so construct a "price mix" that financial and social components might compensate one for the others.

The compensatory formulation is based on a heroic assumption of additivity, which is, of course, open to debate. The terms of the model are additive if and only if each term is independent of the others. On the other hand, if for example, time and lifestyle depend on each other, that is, if, for example, more time spent causes greater change in lifestyle, then the model is multiplicative (interactive) and not additive with respect to those two variables. For a better known illustration, price and advertising are interactive because heavy advertising can often justify selling at a higher price and vice versa. For example, "The parking 'problem' may be interpreted as an implicit decision to keep the money price artificially low (zero or a nickel in a meter) and supplement it with a waiting or time price" (Thompson 1968). Similarly, Christopher Lovelock and Jon Twichell (1974) mention the sacrifice of comfort (from overcrowding in mass transit facilities) that accompanies the adoption of a low-fare program.

Virtually every purchase, whether tangible or intangible, no doubt involves some admixture of both financial and social prices. In fact Adam Smith attached great significance to the latter: "The real price of everything, what everything really costs to the man who wants to acquire it, is the toil and trouble of acquiring it" (in Kotler 1975, p. 176).

The concept of social price is entirely analogous to the economic idea of psychic income, the psychological benefits derived by individuals, benefits considered as substitutes for money, as when one accepts a lower salary for a higher status employment position. The idea that man does not live by bread (or money) alone holds true whether one speaks of (psychic) income or outlay (social price).

FOUR TYPES OF SOCIAL PRICE

Four categories of resources are suggested as those given up by individuals as payment (beyond money) in exchange for product offerings: time, effort, lifestyle, and psyche. Marketers may profitably assume that target consumers are aware of these social "price tags" fastened to every form of exchange (Fine 1981a).

Time

A good many expressions synonymous with the aphorism "time is money" have achieved cliche status. What they all mean is that time expended in an activity represents benefits foregone because that time was not spent in some alternative manner, the economic notion of opportunity loss or opportunity cost. The social price tag labeled "time" is perceived by the consumer to inform him or her of the opportunity loss or benefits to be foregone because of the time spent in making a purchase (at least in a market society; in many societies time is not considered so valuable). It has been said that important intellectual progress occurs at a time when poetry is popular. But adopters of the idea of poetry must pay a time price to write, read, and listen—a price that many harried postindustrial individuals just cannot afford to pay.

Effort

Expending one's effort in exchange for a product offering is merely bartering one's services in that exchange. This can take the form of physical action, as in the case of maintenance assistance by a parent at a cooperative nursery school, or in the travail of participating in an alcoholism program. Continual or repeated payout of effort results in fatigue that is heightened if the effort does not return satisfactory reward. George Homans (1958) points out that a person thereby "incurs *aversive stimulation* or what I shall call 'cost' for short. . . . Fatigue is an example of a 'cost'" (p. 598).

Effort is also sacrificed in giving information in an exchange; information is an important human resource (Dixon 1978). As an illustration, a wholesaler's salesman is welcomed by retailers who accept his knowledge and news of the industry in payment for their allegiance. The salesman is glad to pay this social price, even to the point of making a deliberate effort to amass a store of gossip with which to compensate his clients for their valued friendship. Another example is the exchange of a lighter prison sentence for the police informer who pays for that product with information.

Lifestyle

Modification of one's lifestyle is a price paid in many forms of exchange, as in adopting the idea of marriage, for one example. While some may thrive on diversity and change, most individuals look upon the prospect of disruption of the status quo with at least some trepidation, and this is true whether the anticipated change is for the better or for the worse. The social price of advancement to a better job could be the diminution or elimination of camaraderie with former colleagues. The prospect of having to make new friends is an awesome assignment for some people. A touching example is given by Margaret Mead (1955):

> The iron plough has sometimes been resisted as an assault upon the land. In villages in the United Provinces of India, it threatens established human relationships. A man inherits a relationship to a carpenter family whose task it is to make and repair the plough. This family is always invited to the farmer's feasts, and the women are given saris. The relationship, the "pay," the gifts continue whether ploughs are made or not. . . . Perhaps the farmer can be taught to repair his own plough, but it would mean personal reorientation as well as a change in the valued relationship structure. (P. 192)

One reason for the recent increase in single-parent homes is that many are unwilling to pay the price of lifestyle change in exchange for marriage. As S. Levy and G. Zaltman (1975) expressed it, "A common complaint is that married men dislike paying the price of saying 'I love you,' and in consequence, many marital deals fall through" (p. 42).

Psyche

Part of the price of an exchange often amounts to a forfeit of self-esteem, pride, identity, self-assertion, privacy, control, freedom from fear or risk, or other such losses affecting a person's peace of mind; they are thus grouped under the heading of psyche. When the American Cancer Society undertook to distribute Hemocult kits for self-screening of colon-rectum cancer, two major obstacles were encountered. One was hesitancy to supply a smear of stool as part of the examination. Then too, the program met with a great deal of reluctance to risk the possibility of learning the grim truth of affliction. These two psychic factors are readily seen as making up a high social price to be paid for cancer prevention as an exchange.

Also included in this category is the contribution of one's attention to something—one "pays" attention. Richard Bagozzi (1975) points out that "an exchange can occur between a person and a television program." The "person gives his attention, support, potential for purchase, etc." Earlier, T. S. Robertson

(1970) had carried this idea still further, adding to attention the social price of loss of self-assertion:

> In attending to communication, the individual incurs *costs* and receives *rewards*—an exchange process exists. Costs incurred in attending to mass-media advertising include time and submission to "influence," since it is recognized that advertising is persuasive and one-sided. The reward involved is information, which may be meaningful to the consumer and which may be of value to him in his consumption behavior. . . . It can be proposed that, basically, communication will occur up to the point at which marginal reward from an additional unit of communication equals the marginal cost attached. (p. 52)

ECONOMIC PERSPECTIVES

In all transactions some value is placed upon the commodity being exchanged, and a price based on such value is determined in the open marketplace. In the case of market or economic exchange, the price is explicit in that cash or some other resource convertible into utility passes from buyer to seller. But in nonmarket or social exchanges, the value of the offerings might at first blush not appear to transfer to the seller. Does a marketer obtain utility from a buyer's relinquishment of such resources as time, effort, lifestyle, or psyche? If not, then nonmarket transactions are not exchanges at all, but merely unidirectional doles or gifts.

However, upon reflection, a seller's utility is often increased as a result of the consumer's payment of social price. The transit authority, by deploying fewer trains, exacts a higher social price (of all four types) in addition to the money fare charged its commuters. However, in the process, the authority surely enjoys economies in personnel salaries, fuel, and so forth. In attending to and complying with an antilittering campaign, the effort price paid by a "consumer" is passed on to the "selling" community in the form of utility of cleaner streets. Moreover, there accrues to the seller of social products advantages of consumers' behavior changes, as well as benefits derived when the consumer passes the idea along to others, for example, advocating nonnuclear power, opposing the ERA, continuing to car pool, and so on (Belk 1980).

Reciprocal Trade

Two or more offerings (and their respective prices) are sometimes traded in a reciprocal transaction. For a social marketing illustration, Peter Blau (1955) describes the exchange of advice among agents in a law enforcement agency:

> A consultation can be considered an exchange of values: Both participants gain something and both have to pay a price. The questioning

agent . . . implicitly pays his respect to the superior proficiency of
his colleague. This acknowledgment of inferiority is the cost of receiving assistance. The consultant gains prestige in return for which
he is willing to devote some time. (p. 108)

Thus the consultant's product offering is advice, which is paid for with a forfeit-
ure of self-esteem by the questioner. The latter's product, in turn, is prestige sold
to the consultant at a price of time.

Social Price, Social Cost, and Public Price

Social price as defined above might be confused with two somewhat homo-
nymic terms, social cost and public price. In fact Gerald Zaltman and Nan Lin
(1971) mention "social cost (as) another form of expense" in the adoption of
innovations by individuals, explaining that: "Social cost may come in the form
of ridicule, ostracism, or even exclusion or expulsion from some relevant reference group" (p. 660). While that point is substantively consonant with the thesis
of this chapter, their terminology is believed to be less than accurate. The expression "social cost" has a specific economic meaning quite different from the price
of adoption as defined by Zaltman and Lin. Social costs are not expenditures by
individuals, but, according to K. W. Kapp (1971), refers to the costs imposed
upon other members of the community when those members perceive that they
suffer from the ill effects of the operation of some enterprise—smoke from generating plants, barren mounds from strip-mined areas, and so on. These have
been referred to as "nonpecuniary externalities, such as higher noise levels (as in
the case of air traffic) or in pollution" (Brown, Schary, and Becker 1978).

Public prices, on the other hand, are payments by people within a society
for the performance of such services as police protection and sanitation (ordinarily in tax dollars) and includes license fees for restaurants and taxicabs
(Mushkin 1972, p. 5).

To illustrate the use of these three expressions, assume the product is a
political candidate, or more specifically, the idea(s) espoused by that candidate.
Voters pay social prices in the form of time and effort to cast votes. Election
expenses funded with tax monies constitute public price, and should the elected
official turn out to be corrupt, society sustains a social cost of enduring the evil
effects of corruption.

The Measurement Problem

An obvious deficiency in this inquiry is the absence of yardsticks for
measuring social prices. This is analogous to the measurement problem in cost/
benefit analysis, a problem that has frustrated economists (Mishan 1976). Monetary prices are, of course, measured in terms of cash, a scarce resource. Although
social price is, in general, not readily quantified, it is also measured in scarce
resources. To be sure, the quantity of time available to a person is limited, and

FIGURE 5.1

Time Price vs. Financial Price

Dollars

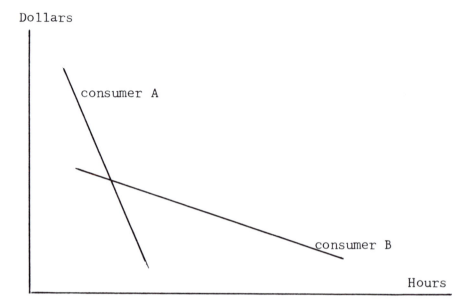

Source: Adapted from Mushkin 1972, p. 99.

similarly, although less measurably, the amount of expendable effort is limited. How much psychological ordeal and lifestyle change can be tolerated without ill effects is an open question.

One could attempt such measurement by self-report questions of the type: "How much more would you be willing to pay if you were assured a polite salesperson?" Resulting measures would of course just be perceptions and hence of questionable quantifiability. But value as measured by financial price is similarly the result of consumers' perceptions. When one leases an automobile, a bonus is paid over and above the cost of ownership in return for the peace of mind that accompanies freedom from repair and replacement responsibilities. The difference could be taken as the exact psychic price paid by one electing ownership in favor of leasing. Such substitute modes of consumption, based on perceptions, offer clues as to how some social prices may one day be measured as the state of the art of consumer psychology is further refined.

On the other hand measurement of the time price has not been overlooked by economists (Dewees 1976, for example). Smolensky, Tideman, and Nichols (in Mushkin 1972) give a reason for this interest: "Time prices also have intuitive appeal because time as such is more equally distributed than money" (p. 95).

They point out, however, that the wealthy often substitute money for time, as depicted in Figure 5.1. The consumer, represented by line A, is willing to pay a relatively high cash price and a low time price for a product, and conversely for consumer B.

Just as differential calculus provided the method for deriving marginal utility from total utility, thus adding deeper meaning to general concepts of price, economic science, and its younger cousin, marketing science, may now be ready for a new calculus, one that will permit measurement of nonmonetary prices discussed in this chapter. A detailed and cogent statement in that direction appears in Edgar Pessemier (1972), discussing what he termed "Measuring the Individual's Judged Worth of Social Alternatives."

IMPORTANCE OF SOCIAL PRICE IN MARKETING

Price, as a controllable strategic marketing factor, is given added importance through the awareness of its nonfinancial component, p_i, in expression (1). In the same way that ordinary prices are "set," so too should social prices be employed by incorporating into the marketing mix those considerations perceived by consumers to constitute their total contribution to the exchange transaction and not just the cash component. This awareness could uncover new promotional opportunities with such themes as "The time you save may be your own," etc. The four price categories outlined above also suggest dimensions for "price positioning" a product offering against competing products, an exercise that could enhance the product planning process.

The concept has particular significance with respect to those exchanges falling within the domain of social marketing. For example, advocates of social change are virtually unanimous about the positive effects of participation in the planning process by those to be affected by the program (see, for example, B. R. Bradshaw and C. P. Mapp 1972). Yet such participation ordinarily means "payment" by target consumers of all four types of social price described in this chapter. It seems plausible to conclude that it is precisely because participation is so "expensive" that it is so desirable. People want to feel that they have some control in the shaping of their destiny. They are willing to invest in such control and indeed are uncomfortable if participation is not available to them for "purchase."

Implications for Further Investigation

Like their financial counterparts, social prices can be psychological prices, that is, those perceived by consumers to be surrogate measures of product quality—the higher the price paid, the higher the quality attributed to the product, and conversely. This area has been well explored in connection with monetary price, and one may conjecture that conclusions ought to be quite similar with respect to social price. Are we not more suspect of the quality of the food at a restaurant if, on a Sunday evening, there is no wait for a table?

Economic principles provide contexts within which social price may be further examined. One of these is the notion of consumers' surplus, the excess of price that the consumer would be willing to pay rather than go without a given product over that price actually paid. Another is indifference curve analysis. The consumer is said to be indifferent as to which of many combinations of goods are to compose an optimum market basket subject to the constraint of a given monetary income. In a similar vein, can one speak of an optimal bundle of adoptable concepts, subject to constraints of available time, effort, and so forth? It is hoped that such threads may be woven by interested consumer researchers into meaningful extensions of concepts expressed in this chapter.

SUMMARY

Price as a marketing factor is presented as possessing an important nonmonetary component in addition to the financial aspects ordinarily considered when one thinks of price. That component for which the term social price is advanced is in keeping with increased social consciousness pervading current business thought. It is a kind of extension of the marketing concept that ever more concern for consumers' needs must guide marketers in constructing the optimal mix of product, price, promotion, and accessibility of product offerings to the market. For expository purposes a broad spectrum of social prices is partitioned into four classes: psyche, effort, lifestyle, and time. Under each of these headings are the resources beyond money that individuals give up in exchange for tangible goods, services, and the "purchase" of ideas and issues.

If a consumer's perception of a product attribute is less associated with the product, per se, and more as being "paid" (in some sense), then that attribute rightly falls within the domain of price, and the perception might be studied in that light. The suggestion is made that marketers employ this concept in the design of the products themselves as well as in framing promotion messages and in other aspects of strategic planning. This would be entirely consonant with trends toward increased interest in psychological aspects of consumer theory.

6

THE COMMUNICATION OF IDEAS

I should not hesitate to prefer newspapers without government, to government without newspapers.

—Thomas Jefferson

Promotion plays a key role in the marketing drama, and promotion is essentially communication. This chapter deals with communication within a framework known as the communication model, which includes the communication's objective, source, message, channel, audience, and effect. Because the source has been covered in Chapter 3, and channels and audience are the subjects of Chapters 7 and 9, respectively, this chapter focuses on the objectives, message, and effects of the communication. First, historical and sociological aspects of communication are discussed.

The very root of the word communication implies community. The Latin origins of the word community, moreover, mean "to build a wall or fortifications around a town or city." While we usually think of community as inclusion, it also involves the idea of exclusion. Communication has the same conceptual difficulty. When we "build community" or "offer a communication," we include insiders and exclude outsiders. The discipline of marketing encounters a parallel

This chapter has benefited from collaboration with Dean Charles Nanry of Rutgers University, a sociologist, for whom the topic of communication holds a more than passing appeal. The author trusts that readers will find refreshing this interdisciplinary perspective in the otherwise strictly marketing orientation of this book. In point of fact, "interdisciplinary" is increasingly becoming a byword within the marketing field. What is perhaps the foremost scholarly vehicle read by marketers, the *Journal of Consumer Research*, bills itself as "an interdisciplinary journal." Marketing has become a richer and more exciting subject as a result of its eagerness to welcome thinking minds from its neighboring social sciences.

problem in assessing patterns of acceptance and rejection of goods, services, and ideas.

The social marketer sees the market itself as a mechanism by which transactions occur. Sociologists, among many other social scientists, regard the business exchange process as one in which communicators take advantage of the symbol-creating, and hence symbol-reacting, nature of humans.

The advertising industry has long understood this characteristic: the tendency of human beings to personify and to symbolize. From the aura of affluence of the person who owns a Packard to the cuteness of the Pillsbury doughboy, symbols are being loaded onto car frames and wheat flour. Putting buyers and sellers together is the function of marketing and the sine qua non of the marketing society. Symbol manipulation is one of the tools of this activity and, of course, symbol manipulation is accomplished through communication. The goal of any promotion campaign is to create a "community of buyers"; the goal of idea marketing is to create, through appropriate symbol manipulation, a community of convinced adherents to some cause or plan of action.

A HISTORICAL PERSPECTIVE

Everett Rogers and F. F. Shoemaker (1971) point out that the essential basis for the modern sociocultural approach to communications resulted from clues out of rural sociology in the early 1940s. One concern, for example, of agricultural researchers in this period had to do with the adoption of new hybrid corn strains by midwestern farmers (Ryan and Gross 1943). It was found that hybrid corn salesmen reached a few farmers who were willing to experiment and that these early adopters then either did or did not (for a variety of respectable sociological reasons, such as their status among fellow farmers) persuade neighbors to adopt the new strains of corn. The adoption of innovations in a variety of nonagricultural fields also built up a body of theory and research. The work of William Fielding Ogburn, a pioneer American sociologist, himself well aware of rural sociology, had an impact. His theory of cultural lag—based on a large body of empirical work that ranged from agriculture to aviation—suggested that cultural adoption, a group process, always lagged behind technical invention and innovation (see Chapter 9).

In the 1950s the work of a group of researchers out of Columbia University's Bureau of Applied Research made an important additional contribution to the innovation and diffusion of social communication literature. These studies, summarized in *Medical Innovation* (Coleman, Mendel, and Katz 1959), focused on the adoption by physicians of a new wonder drug. The researchers found that in each research setting certain doctors who held positions of influence based, for example, on their roles in medical societies, served as gatekeepers in persuading other doctors to adopt the new drug. The methodological breakthrough represented by these researchers, however, stemmed from the source of data used, namely, the study of pharmacy records that revealed which doctors ordered what drugs for their patients. Thus an objective source of data rather than subjective self-reporting by doctors themselves provided more credible information of the diffusion-adoption process.

In the 1960s and 1970s a great deal of information accumulated in the area of sociological research on communications. Sociologists have been both eclectic and quick to pick up on the work of psychologists and others in the field. Much of this research is well summarized in the work by Rogers and Shoemaker (1971) and in *Theories of Mass Communication* by Melvin DeFleur and Sandra Ball-Rokeach (1975). On the empirical side one might summarize most of the empirical findings of the last two decades by suggesting that the diffusion-adoption process follows a J-shaped curve until saturation occurs or there is an interruption by some new innovation, at which point S-shaped models fit the data best (DeFleur and Ball-Rokeach 1975, p. 15). The hybrid corn and medical innovation studies established the empirical models that have held for some time now.

As Rogers and Shoemaker (1971) point out, the empirical tradition in the area of innovation-diffusion-adoption has been dominated since the 1960s by researchers in marketing (pp. 68–69). An excellent integrative summary of this research exists in Rogers (1976). But one must exercise caution in interpreting and applying the vast fund of empirical research in this area from the field of marketing because most of it applies to actual products produced for profit. Nonbusiness applications, and especially the marketing of ideas, will likely demand creative rethinking and experimentation.

Theories of Communication

Rogers (in Pool 1973, pp. 290–312) suggests that the process of communication can be reduced to a few basic theories. The first is the hypodermic needle theory, which holds that messages move from one single source to a destination sequentially; it is not very useful outside carefully controlled laboratory settings because it ignores group process. The second is Joseph Klapper's (1965) two-step flow hypothesis in which an opinion leader filters and interprets information for his or her followers. Groups and group dynamics were brought into communications research by Klapper, an important advance.

Rogers goes on to suggest that many theories based on one-way mass media communication, that is, communication that is noninteractive, can be described as disguised one-step flow models. The key to understanding one-step communication flow is that individuals are "atomized," separated, and do not communicate with one another about the content of the communication. This is mass communication in the limiting case of the truly mass society (Kornhauser 1959). In mass society each individual may be thought of as compartmentalized, cut off from balancing sources of information and subject only to those officially communicated. All large-scale modern societies are massified to some extent—the issue revolves around how near the average citizen is to Winston in Orwell's *1984*. The one-step flow notion may apply to totalitarian societies and to "cut-off" segments of other societies, but not to most modern social systems.

The final pattern suggested by Rogers is the multistep flow model. In this model the exact number of steps involved in any communication process depends on the intent of the sender, the availability of mass media to the sender, the extent of exposure to the message by individuals, and the nature of the message and its salience to the audience exposed to it. His formulation represents an attempt to marry process and structure. It also incorporates the possibility of interaction among those receiving messages. This final model, Rogers claims, now dominates communications research and theorizing. It also bridges a gap between psychology and sociology.

Idea Marketing: A Special Case

In a recently published article, Michael Rothschild (1979) suggested that marketing communication techniques for public and nonprofit sectors create a unique set of problems. For individuals, involvement is either very high or very low (one is in the movement or not), benefits are often hard to perceive (why should I drive more slowly if I can afford the gas?), and the cost may be high (why should I go out of my way to look for recycled paper products?):

> Problems more prevalent in nonbusiness cases include the intangibility of nonbusiness products, the nonmonetary price of purchase, the lack of behavioral reinforcers, the need to market an entire but heterogeneous society/market and the extreme levels of involvement, varying from very low to very high. Because of these factors, the transference of marketing principles to nonbusiness is far more complex than had originally been thought. (Rothschild 1979, p. 1)

Very often only weak personal benefits can accrue from doing things that will benefit the commonweal. The issues involved in the marketing of ideas may be quite intangible and hard to demonstrate in, for example, an advertising campaign. The work of Rothschild and others suggests that in the nonprofit/nonbusiness area, where most products are ideational in nature, much greater concern must be given to the milieu in which the target of marketing techniques exists. It is in this area that even closer attention to the traditional concerns of sociologists must be given.

IDEAS AND GROUPS: THE NEED FOR GROUPS TO ACT

Key questions arise from the sociological perspective that determine the real goal of such things as advertising campaigns. Is a target group open or closed to outside communication? What is the position of the communicator vis-a-vis the target group? What is the status of the sender? What is the power relationship existing between sender and receiver?

The answers may turn on a series of insights in a neglected sociological classic, *Improvised News*, by Tamatsu Shibutani (1966). Shibutani suggests that the way in which communication really takes place is not through some "hypodermic needle" or even one-step flow, but rather through a group process. Each and every group has a need to act as a group. In order to act as a group, the members of the group must have group-relevant information. If there is a lack of information, the group will either take whatever information it can get or it will create it. Rumor becomes not an evil thing but merely the work of a group to supply itself with the information it needs to act. Thus the task of idea marketing becomes one of supplying the best and most humane sorts of information to groups that will, in the long run, act. The only hope is that situational conditions will make it reasonable to act, in the long run, in the best interests of the society as a whole.

Let us look at the task of the idea marketer in "selling" an alternative thought pattern and course of action to someone at the end of either a link or chain of communications. We take as given the Shibutani principle, that a group will form some basis for acting or not acting. The social always precedes the individual, that is, ready-made units beginning with the family are already in place when social awareness occurs sometime in the first year of life.

This principle can be extended to basic sociological categories, such as class, ethnicity, nationality, sex, and so on. It can also be extended to "artificial" (socialized) categories that constitute opinion groups, associations, and other social forms that we recognize as "real" social forces in the real world. As we age, any communication flows and eddys around contours of opinion and behavioral patterns that exist a priori. Individuals are entrapped by some groups by virtue of birth, and must, if they are so inclined, escape them only with great effort. Some groups are joined and resigned at will and with varying degrees of ease. Just as the shark must always swim and never rest in order to exist, groups must always have an agenda else they will fade and die *as groups*. (Individuals may certainly live to join another group.)

Getting on the agenda for a product made attractive through advertising to a consumer with discretionary resources is relatively easy. Getting an idea on the agenda of some group to the point where that idea is deemed to have group value is most difficult, unless that idea is part of the very fabric of group life. Thus the marketer of ideas must find an idea "whose time has come," that is, articulate a notion that is already passively a part of the normative structure of some group (saving the saved). An idea whose time has not come must be "sold"; it is not readily bought.

It is a truism that people live in groups. Group characteristics from the biological to the normative form the very essence of the individual self. Yet some groups to which an individual belongs are more salient, more powerful, than others. There are levels of group participation and influence. The very existence of a group as a group depends upon the creation of "we-feelings" by the members of the group itself. For some members the maintenance of the group may be of grave concern; for others it may not.

For the purposes here we can think of a group as having a core of members characterized by their intensity of interaction, that is, the core members communicate with one another often and with outcomes that have behavioral and attitudinal import for each other. Beyond the core may be still others who, in varying degrees, are active participants in group life. Meanings and plans of action for this second level of group members are affected by the group. They experience attitude and behavioral changes along with the core members of the group but with less intensity and with less far-reaching effects on other aspects of their everyday lives. They may be those who support group activity with contributions of either time or money or both. A third level of group life involves those who may be thought of as passive participants: They usually follow the "party line" but without major involvement in the life of the group. Passive participants, for example, make up the bulk of membership in American political parties.

In most cases the idea marketer will be asked by some core group to expand the core itself along some axis represented by a key idea, which, in turn, represents a plan of action for an even larger constituency of active and passive participants. At other times the idea itself may constitute the focal point for the creation of a core group. In either case the marketing of ideas represents an intelligent use of knowledge about how groups behave and the employment of that knowledge to bring about some desired social change.

The concept of disseminating an idea is predicated on the notion that groups seek plans of action. Core members of any group are in the business of supplying paradigms (models) of behavior and attitude to other members and to those who constitute the audience for the group, consumers. If the model of communication outlined below represents the formal structural aspects of the flow of ideas, group life and its constituent elements represent the process whereby that structure is brought to life.

In the context of communication two factors help define the impact of group life on the communication process. One, with a long tradition in social psychology, is the notion of commitment (Kisler 1975). Getting a core group to focus its activities on some idea and bringing about a set of conditions where the group devotes its efforts to "selling" that idea to others tends to galvanize the sense of we-feeling within the core group. This "missionary effect" submerges doubts, and the level of commitment to the group rises as an individual preaches the party line. Speaking out, especially in public, brings about a kind of benign brainwashing that leads one to firmer conviction.

A second factor, which also spreads ideas, is "the strength of weak ties." This concept has grown out of sociological research on social networks. It is a fact that one's particular communication network consists of friends and acquaintances usually made up of persons like oneself (it is, in other words, homophilous or similar). Close attraction facilitates effective communication. There is cohesive power in weak ties of friendship and acquaintance, although the commitment to ideas from such networks may be quite shallow and may lead to compliance only when countervailing forces are either very weak or nonexistent (Rogers 1976, p. 299). A brief example from the research literature may clear up the meaning of these two limiting factors on the process of group communication.

A Case in Point: The WCTU

In his book on the temperance movement, *Symbolic Crusade*, Joseph Gusfield (1963) points out how several small, very committed core groups such as the WCTU (Women's Christian Temperance Union) went about the business of gaining wider support in the latter half of the nineteenth century for anti-alcohol sentiment in the larger American population. Historical forces, such as resentment against immigrants (especially the Irish) and the growth of Protestant fundamentalism, conspired to strengthen their position. Gusfield then poses an interesting question about the failure of the movement after it had gained its greatest success: the adoption of Prohibition through an amendment to the U.S. Constitution.

It is clear from his analysis that the strength of weak ties became so stretched that the central idea of Prohibition got lost. Such a broad coalition was formed in order to get the Eighteenth Amendment passed that the members of that coalition began to fall apart almost immediately, once that limited goal was reached. Such widely diverse groups as the Anti-Saloon League and the Ku Klux Klan found themselves in coalition. After 1920 it was impossible for them to get congressmen elected or to have any real political effect. The temperance concept meant too many things to too many people, and the shallow ties across competing core groups led to the downfall of the movement.

Ideas live or die in a particular group context (market segment) and prepare for the weakening of support at the very moment that support grows. Linkages across groups can cause problems, as Martin Luther King found when he came out in opposition to the war in Vietnam and lost support for his civil rights positions. Coalitions are risky because they involve the linking of core groups that may be less able to take advantage of the weak ties phenomenon. For marketers of ideas nothing can substitute for a clear sense of the normative and likely network ties of market segments lending support to some position being sold and to understand the compromises necessary in order for the idea to remain sold.

THE COMMUNICATION MODEL

These historical and sociological perspectives provide a backdrop for a discussion of the communications model. Its six components are:

Objective: The objective of a communication refers to the purpose for which some message is created. It is the attempt to sell some idea to others and to frame a way of expressing that communication so that it has an intended effect.

Source: The source of a communication refers to the person(s) or organization placing a communication "out there" in order to convince, warn, or persuade some audience about the benefits, dangers, or existence of some product or idea (see Chapter 3).

Message: The message is the communication itself objectified in some way so that it is accessible to others. It may be an object, words, or an image that is used to describe or personify an idea.

Channel: A channel is the medium through which communications flow. If I talk to you about something, the channel is word of mouth; if I place a public service announcement on television, the channel is the mass media (see Chapter 7).

Audience: The audience refers to the receivers of the communication; the audience may vary in size from one to many. It may be targeted by communicators (segmented advertising based on demographics, for example) or it may be quite general—the scattergun approach.

Effect: This component refers simply to what happens as a result of the communication process. Do people do something because of the communication? Do they do it now or later? Is the change in attitude or behavior or motivation lasting or only passing (impulsive)?

The objective, effect, and message are taken up below.

The Objective of the Communication

An idea marketer must first decide the objective, the purpose of a communication program. In some cases the purpose will be to teach or to inform an audience. In some other cases the purpose may be simply to pose questions that an informed citizenry ought to have before it. Some communications, such as those sponsored by a mental health association, may be to convince people that their behavior (anxiety) may be quite normal and that anxious feelings are experienced by nearly everyone. Here the message may be very subtle, that is, teaching someone to discriminate between normal feelings and those that move one beyond the normal category.

Still other communications may be of the imperative type, telling people the law, for example, in order to warn them of their potential liabilities. The various campaigns to get aliens to register every January or to get young men to register for the draft are of this type. Some campaigns may have the purpose of creating new role models for people to either follow or recognize. The conscious attempt to employ black actors in TV commercials may be even more important than the actual objective of the message itself. The idea that is marketed is carried within the context of product marketing, but may surpass it in importance.

The Adoption Model

The marketing approach to goal setting in communication planning is synthesized in what has been terms the adoption model:

> Awareness
> Interest
> Desire
> Action

That approach asks: How far down the adoption model do we wish to take the consumer? The adoption model is not only a set of objectives to be achieved but is at the same time the possible effects to have attained if the campaign is successful. The theory holds that until the audience is aware, it cannot become interested; only then can desire be generated, and only then can action be expected. If we set out only to stimulate interest, and end up achieving cooperative action, we have indeed been successful beyond our expectations. On the other hand, let us say our objective is to develop desire among consumers and we have only gained their awareness, then we have fallen short in carrying out our strategic planning. Thus the adoption model provides a checklist from which to select objectives for a social promotion campaign, as well as a yardstick with which to measure effects of the effort. For that reason the adoption model has often been called a "hierarchy of effects."

It is generally felt that "mass media rarely have direct effects; they influence change only through interpersonal processes" (Westley in Zaltman 1973, p. 224). Mass media advertising creates awareness and interest, while word-of-mouth communications must be called into play to complete the job of actual adoption (action). This is a vast simplification of the two-step-flow model of communication but it has been validated in many empirical studies.

Communication Effects

In addition to communication effects specified in the adoption model, several other effects may be anticipated from promotional efforts in social marketing. For one, Rogers and Shoemaker (1971) refer to the "diffusion effect." They describe a cumulative effect whereby an increasing amount of pressure is exerted on nonadopters to adopt as the level of knowledge and adoption increases in the population. ". . . as the rate of awareness and knowledge of the innovation increased up to 20–30%, there was almost no adoption. Then, once this threshold was passed, each additional percentage of awareness-knowledge in the system was associated with several increases in the rate of adoption" (p. 163).

Another effect of social cause communication is that messages are most readily received by target segments having least need for them and most slowly received by segments having greatest need. For example, pamphlets and other media employed in nutrition and birth control promotion typically reach higher class, more literate segments and neglect the rural poor who have a more compelling need for such information. Describing nutrition education in India, F. J. Levinson (1972) reports:

> The annals of well-meaning educators are filled with episodes of neatly arranged demonstrations attended only by the well-to-do. The educators track down the lower income mother and deliver their message to a nodding, acquiescent woman who then totally ignores it. The educator throws up her hand in horror and stomps away to write another report about the ignorant villager. (p. 78)

As a result, a situation evolves something like that described by the adage, "the rich get richer and the poor have babies." P. J. Tichenor et al. (1970) called this the communication gap hypothesis (pp. 159-70), explaining that "one effect of mass communication is to widen the gap in knowledge between two categories of receivers" (high and low in socioeconomic status).

Rogers proposed extending the scope of this hypothesis to deal not only with the cognitive (knowledge) effects of communication but with the affective (attitudinal) and connative (behavioral) as well. He (1976) suggested the more encompassing name "communications effects gap" (p. 233).

Another communication effect to be sought is the absorption of the message by means of a kind of spontaneous intuition among target individuals. It becomes stylish for target individuals to talk about a concept, such that awareness virtually permeates the atmosphere. It becomes the "in thing" and is accomplished through careful strategic planning.

Better known in marketing is the carry-over effect over time and space, according to which one may expect greater impact on an audience as time passes. Closely related to the carry-over effect is the sleeper effect, holding that delayed responses can be expected to result from repetitions or "pulsings" of message exposures over time more than from the immediate stimulus. William McGuire (1976) describes it as causing a "gradually increasing persuasive impact" (p. 309). Finally, although by no means exhaustively, the halo effect ensures acceptance of an idea related to one's larger sphere of interest. Thus an audience known to be fond of outdoor living is likely to approve of a bill for nature conservation.

Although these communication effects are difficult to measure, their careful consideration during the planning stages of a social promotion effort has obvious long-term importance.

The Communication's Message

Messages designed to promote social causes should conform to certain general principles if campaigns are to enjoy maximum effectiveness. Marshall McLuhan's technological reductionism—the medium is the message—is of little help, as in that formulation, message/symbol is simply combined with medium/symbol. In general, the design of a promotional message requires: (1) A decision as to the basic appeal or theme about which the message is to be structured. This theme underlies all other aspects of message design. (2) Determination of a suitable approach, that is, whether the appeal is to be rational or emotional. (3) Creation of the actual copy.

Messages may be designated according to type of persuasive appeal:

> Logos (logic of the claim)
> Pathos (emotion, need)
> Ethos (emphasis on the source)
> Fear appeal

Studying 23 public service announcement (PSA) commercials for ideas and issues, Jerry Lynn (1974, p. 629) found most positive attitudes toward PSAs using emotional appeals.

Choice of appeals in social cause promotion should match cultural and intellectual characteristics of the target market. This point was made clear in recent failures of attempts to promote birth control in India. Appeals were made to patriotism, common sense, and intellect, among a population "constantly beset by internecine quarrels among at least 14 major cultures" (Martin 1968, p. 54). These appeals fell on deaf ears of people who were more concerned with health, appearance, longevity, and having enough children to provide security in later years.

Several writers have focused on pros and cons of fear appeals in messages designed to bring about behavioral change. A fear appeal may cause anxiety, which can have either of two opposite effects. The anxiety can evoke hostility, withdrawal, and a negative response to the message, or it can produce a driving motivational effect that can spur a recipient on to opinion change and adoption behavior. McGuire (1976) takes the former position, arguing in favor of messages that suggest solutions to problems rather than appeals to fear about problems (pp. 304, 7, 80). A middle-of-the-road stance is probably the best approach, with a modest amount of fear to be employed.

The order of presentation of arguments in a message deserves some attention. Should the most potent point appear first or last in a communcation? Put another way, will the earliest observed part of the message carry the greatest impact (primacy) or will the last (recency)? Research findings seem divided but agree that either extreme is more effective than placing the strongest arguments in the middle of the message (Kotler 1975, p. 207).

What is important in message design is that a match be effected between the words and those for whom the words are intended: "For example, a state university might appeal to alumni on the basis of their loyalty and emotional attachment, to parents of students on pride in their children, to individuals on state pride and lower taxes, and to businesses on the basis that the university improves the economy of the state and produces well-trained employees" (Shapiro 1973, p. 126). In social marketing, message design is even more crucial an undertaking than in conventional selling:

> If one builds a better mousetrap, it will probably be taken up rather quickly—given enough advertising and adequate retail distribution. A new mousetrap requires no great revolution in anyone's life style or identity; the consumer simply substitutes the new mousetrap for the old one and life goes on unchanged. But a new social form is not introduced so easily. An innovative kind of school, a new way of dealing with poverty, a new procedure for resocializing delinquents, a new technique for rehabilitating the schizophrenic—all are likely to disrupt complex and valued roles, identities, and skills. The disruption may have widespread and ramifying effects, so that whole communities may be challenged and angered. Under such circumstances the new social invention may die of malnutrition, may be forcibly ejected, or may be so changed that it loses its essential character. (Taylor 1970, p. 70).

Message Design and the Law

The wording of the message used in the promotion of a concept could have legal implications. In fact, American law distinguishes between ideas and issues (a distinction also drawn in Chapter 1) in the following way: An idea message must be factual and its advertising expense is tax deductible; but the message in an issue ad, while it may contain biased statements, involves costs that might not pass as a legitimate business deduction. Prakash Sethi (1979) has analyzed this matter in detail, calling the former image advertising and the latter advocacy. Thus, to use the illustration discussed under the topic of advocacy in Chapter 2, if a meat packer promotes its good name, that is an idea. The message may not exaggerate and campaign costs are tax deductible. However, if the same firm were to espouse meat consumption as an efficient source of protein, it is taking a position on a controversial issue. A one-sided point of view may be taken, but in the strictest sense, the firm must pay for the program with after-tax dollars. The line between product and idea is obviously vexing to the courts as well as to philosophers and idea marketers.

SUMMARY

Following some historical and sociological insights into the promotion of concepts, three components of the communication model were discussed. These were the objective and effects of the campaign and the nature of its message. The message is tied to group concerns and the problem of making real something that is abstract to the concerns of diverse groups. The key here may be the literature on adult socialization, which stresses the notion of relevance. It is crucial to realize that any message must be translated into the language of the groups to whom a communication is directed. All communication is a translation exercise. The medium is not the message; the message is a telescoped version of group norms that may or may not capture group norms—or change them if it is powerful enough to break one set of norms in favor of another superseding set. You sell neither sizzle nor steak; you sell biodegradable packaging and humane slaughtering.

7

CHANNELS OF DISTRIBUTION IN SOCIAL MARKETING

To emphasize the importance of choosing the best medium for a particular message, "we can call to mind the simple thought that one cannot whistle an algebraic formula."

—Whitney J. Oates (in Bryson 1948, p. 28)

This chapter deals with channels of distribution in the marketing of ideas. The subject is approached by discussing channels in conventional marketing and extending the concept to apply to ideas as products.

Rarely, if ever, does an institution by itself carry out all of the operations necessary for the satisfactory completion of the marketing process. Instead, those operations—packaging, labeling, warehousing, pricing, display, delivery, service, and so forth—are usually performed by various organizations. The entire system of institutions involved in the marketing of a given product is called the channel of distribution for that product and is typically depicted as follows:

Producer
Wholesaler
Retailer
Consumer

Channel middlemen include wholesalers, brokers, agents, and so on, and each is assumed to be knowledgeable not only about its particular role, that is, which marketing functions it is expected to perform, but also how best to perform those tasks. The question of which functions are performed by which members of the channel is of lesser consequence than the strict requirement that all functions actually be performed. If a particular task is neglected by one member, then either that task is assumed by another or the overall marketing process suffers because of the neglect.

An important objective of the channel is that the product offering be made available at a time and place convenient to consumers. In fact, the distribution process is referred to as the "place" component of the marketing mix. Place is a measure of whether, and to what extent, the product will be accessible to the customer when purchase is to be effected. With any product offering, no matter how well designed, attractively priced, or elaborately promoted, the strategies and tactics leading up to the point of purchase are to no avail if the product is inaccessible to the consumer at the crucial point in time and at the proper place to suit target consumers' needs and wants.

In economic terms, place imparts time and place utility to the product offering, just as the physical characteristics of goods add form utility. Furthermore, place adds value to a product. That is, accessibility enhances the price that consumers are willing to pay for the offering. A consumer derives more utility or satisfaction from an exchange if it is available for purchase at a desired time and place and with minimum difficulty. For example, under many circumstances, an individual will perceive an object to be more valuable if it is on hand at the point of purchase than if it must be "special-ordered."

IMPORTANCE OF THE STUDY OF CHANNELS

Examination of a marketing channel provides insights as to just which institutions are involved in the distribution process, what their roles and functions are, and whether these are being adequately carried out. Any particular channel arrangement might upgrade the place utility that customers enjoy for a product, that is, marketing through either a larger or smaller number of middlemen could increase efficiency of deliveries. So channel choice has a direct bearing on accessibility. Another reason for studying channel structure is to explore alternative modes of distribution, or alternative channels. For example, a producer might wish to sell through several middlemen because each makes a unique and necessary contribution. Or he might wish to shorten the channel by selling directly to consumers. Each arrangement affords a set of advantages and also imposes certain constraints upon the producer who ordinarily designs channel structure believed to be optimal to situational requirements.

Marketing theorists have also examined channel theory in the distribution of services (Rathmell 1974). Louis P. Bucklin and James M. Carman (in Sheth and Wright 1974) present an especially clear application to the health maintenance organization (see too, Venkatesan in Zaltman and Sternthal 1975). Interestingly, the topic has drawn the attention not only of marketers; practitioners in the services sector are also aware of the importance of distribution. For example, Neil Gilbert (1972) discussed the channel for the delivery of welfare services, and James Taylor (1970), describing a psychological rehabilitation project for the poor, highlighted a network of organizations involved in the delivery of that social cause. He explained the success of that network by what he termed the "principle of coaptation," or an "interpenetration of personnel from other groups and agencies" (p. 74), such as local offices of the Division of Vocational Rehabilitation, the Office of Economic Opportunity, the Urban Renewal Agency, as well as health, school, and correction institutions.

Ideas and social issues must similarly be "handled" by various institutions making up a distribution channel in order to ensure smooth delivery to potential adopters at a propitious point in time and at a convenient place. Inviting involvement by community-based organizations may be a large step in that direction.

Channel Leadership and Control

Examination of channel structure also reveals the nature of leadership and control exercised within the system. Organizational control and the concomitant degree of harmonious relationships pervading the channel have a direct effect on the manner of delivery of the product to the customer. It has been shown that a cordial atmosphere within an institution is usually manifest by more considerate treatment to clients (Schneider 1973). The four Ps are presented in the marketing literature as controllable variables, yet control is not automatic. The institution can control distribution only if it sets out systematically to do so (similarly for control of product design, pricing, and promotion planning). Otherwise control is left to chance. Lamenting the lack of control over the distribution of health care, a hospital administrator stated:

> between the hospital provider and the health care consumer stand layer upon layer of intermediaries—physicians, insurers, citizens planning groups, and government agencies—that in fact control the choices, exercise the options, and make the decisions that are accomplished on more or less a one-to-one basis in virtually any other consumer-provider exchange. (Yedvab 1974, p. 58)

Long channels are not exclusive to hospitals. They are also seen, for example, in the travel industry where the provider-consumer exchange involving hotels, airlines, limousines, and so on, may take place oceans away from the travel agent's offices. With tangibles, too, the producer-consumer relationship is affected by the presence of a large number of middlemen, as for example, with such convenience goods as tobacco and most food products.

Competition and Conflict

A marketer is constantly sensitive to competitive forces—"noise in the system"—tending to distract the attention of the target audience from the message intended for that audience. Because competition is ever present, one seeks to maximize the signal-to-noise ratio. One must take cognizance of competing influences, such as campaigns by other organizations for the promotion of offerings that compete for consumers' funds, time, attention, interest, and other scarce resources. At a time when other campaigns are in progress, the level of advertising clutter could be so high as to diminish the effectiveness of any one promotional effort. So it behooves the marketer to scan the competitive environment for temporal, media, geographic, and other factors influencing message delivery.

On the other hand, Leon Festinger and Nathan Maccoby (1964 in Petty et al. 1976) demonstrated that, in cases where the message is likely to elicit unfavorable thoughts from the audience, distraction can actually enhance persuasion because the "noise" could inhibit concentration needed for effective counterargument.

But there is another form of conflict, quite apart from the standard variety of competition, that exists in virtually every channel of distribution, and it is called channel conflict. One might assume that the institutions in a channel for a given product are unified by the common objective of consumer satisfaction. However, these institutions are by definition autonomous and independent of each other, and quite often commonality of goals gives way to the service of self-interests of individual members. What results is channel conflict (Mallen 1977, pp. 224-25). Then too, because interorganizational relationships inevitably amount to interactions between people, a channel becomes a sociopolitical arena in which some personalities (and hence the institutions to which they belong) emerge as dominant. Indeed, one member may be accepted by the others as the "channel captain" who is then looked upon as leader, arbiter, and influencer of major decisions within the structure (Stern and El-Ansary 1977, p. 448). While satisfaction of customers' needs is the ultimate goal in any marketing process, channel members also have needs that must be met in order that the distribution operation runs smoothly. The good offices of the channel captain are often called upon to bring about harmony within the system.

Channel members are motivated by different forces—profit, humanitarian or altruistic goals—yet their activities could nevertheless mesh very well. For an example of an idea marketed by a private sector firm, consider a manufacturer of fluorides and the idea of fluoridation. Motivation for the firm is profit maximization, yet it becomes involved in a channel for distributing the idea of fluoridation. Also present in the channel are the American Dental Association and various public health agencies, whose motivation might be either altruistic, or image creation, or both. Although each organization is driven by forces to suit its own ends, the channel could be highly efficient and effective in achieving its overall purposes.

It should be noted that the channel belongs to the product, not to the institution. One does not speak of the channel of a hospital, of the Department of Health, Education, and Welfare, or of a physician; one refers instead to a channel for health care. Every product offering has a channel of distribution through which it is marketed. Whether the product is a tangible, a service, or an innovation, some system of institutions is involved in the process of distributing that product.

CHANNEL STRUCTURE FOR CONCEPTS

As with marketers of conventional goods and services, advocates of social products must concern themselves with the place component in the marketing mix. The channel of distribution for an idea or a social issue, although more abstract, is quite analogous to the channel structure for an ordinary product or service, for it is just a network of institutions involved in the distribution or dissemination of the social product from originator to adopter. The optimal set of such institutions is that which involves only those organizations making a meaningful contribution to the most efficient and effective dissemination process. This implies the presence in the channel of only those organizations performing useful functions. As in the case of ordinary products, the channel elements acting in concert make up a team for optimal delivery of the social product to the intended market.

An Action Network

A system for the delivery of an innovative idea to potential adopters is a network of outlets to which individuals can turn for information about the idea. With specific reference to social marketing, Philip Kotler and Gerald Zaltman (1971) point out that ". . . place means arranging for accessible outlets which permit the translation of motivations into actions. Planning in this area entails selecting or developing appropriate outlets, deciding on their number, average size, and locations, and giving them proper motivation to perform their part of the job" (p. 9).

Once the outlets of a channel for ideas are delineated, members' roles must be specified. For example, in the realm of public opinion, John Ferguson and Dean McHenry (1973) asked rhetorically: "What roles are played by parent, peer, teacher, clergyman, pressure group, mass media, and others? What relevance do public relations have to policy formation? How effective are social controls? Is there free competition of ideas in the marketplace?" (p. 224)

These are among the many questions that must be addressed in attempting to formulate a channel theory for social marketing. As with channels generally, the component institutions making up a channel for ideas may be divided into three classes, corresponding to producers, middlemen, and consumers. These are, respectively, the sponsors from which ideas and issues emanate, intermediaries of various types, and the target audience. Sponsoring institutions were discussed in Chapter 3 and their ultimate consumers will be taken up in Chapter 9. The middlemen for concepts constitute the subject matter of the remainder of this chapter.

The institution sponsoring a concept is generally positioned in the distribution channel superordinate to the other parties to the process and often assumes the role of channel captain usually setting policy not only for itself, but often dictating terms and procedures under which other channel members are to operate. (But not always. Sometimes organizational size determines the locus of channel power and leadership. For example, such middlemen as fund raising consultant, ad agency, university, or political body could dominate the activities of an idea sponsor, especially a smaller one.)

INTERMEDIARY DISSEMINATORS OF CONCEPTS

A host of community-based organizations (CBOs) participate in many ways in programs related to the spread of social causes. Too numerous to attempt to list comprehensively, they include the entire gamut of private, governmental, and religious bodies, grass-roots movements, and a near-infinitude of associations. Many are at the same time intermediaries as well as sponsors of ideas and issues; in social marketing it is often difficult to distinguish the producer from the wholesaler. The important consideration for the concept marketer is to determine which institutions are to be formally and appropriately included in the distribution scheme for a particular offering.

CBOs play a unique middleman role in social marketing as gatekeepers. In that role, they can increase (or decrease) the credibility of the concept "depending on the credibility which the organization itself has with the target market. This ability to directly or indirectly affect the offering, makes social intermediaries quite different from the wholesalers we think of in business marketing" (Novelli 1980b).

For the most part, intermediary elements of distribution channels for ideas are the media through which information flows. In a sense, the media are to concept marketing what wholesaler middlemen are in traditional marketing channels. In the latter realm, the media carry information *about* the product, while in the present context, information *is* the product. In fact, because a newspaper or a television screen cannot deliver an actual product, media are entirely in the idea business. The most tangible good at most is reduced to two-dimensional ideas on the printed page. Media carry ideas only.

Communication theorists generally class information channels into two broad types, mass media and interpersonal media. Mass communication channels, or what are typically referred to simply as media, include print (newspapers, magazines) and broadcast (radio, television) media, while personal channels subsume all types of personal selling and word-of-mouth processes. Parenthetically, the dichotomy mass versus personal media is a recent oversimplification. In the 1940s a communications scholar wrote, "There are many media of communications—speech, poetry, prose, music, gesture, painting, the dance, scientific formulae, and so on" (Oates in Bryson 1948, p. 28). A generation later, as

Western society hurries along toward the era of future shock, emphasis seems to shift from these aesthetic media to a communication dichotomy—either mass or personal—either one-to-one or one-to-many.

Mass Media

Print media, and newspapers in particular, play a more prominent role than radio and television in idea and opinion advertising (Wedding 1975). For one thing, television has not been too successful as a channel for ideas, as for example, the recent failure in campaigns to promote seat-belt use. Then, too, newspapers seem to feel a stronger obligation to serve as "common carriers of public discussion" (Commission on Freedom of the Press 1947, p. 23). As stated by the *New York Times* in an editorial: "The guarantees of the First Amendment are not merely guarantees of the publisher's right to publish. They are, more importantly, guarantees of the public's right to know. We consider that is what a free press truly means: the maintenance of open communication in the realm of ideas" (December 20, 1963, p. 28).

Moreover, marketers of ideas have been attracted to print media because of relatively lower costs, as well as the desire for a high degree of audience involvement in an idea. Print advertising, by permitting repetitive reading affords potentially deeper understanding of ideational messages than would be possible in a 30- or 60-second broadcast. In Figures 7.1 and 7.2 several print ads for concepts are reproduced. (See Figures 7.1 and 7.2 at end of chapter.) The exhibits in Figure 7.1 typify idea ads; those in Figure 7.2 show ads for social issues.

That print media are better suited than electronic media as channels for the communication of ideas was dramatically argued by Joe McGinniss (1969):

> Television seems particularly useful to the politician who can be charming but lacks ideas. Print is for ideas. Newspapermen write not about people but policies; the paragraphs can be slid around like blocks. Everyone is colored gray. Columnists—and commentators in the more polysyllabic magazines—concentrate on ideology. They do not care what a man sounds like; only how he thinks. For the candidate who does not, such exposure can be embarrassing. He needs another way to reach the people.
>
> On television it matters less that he does not have ideas. His personality is what the viewers want to share. He need be neither statesman nor crusader; he must only show up on time. Success and failure are easily measured: how often is he invited back? Often enough and he reaches his goal—to advance from "politician" to "celebrity," a status jump bestowed by grateful viewers who feel that finally they have been given the basis for making a choice. (p. 29)

Although newspapers are more appropriate communication vehicles for ideas, by selecting some news stories and omitting others, newspaper editors decide which ideas they will market and which they will demarket. Such editorial discretion is one way that owners and publishers influence public opinion (Ferguson and McHenry 1973, p. 234).

Radio and television media are less biased than newspapers in the dissemination of ideas, for they must conform to the FCC's doctrine of fairness and balance, according to which broadcasters are expected to present a balanced mix of entertainment, news, and public service programming. While no formulas are specified, the FCC does keep tabs on the number of public service announcements (PSAs) aired by the electronic media without charge to concept advertisers (Kitaeff 1975). These are brief, usually 10- to 30-second broadcasts of messages in support of ideas held to be in the public interest on behalf of such marketers as the American Cancer Society and local YMCAs.

A large number of PSAs broadcast by a station in the course of a year is one positive factor in the renewal of its license by the FCC. Moreover, the fairness and balance doctrine dictates that in any controversial issue a broadcaster is obligated to make time available for the airing of opposing viewpoints by bona fide spokesmen. Because many ideas, opinions, and issues might have a large number of views, each of whose proponents could demand air time, broadcasters are reluctant to adopt an open policy toward idea advertising. This is particularly true in the case of support for a political candidate. Here the requirement is that equal time be made available to all opponents.

In 1965 the American Civil Liberties Union undertook a crusade to convince mass media channels to accept concept advertising on a nondiscriminatory basis. Five years later a study by Robert Gwyn (1970) of a cross section of both print and broadcast vehicles revealed hardly any progress resulting from the ACLU efforts.

Quite apart from PSAs, broadcast media are also used in programming messages of longer (15- to 60-minute) duration, talk shows, interviews, editorials, and so forth.

Other mass media have been used in social marketing. Paul Placek (1974) found that a direct-mail campaign greatly increased interest and participation in a family planning program and fostered informal discussion about family planning—the "diffusion process" (p. 560). Several firms have made a specialty of direct-mail campaigns for the dissemination of social products, including fund raising for politics and other causes (Haggerty 1979). Quoting an executive of one such firm: "For example, a mailing prepared for Handgun Control Inc., carries on the envelope, in large type, the words: 'ENCLOSED: Your first real chance to tell the National Rifle Association to go to hell!'

"The letter inside begins: 'Dear potential handgun victim:'" (Dionne 1980, p. F9).

The motion picture is another medium through which ideas are spread, although it is often characterized by "a strong proclivity to glorify wealth, elaborate homes, and well-dressed people" (Ferguson and McHenry 1973, p. 237), as well as ideas related to sex, crime, and violence. There is some evidence negating the effectiveness of films as idea channels (Brembeck and Howell 1976, p. 39). On the other hand, in Japan, which has the highest per capita consumption of cigarettes in the world, government-sponsored posters and comic books carrying messages illustrating adverse effects of smoking have met with some positive effect. Posters have also been successfully used in India's population control program. Nutrition messages were publicized in comic books and distributed in India, where use has also been made of ". . . traditional folk media such as the jatra (traveler's talk), puppet shows, folk songs and folk dances. The attempt is to move from the somewhat urban-elitist approaches of the past into a much more imaginative approach" (*Population and Development Review*, June 1976, p. 312).

Bumper stickers as a mass medium for concept marketing have become popular. In a whimsical article, L. N. Daniels (1973) applauds motorists for using their vehicles as communications carriers to the extent that "the mass audience itself, whether it realizes it or not, is now in control of a communications medium of considerable potential" (p. 12). He lists scores of ideas and issues channeled by bumper stickers. The list includes

Keep America Beautiful. Don't Litter. Give the Indian Back His Land. Speed Kills. Try a Little Kindness. Good Neighbors Come in All Colors. Honk if You Love Jesus. Register Communists, Not Guns. Be Kind to Animals, Don't Eat Them. America, Love It or Leave It. Support Your Police. Hate Cops? Next Time You Have Trouble, Call a Hippie. Make Love, Not Babies. Warning, I Don't Stop for Iranians. Stamp Out Poverty—Work. Switch to Rice. Go Metric. Join the Peace Corps. (Daniels 1973, pp. 11, 12)

Finally, although by no means exhaustively, a recent addition to the list of mass media for causes is the imprinted T-shirt.

The promotion of ideas and issues via the mass media has increased in recent years largely through the activities of the Advertising Council. The Ad Council is a nonprofit organization through which American businesses join with advertising professionals to contribute talent and other resources in the promotion of social causes. It has two principal objectives: to improve societal welfare and to enhance the public image of the advertising industry. Harnessing enormous volunteered creativity of advertisers as well as agency personnel, the Council annually produces an estimated half a billion dollars worth of ads, or about 1 percent of total U.S. advertising volume. No other nation in the world has any such program for the promotion of social goods.

Among the better known causes fostered by the Ad Council are energy conservation, forest fire prevention (the Smokey Bear campaign), nutrition, population control, antipollution, and the value of health and education, to mention only a few. The Council, however, is entirely in the advertising business and has been criticized for omitting other marketing activities from its programs. T. V. Greer and W. G. Nickels (1975), for example, have argued that the Council should consider all components of the marketing mix before jumping on the promotion bandwagon. Without an overall marketing plan, advertising resides in a vacuum.

One of the most successful uses of mass media in social marketing is the MDA (Muscular Dystrophy Association) telethon hosted by Jerry Lewis. Through

TABLE 7.1

Possible Media, Channels, and Vehicles

1. TV—PSAs	30. billboards
2. TV—talk shows	31. posters
3. TV—editorials	32. taxi signs
4. TV—news shows	33. transit cards
5. TV—short films	34. truck signs
6. TV—interview shows	35. roadside signs
7. TV—station break slides	36. theater shorts
8. TV—paid commercials	37. films/filmstrips
9. TV—documentaries	38. bumper stickers
10. TV—children's shows	39. litter bags
11. radio—PSAs	40. matchcovers
12. radio—phone-in shows	41. telephone hot line
13. radio—editorials	42. restaurant placemats
14. radio—news shows	43. restaurant "tent cards"
15. radio—interview shows	44. decals
16. radio—station breaks or DJ tag lines	45. key tags
17. radio—paid commercials	46. shopping bags
*18. newspapers—news stories	47. calendars
19. newspapers—feature articles	48. road map imprints
20. newspapers—editorials	49. dashboard stickers
21. newspapers—interviews	50. stamp cancellation imprints
22. newspapers—public service ads	51. speed/distance "calculators"
23. newspapers—paid ads	52. gas consumption "calculators"
24. newspapers—cartoons	53. exhibits
25. newspapers—letters to editor	54. speeches
26. newsletters	55. letters (direct mail)
27. brochures/pamphlets/reprints of articles	56. personal visits
	57. package imprints
28. flyers/mailing inserts	(for example, milk cartons)
29. coloring books/comic books	58. CB radio

*Items 18–25 also apply to magazines whose circulation is limited to one state or to a particular city.

Source: Department of Transportation 1978, p. 4.

the use of a plethora of talented show business personalities, Lewis has shown many corporations that it is beneficial to become associated with the MDA campaign (Robinson 1978, pp. 72-74).

Table 7.1 contains a comprehensive list of possible media, channels, and vehicles for messages in the promotion of the 55 mile-per-hour speed limit. It can serve as a checklist for many other social promotions.

Interpersonal Channels

Mass media such as the print and broadcast vehicles discussed in the previous section constitute channels for rapid dissemination of innovations among large audiences in a one-to-many manner. The term mass media is synonymous with impersonal channels. By contrast, marketers are very aware of highly effective personal channels, alternatively referred to as word-of-mouth (WOM), informal, or interpersonal media (Turow 1974) for information flow, and about which a sizable literature has accumulated. Jacob Jacoby (1976), reviewing this area of research, reported that WOM is especially useful to the change agent because favorable information is more likely to be transmitted than unfavorable (p. 1036). Furthermore, WOM is more trusted than mass media because it is a two-way communication form. (This is particularly true in less developed societies, where the "interpersonal channel totally predominates in the diffusion of innovations" [Rogers 1976, p. 227].)

But WOM is an expensive medium, and because it is a "push" method of communication, the marketer is at the mercy of intervening salesmen to relay the idea effectively to the target audience. This poses difficulties, such as those encountered by Paul Bloom and William Novelli (1979):

1. The Federal Flood Insurance program has had difficulty getting insurance companies' agents to add flood insurance to their product line. The agents have seen this insurance as being hard to learn about, hard to sell (with Government forms and regulations to worry about), and low in profitability.
2. A program designed to motivate physicians to teach their patients smoking quitting skills ran up against the problem that, although the physicians wanted to cooperate, they did not know how to be teachers. It, therefore, became necessary to teach physicians how to teach patients—a task that was complicated by the natural inclination of many physicians to be know-it-alls and not want to be taught anything. (p. 10)

A pivotal role in the WOM communication-influence process is played by certain individuals called opinion leaders, a term usually ascribed to persons within a community whose opinions are respected, trusted, and sought out. Often the opinion leader is not a formal leader, such as a political figure, but someone with no special station at all. More likely he or she is a well-informed, well-liked individual who is sociable and keeps in touch with sources of information. In fact, the opinion leader is to the distribution of ideas what the channel captain is to the marketing of goods and services. Both are intermediaries who, because of a dominant position, command a strong following of those above and below themselves in the channel hierarchy. Thus a nurse having a charismatic personality could emerge as a more important intermediary in the health-care channel than the doctor. Her advice, her clarifications, and her interpretations of information will be taken as authoritative by hospital administrator and doctor, as well as patient. Again, a county agricultural agent is an official adviser to farmers but his position may well be preempted by a knowledgeable tractor mechanic who, *en passant*, transmits valuable farming ideas to his customers. The challenge to the idea marketer is to locate appropriate opinion leaders, to cultivate their interest in the cause to be promulgated, and to maintain satisfactory relationships with them.

Situated between mass and personal channels of idea distribution are pressure groups (special-interest groups, lobbyists, and so on) and advocacy groups. Ideas transmitted along these channels do reach mass audiences but more personally than via print and broadcast media. Pressure and advocacy groups are alike in that each is organized to foster some cause benefiting the special concerns of its members or of constituents for whom the group serves as chosen representative. They differ principally in the direction taken by their respective efforts. Advocacy groups offer advisory service downward and outward to consumers and others seeking advice. (In the history of English and German law, the advocate was a special kind of lawyer who advised other lawyers in the preparation of cases.) Pressure groups representing individuals or institutions set out to systematically cajole government to enact laws favoring their causes (see Figure 7.3). Pressure groups are macro in nature because they seek to bring about social change, while advocacy is a microprocess in which ideas are transmitted to individuals. These channels for concept diffusion were included in the discussion of various types of exchange transactions in Chapter 2.

The advocacy group may be seen as a "top-down" channel for ideas, as exemplified by Consumer Reports, the Center for Automobile Safety, the Association for Rating Charitable Organizations, and the Better Business Bureau, as well as groups providing advice for the elderly, apartment dwellers, and so on. On the other hand, pressure groups are "bottom-up" in that they attempt to influence legislators on behalf of individuals or groups. Examples include the several well-known civil rights and feminist groups and lobbies sponsored by trade organizations. A prominent pressure group is the organization Common Cause, which has attracted a following of nearly a quarter million members. It is a citizens' action lobby organized to bring Americans to bear pressure upon politicians regarding various issues (listed in Chapter 4) in the public interest. Excluded from this discussion are corporate political action committees functioning primarily to contribute funds to political candidates. Their roles as middlemen

FIGURE 7.3

A Generalized Channel of Distribution for Concepts

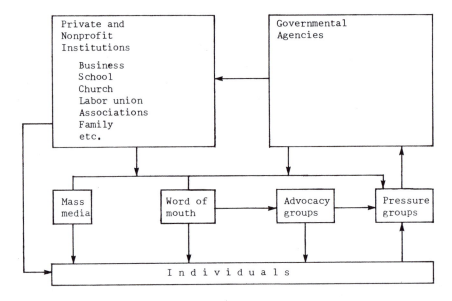

Source: Constructed by the author.

of specific ideas are secondary to the purpose of exerting broad influence on behalf of their sponsors.

Private business firms, cited earlier as initiators of ideas, also play intermediary roles in the diffusion process. Wholesalers and retailers are strategically situated to act as conveyers of ideas and social issues, at the same time that they serve in their roles as middlemen of goods and services. Pharmacists have always given customers advice on health-care matters and even rendered minor services such as removing cinders from people's eyes. The pharmaceutical industry also takes part in such health activities as the National High Blood Pressure Education Program which promotes detection and treatment of hypertension. Retailers of electronic and hi-fi apparatus have long realized the benefits of marketing relevant ideas and advice along with their tangibles. It is surprising that book publishers are not widely involved in the promotion of reading improvement domestically and in the upgrading of literacy worldwide. Justification for involvement of business firms in idea marketing may be found on altruistic grounds, or motivation could be purely economic, that is, profit maximizational. Consumers are more eager to patronize those establishments where needed information is readily available. At the same time, participating in social programs enhances the firm's public image.

Food establishments are a prominent forum for the exchange of nutrition information. They are in an enviable position to convey ideas about sound nutrition and in the long run would benefit from such activities. Nutritionally educated consumers must be healthier and hence better customers. Of course, they will be better customers not for packaged snacks, junk foods, but for more wholesome items, such as vegetables, fruit, bulk grains, unseasoned nuts, fish, and other basic foods. The channels employed here would be primarily word-of-mouth between staff and customers, posters, in-store loudspeaker announcements, and ads in the mass media. If by promoting the idea of sound nutrition the merchant is thereby to lose sales in the snack department, the loss should be offset by increased interest in healthier food items. At the same time the store creates goodwill with a sizable health-food segment that otherwise searches for specialty shops outside the community.

At the higher rungs of the food distribution channel, wholesalers and producers could respond to such a shift in demand by themselves introducing more nutritious product lines. If successful, no economic losses need be endured overall, while large societal benefits might accrue. Television watching can be just as pleasing while munching fruits, carrots and other raw vegetables, cheeses, or whole grain crackers without cancer-suspicious additives as those found in salted pretzels, candies, and so on.

A populace more aware of healthful nutrition habits must in the long run comprise broader markets for the food industry. This is especially true in third world countries, where advertisements are now luring people to spend meager funds on packaged vitamins. Here industry as well as government could divert such promotional effort into the marketing of healthier eating habits. One wonders why food merchants seem to sidestep the inclusion of this most important "line" into their product mix. It is easy to predict that some standard bearer among food chains will one day capitalize on these virgin promotion possibilities. The food industry has a stake in advancing education designed to develop nutritionally concerned customers.

The most obvious middlemen of ideas are the institutions within the educational sector. Students who attend schools (above the compulsory grade) have already purchased the idea that education is a good thing. But they are also being sold large packages of knowledge in various subjects, as well as extracurricular concepts. It is no wonder, then, that many sources of ideas have sought out educational institutions to act as intermediaries for ideas, for example, the U.S. Agricultural Extension Service, which operates under university auspices.

Fraternal and service organizations like the Kiwanis and the League of Women Voters usually have, in addition to the objective of socialization for members, one or more altruistic goals, such as service to the community. Often they choose to market ideas as well as services, in some cases purporting to be primarily forums for the discussion of social causes and to be vehicles for dissemination of issues on which the organization takes a stand. These groups adopt ideas they deem important and usually perform an efficacious job of promoting their adopted causes, often by sheer weight of numbers of well-motivated volunteers. Some fraternal organizations are engaged in the marketing of more tangible ideas, including insurance plans of various kinds.

THE CONSUMER'S PLACE IN "PLACE"

Channel theorists are divided on the question of whether the ultimate consumer is or is not to be considered part of the distribution structure. Typically, the consumer appears at the lower end of channel diagrams as the recipient of the product, below all of the other members who ostensibly have performed their assigned functions in the marketing scenario. But the consumer is by no means an insignificant actor in that process. The adopter of an idea meets all the qualifications for channel membership: a party to the process, an independent entity, a performer of one or more marketing functions. Including the target consumer as an integral part of the channel structure places the marketer on notice for consideration of consumer wants and needs. Like the traditional product, the idea must find a satisfied market; consumers' dissatisfaction with a social good implies a need for product modification (as with fashion trends) or portends early obsolescence, as occurred with the idea of the Susan B. Anthony one-dollar coin.

The crucial dependence upon consumer acceptance raises the question about the extent to which consumer participation in the planning process should be encouraged. J. O. Yedvab (1974) advocated representation in programs (p. 56) but only to the extent that consumers be invited to committees, boards, and so on. He cautioned that no operational responsibility should be given them; that actual decision making should be relegated only to administrators (p. 60). Other sociologists have studied conflicts arising from client membership on advisory bodies as well as on staff. It is perhaps an elitist view, but most of these studies conclude that, where such integration has been attempted, ideological and cultural differences between marketer and client brought more damaging than advantageous outcomes (for example, Schwartzman, Kneifel, and Krause 1978, p. 93).

Yet this is an era of consumer enlightenment. Individuals seem increasingly to be demanding that their voices be heard by marketers of products they buy and services rendered to them. Purveyors of ideas must also attach credence to consumer feedback, and in some cases, consumers of ideas should have input into the formulation and dissemination processes. Involvement can go a long way to build trust.

DESIGNING AND ORGANIZING THE CHANNEL

The structure of the channel itself might vary from that of a loosely knit group of separate entities to a highly cohesive network that might in many ways resemble a single organization. An idea channel may be designed by listing all organizations interested in the promotion of the idea, or having some capability useful to its marketing. These are then sequenced hierarchically in flowchart format, and what results is the channel. A generalized channel of distribution for ideas is schematized in Figure 7.3.

Louis Stern and Adel El-Ansary (1977) described the design of a channel for a defensive driving course (DDC) marketed by the National Safety Council. They recognized that

> Because such efforts on the part of the Council really involve the marketing of an idea—the concept of defensive driving as a deterrent to highway accidents—it is clear that there must be an effective

FIGURE 7.4

Channel of Distribution for the Idea of Safe Driving

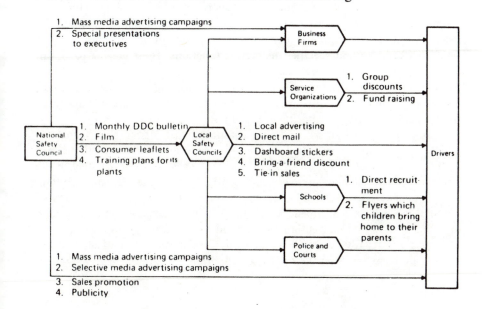

Source: Kotler 1975, p. 299.

merging of distribution and promotion in its program. The use of specific agents who can carry out the idea and enforce it must be blended with such vehicles as advertising, press releases, and other promotional tools. Clearly, no marketing program can rely on any one element of the marketing mix; each must use all elements in combination in order to achieve its goals. (p. 560)

The National Safety Council's DDC channel is reproduced in Figure 7.4.

The very process of channel design encourages zero-based planning of the roles and functions of institutions participating in the program and suggests reappraisal of an improvement in day-to-day operation of these institutions with respect to the objectives of the entire channel. The process also addresses a frequently encountered dilemma as to whether the marketer should perform a given function internally or contract it out—the make-or-buy decision familiar to producers of goods. Such decisions are usually made on the basis of which organization is most experienced or most efficient at the particular task. Often, contracting out to an intermediary makes sense.

SUMMARY

Ideas and issues, like conventional products, must be accessible to potential adopters at the time and place and in a manner that will facilitate adoption. To accomplish this, the marketer constructs a network of institutions, each of which performs certain specified marketing functions. These are the parties to the marketing process; each makes a contribution. A typical network for concept marketing includes the organization initiating the particular cause, community-based institutions, mass and personal media, pressure and advocacy groups, private firms, government, and finally the consumer.

Just as no ship can sail smoothly without a chief officer, the channel too usually operates under a channel captain who is responsible for smooth delivery of the concept from its source to those whose needs are to be satisfied in the transaction. The channel must be sufficiently "long," that is, must contain enough members such that all tasks necessary for the successful execution of the total job will be performed. At the same time it must not be too unwieldy. In the same way that conventional goods and services have greater utility when they are made readily accessible to their buyers, the availability of ideas at the point of purchase increases their potential adoption.

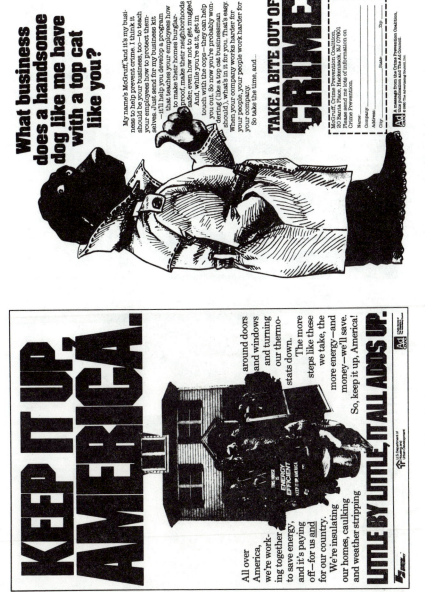

FIGURE 7.1. Idea Ads. (A) Energy, (B) Crime.

It's hard to decide who needs your gift the most, isn't it?

A LOT OF THE ABUSES CHILDREN ENDURE ARE EVEN WORSE THAN BROKEN BONES.

Broken bones are what most people think of when they think of child abuse. Unfortunately, battered children are only part of the problem. About one million children in America are abused every year.

Some are emotionally abused. Belittled, constantly teased or in some way made to feel inferior because they are not capable of performing up to their parents' unreasonable expectations.

Others are sexually abused. Not by a pervert off the street, but by an adult who is usually a trusted friend or a member of the child's family.

Still others suffer from neglect — the lack of food, clothing, shelter or medication when necessary.

All of these abuses can and do kill. About five children die from child abuse every day. Those who somehow manage to survive are scarred for life. They often end up in mental institutions and jails. Abused children may grow up to abuse their own children.

The situation is desperate but not hopeless. Over 80% can be helped. We know what to do but we can't do it alone. Please write and find out how you can help prevent child abuse.

Abused children are helpless. Unless you help.

United Way helps you do the right thing.

You give so generously. And yet, you can't help wondering if you're helping all the people you can.

When you give through United Way, you support a wide range of human services. Needs and distribution of funds are reviewed by local volunteers. People like you, who visit agencies, go over budgets, check for duplication.

All to make sure your one generous gift does all you want it to do.

Thanks to you,
it works.
for all of us.

United Way

FIGURE 7.1   (continued), (C) Child Abuse, (D) United Way. Courtesy of the Ad Council.

122

You're 15... going steady. Should you put yourself on the pill?

That we can seriously ask the question here indicates the extent of the sexual revolution. That you—teenage girl, boyfriend, or apprehensive parent—are eagerly reading on indicates the importance of the question.

But sorry... we don't have a simple yes or no answer. The matter is too personal, too complex. Moral values are involved. So is peer pressure. And the desire to express love through sexual activity is deep, strong and very human.

Sex without birth control can create big problems— unwanted pregnancy, terminated schooling, unwise marriages. But the Pill is no cure-all either. There can be hazards to health as well as damage to self esteem and personal relationships.

We will make two suggestions. First, keep the lines of communication and trust open between yourself and the older generation. You are not alone. Second, get professional guidance. There's help available from clergymen, family, doctors, teachers, family friends, and official health agencies.

What do you think?

Your opinion makes a difference, but to reach an informed opinion you need facts and viewpoints. That's where we come in. As your daily newspaper, we give you the information you need. Breaking news. Editorial opinion. Columns. Letters to the editor. We keep you on top of issues like the sexual revolution—issues that affect your life.

So read us regularly. Don't miss an issue.

(NEWSPAPER LOGO)

DON'T YOU HATE NOT KNOWING?

FIGURE 7.2.A Social Issue Ads. (A) Pill at Age 15, (B) Social Marriage, (C) Capital Punishment, (D) Gun Control. Courtesy of the Newspaper Advertising Bureau.

FIGURE 7.2 B (continued)

How many people should you marry?

Don't laugh.

For most people, marriage is "till death us do part." But that's not the only idea in town. Some social thinkers have proposed the idea of "serial marriage:" that is, only one mate at a time, but with a number of changes over a lifetime as partners change and develop and needs change with them. Others propose "contract marriage" for a specified period of time, renewable like a lease, with the rights and duties of each partner spelled out.

Another idea is "open marriage," with both partners free to explore extra-marital relationships as long as they don't interfere with mealtimes and laundry. "Group marriage" would provide safety in numbers... while still other voices claim that marriage itself is an idea whose time has come...and gone.

What do *you* think?

Your opinion makes a difference, but to reach an informed opinion you need facts and viewpoints. That's where we come in. As your daily newspaper, we give you the information you need. Breaking news. Editorial opinion. Columns. Letters to the editor. We keep you on top of issues like marriage—issues that affect your life.

So read us regularly. Don't miss an issue.

(NEWSPAPER LOGO)

DON'T YOU HATE NOT KNOWING?

FIGURE 7.2 C (continued)

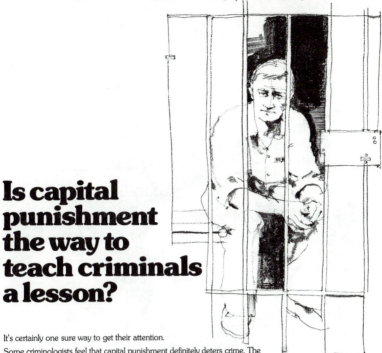

Is capital punishment the way to teach criminals a lesson?

It's certainly one sure way to get their attention.

Some criminologists feel that capital punishment definitely deters crime. The holdup man may not squeeze the trigger if he knows it could cost him his life. Other experts say the death penalty doesn't deter because criminals don't expect to get caught. Unfortunately, statistics are scarce and ambiguous.

Another problem: there's no way to make amends if a mistake is made. Enough innocent people have been convicted of crimes—with the truth surfacing only years later—to make this a very real concern.

Finally, many people feel that the taking of human life is an act that demeans the state to a degree that is unacceptable in a civilized society.

What do you think?

Your opinion makes a difference, but to reach an informed opinion you need facts and viewpoints. That's where we come in. As your daily newspaper, we give you the information you need. Breaking news. Editorial opinion. Columns. Letters to the editor. We keep you on top of issues like crime and capital punishment—issues that affect your life.

So read us regularly. Don't miss an issue.

(NEWSPAPER LOGO)

DON'T YOU HATE NOT KNOWING?

newspaper
readership
project
np

(continued)

FIGURE 7.2 D (continued)

Is happiness a warm .30-06?

For some it is.

It is for the sportsman, warmed by memories of silent, snowy woods. It is for the collector, handling the perfection of finely-crafted blued steel and oiled walnut. It is for the target shooter, breaking his personal record for consecutive bullseyes, reaching out beyond himself.

These "gun nuts" deserve to be heard. Last year they spent $250 million for hunting licenses and taxes, all of which went to wildlife conservation. Largely because of such conservation efforts, experts believe there are more deer in America now than in Colonial days.

From the other side, however, sincere voices argue that widespread ownership of guns complicates the problems of crime and violence. They say that the handgun and the high powered rifle have no place in an increasingly urban America...that the rifleman rightly belongs to yesterday and to legend. And they deplore that trait in man which takes pleasure in killing animals for sport.

What do you think?

Your opinion makes a difference, but to reach an informed opinion you need facts and viewpoints. That's where we come in. As your daily newspaper, we give you the information you need. Breaking news. Editorial opinion. Columns. Letters to the editor. We keep you on top of issues like gun control—issues that affect your life.

So read us regularly. Don't miss an issue.

(NEWSPAPER LOGO)

DON'T YOU HATE NOT KNOWING?

newspaper
readership
project

8

SOCIAL MARKETING APPLIED: A STRATEGIC PLAN FOR CETA

A mighty maze: But not without a plan.
—Alexander Pope, *Essay on Man*

Although as Kurt Lewin remarked, "Nothing is as practical as a good theory," it is time in this book to apply its theoretic precepts. To demonstrate an application of social marketing, this chapter presents a synopsis of a marketing plan drawn up for an agency charged with administration of a new concept in government-sponsored manpower programs. For any product, whether tangible or abstract, a marketing effort benefits from the preparation of a written plan, a road map. A strategic framework so prepared guides resource allocation where it will do the most good and serves as a basis for monitoring results and reshaping policy where necessary.

The plan discussed in this chapter attempts to achieve these purposes by first discussing the background of the sponsoring institution—"where we are now"—and then its objectives—"where we want to go." Next, strategies are explored for fulfilling these objectives—"how we'll get there"—as well as the tactics or actions for carrying out the strategies—"what we must do to get there."

The acronyms to be employed here are

CBO—Community-Based Organization
CETA—Comprehensive Employment and Training Act
CT—Classroom Training
NAB—National Alliance of Business
OJT—On-the-Job Training
PIC—Private Industry Council
PSA—Public Service Announcement
PSE—Public Service Employment
PSIP—Private Sector Initiative Program
TJTC—Targeted Job Tax Credit

BACKGROUND: WHERE WE ARE NOW

The full-scale marketing plan of which the present chapter is a synopsis was prepared by the author (Fine 1979a) for a regional Private Industry Council (PIC) operating under the Comprehensive Employment and Training Administration (CETA). At about that time, a fork had been reached in the road to government-sponsored manpower programming. One branch continued the philosophy of the past, namely, that of maximizing the *quantity* of structurally unemployed placed in jobs. That approach served the objective of immediate reduction of unemployment figures and thus provided attractive statistics. Moreover, many saw the chief purpose of government-funded programs as simply to fill entry-level jobs with workers qualified for little else—on the surface, a not unreasonable goal.

The drawback here was that such programs did not ameliorate, but instead perpetuated, the hard-to-employ situation, while not going far enough to upgrade the marketability of these individuals. Still worse, employers had been left with a poor taste for virtually all government-sponsored manpower programs (Carlson et al. 1978, p. 1): ". . . the publicly-financed employment and training system has become so expensive, so complicated, and so ingrained in and out of society, that past business attitudes and institutions must be substantially altered. . . ." (Special Report No. 31 1978, p. 11)

Needed: Quality as Well

Branching sharply from the road to immediate placement is an approach that seeks to provide an improved supply of labor by enhancing the long-term *quality* of the economically disadvantaged. Instead of instant gratification of manpower needs, this approach addresses the problem with a more enduring philosophy, saying in effect, not "Let us employ the hard-to-employ," but rather, "Let's help the hard-to-employ become easier to employ."

Faced with growing disenchantment on the part of business, the government in January 1978 inaugurated a new CETA program, Title VII, called the Private Sector Initiative Program (PSIP), under which businesspeople were given wide latitude to run the CETA show. This was to be accomplished by establishing regional Private Industry Councils (PICs) dominated by the private sector rather than by government. One of these PICs ordered that a marketing plan be drawn up because it viewed itself not as a group of individuals who were to devise programs dealing with employment and training activities, but as businesspeople starting up a firm to sell a product.

OBJECTIVES OF THE PIC: WHERE WE WANT TO GO

The objective in any marketing endeavor is to satisfy one or more target markets by supplying products most acceptable to those markets. That objective is the mission, or product, of the firm. It answers the question, "What business are we in?" In conventional marketing the attainment of that objective hopefully yields financial profit, but in social marketing what is sought is widespread adoption or utilization of the idea being propounded, in a manner that most benefits the target markets intended to be served.

In the case of the PIC, at first blush the objective is seen as providing jobs. However, after serious discussion with council members, it developed that their objective was to increase productivity in industry through improvement in the quality of that class of labor supply consisting of the economically disadvantaged. As marketers, the PIC serves not one, but two distinct target markets, and must design a unique product offering for each one.

Participating Firms and Productivity

One market consists of participating firms, and for this market, the product designated is *productivity*. The PIC must "sell" client firms on the idea that the PSIP is aimed at increasing productivity—something that all businesses are eager to buy. Economic systems throughout history have set improved productivity as an important industrial objective, where productivity depends, at least somewhat, on the employment of conscientious and efficient workers. So it is fitting that a plan for marketing the idea of innovative manpower recruiting, should consider the idea of improved productivity as its product.

Employment Recruits and Earnability

The other market served by the PIC is made up of potential enrollees for job training programs. These recruits typically have a history of poverty, low educational attainment, weak vocational skills, social problems, and inability to hold a job. They are likely to have antisocial habits, be unsure of themselves, and often must take time out from work to resolve family problems. In general, they desire immediate gratification and may have difficulty waiting for payday. Many possess innate talent that is wasted because they lack the self-esteem needed to sell themselves. Some are convinced of their worthlessness and are afraid to say otherwise. Perhaps their greatest need is to acquire the ability to earn regular income.

The social marketer seeks to translate the satisfaction of consumer needs into the design of a specific offering. In the present case, the social product to be marketed to the recruit market is designated as earnability—the capacity, as stated above, for earning regular income.

Two objectives are thus isolated for the PSIP, corresponding to the needs of its two markets. Each objective identifies a product to be marketed—productivity for the market of participating employers, and earnability for potential enrollees. They are the two product lines within the product mix of the PSIP.

FIGURE 8.1

Fiscal Year Media Plan

Description	Oct.	Nov.	Dec.	Jan.	Feb.	Mar.	Apr.	May	June	July	Aug.	Sept.
Local Newspaper (250-line insertion)	RRR	R	B	R	RRR	FR	FR	R	FR	R	R	FR
Flyer Mailings, all F (%)	5	3	10	2	5	25	15	10	10	5		5
"Out of Home" Posters, all R (%)	3	10	2	5	25	15	10	10	5		5	5
PSAs on Local Radio	RRR	R	R	R	RRR	FR	FR	R	FR	R	R	FR
					Industry Concentrations							
Lumber and wood products	X											
Retail trade												
Transportation												X
Finance, insurance, and real estate								X				
Construction contracting							X					
Mining, agriculture						X						
Textile mill products						X						
Apparel and needle products										X		
Furniture and fixtures							X					
Chemical and allied products					X							
Petroleum and coal products						X						
Rubber and miscellaneous plastics					X							
Leather industry									X			
Stone, glass, and ceramics									X			
Machinery (excluding electric)							X					
Electric goods and machines						X						
Automobile industry								X				
Aircraft industry			X									
Instruments and clocks			X									

Note: F = Promotion to the audience of participating firms; R = Promotion to the recruit audience.
Source: Constructed by the author.

STRATEGIES AND ACTIONS: HOW TO GET THERE AND BY WHAT METHODS

The plan appears in five parts, each representing a strategic marketing factor—market segmentation, product design, distribution, pricing, and promotion. Strategies are discussed for each of the two focus products/markets.

Market Segmentation

Segmentation by Seasonality of Demand

The choice of a segmentation criterion for the market of client firms was motivated by the realization that companies have differential hiring needs depending upon the time of the year. In the marketing of productivity to these firms, the most relevant criterion appeared to be time of the year of peak need for workers—segmentation by seasonal demand. Strategy was suggested to time the promotional effort for PSIP to conform to seasonal requirements of potential employers—what might be called segmentation by seasonal demand. Given the constraints on such resources as the amount of time available to job development staffers, mailing facilities, and so on, it makes sense to contact firms at the time of the year when they are likely to be most receptive. An analogy is seen in the manner in which savings and loan associations usually time advertising programs to conform to quarterly interest payment periods. Thus, for example, construction contractors seek extra workers in March, the apparel and needle trades in April, and the leather industry in June. While some industries show no apparent particular seasonality, those that do are listed in Figure 8.1, indicating periods of the year in which promotion to each industry may be best directed.

Other approaches could have been used. Apart from the seasonality criterion, firms could also have been segmented on the basis of near term/long term need for workers, degree of skill required, or geographic location, for example. Each criterion implies a different segmentation scheme.

Segmentation by Employment Readiness

A second segmentation strategy was proposed, this time for the recruit market, based on the readiness of the recruit for employment. It is explained by a two-dimensional model, containing four cells (Figure 8.2). The first dimension considers achievement in vocational skills, and the second considers the degree of personal and/or family stress affecting the recruit. The model offers a basis for planning the placement of recruits. It is employed to suggest a differential product design unique to each category.

Recruits belonging in cell 1 are in possession of sufficient vocational skills and at the same time are relatively free from personal and family stress. Cell 2 in the model defines a submarket enjoying freedom from stress but in need of

FIGURE 8.2

Segmentation of Recruits by Employment Readiness

| | | Recruit's Vocational Skills | |
		GOOD	POOR
Personal/ family stress	MILD	CELL NO. 1	CELL NO. 2
	SERIOUS	CELL NO. 2	CELL NO. 4

Source: Constructed by the author.

vocational training. Cell 3 recruits have some vocational skill but suffer from personal and family problems. Recruits in cell 4 are doubly disadvantaged, enduring both types of difficulty.

Having proposed segmentation of the private sector market according to seasonal demand, and the recruit market according to employment readiness, the actual products for these respective markets are discussed below.

Product Strategy

Within the two specified product classes, the PSIP spawned several programs that in marketing parlance may be viewed as product forms:

1. On-the-job training (OJT) under which the employer may be subsidized at a rate upwards of 50 percent of starting wage.
2. Classroom training (CT) in either clerical or vocational skills.
3. The Targeted Job Tax Credit (TJTC) program, permitting private for-profit employers to be eligible for tax credits upon hiring disadvantaged individuals from among specific target groups, including welfare recipients, handicapped, poor youth, poor Vietnam veterans, cooperative education participants, and ex-convicts (Special Report No. 31, p. 14). An employer may obtain the training subsidy as well as the tax credit by both hiring and training the disadvantaged.
4. Work experience programs encouraging recruits to gain practical exposure to job settings on a part-time basis, for example, while still in school.

Productivity

Productivity, according to economists, may be increased by improving the quality of the labor force, investing in more efficient capital equipment, or automation (Lovelock and Young 1979, p. 168). This study is obviously concerned with only the first of these alternatives, and product strategy for productivity then amounts to design of programs for optimally equipping PSIP recruits to become productive workers. This means not only vocational training for recruits but also enhancing their capacity to report to work on time and consistently.

Strategy for product improvement must consider the following areas of disillusionment with government manpower programs, experienced in the past by industry:

1. Red tape and overregulation
2. Adverse publicity
3. Bias against business participation on the part of some government officials
4. Unreliability of employees
5. Termination after training
6. Lost productivity of trainers
7. Poor return on training investments
8. Employees taking unfair advantage of unemployment and compensation privileges

An agenda of steps for ameliorating product deficiencies is an integral part of a marketing plan. In the present case, one would include (numbers correspond to the items listed above) the following:

1. An official to be designated as an ombudsman or "red tape cutter" for participant firms, with a "hot-line" phone number for the purpose.
2. The theme to be emphasized is that the PIC represents a new brand of CETA. Indeed, PIC should be made a brand name, which will be promoted with the goal of making it well known, respected, and hopefully rendered generic. The producer of a branded item tolerates nothing but quality output for long-term welfare of the firm.
3. Private sector participation is now mandated by law. At least 50 percent of the PIC membership must be drawn from the business community, and there is every reason to believe that businesspersons are answering the call with the intention of becoming actively involved.
4-8. Expansion of programs designed to improve the quality of the PIC recruit. Before "selling" the recruit to employers, care must be taken that he or she is indeed "salable."

Earnability

The social product, earnability, is the capacity of an individual to earn money in steady employment. A recruit acquires earnability by attaining at least some of the following:

1. A feeling of investment in the commitment to a job preparation program
2. Basic and vocational skills
3. Employment habits such as promptness and regularity of attendance, getting along with others, proper dress and hygiene, and so on
4. Self-confidence
5. Assurance that personal problems need not hamper job performance and that sources of help are readily available
6. Understanding and utilization of his/her capabilities

Earnability is secured by most people through education or from work habits developed early in life, but for many who were deprived of these privileges, CETA programs can fill a serious void. However, earnability is not the same thing to all target individuals. As with many products, it must be differentiated.

Earlier, a model was proposed for segmenting the recruit market into four groups according to employment readiness. If that segmentation strategy is to be useful, then a package of earnability (product form) should be defined to suit each of the four submarkets. Referring to the model in Figure 8.2, the following (product differentiated) product forms are suggested:

Cell 1: These recruits are ready to be assigned to available positions under Title VII arrangements, except that some may require orientation into world-of-work habits.

Cell 2: Here, too, applicants may be placed into job slots but will also be enrolled in some form of training, OJT or CT. Their employers are thus eligible for a combination of Title VII and TJTC support.

Cell 3: The product form for these recruits consists of job placement together with counseling or referral to an appropriate CBO. The employer should be made aware that although he or she is obtaining a trained worker, some patience will be necessary to deal with the stress factor.

Cell 4: Earnability in this cell is made up of OJT or CT type placement along with personal/family help as in Cell 3 above. Should need for this product form exist among large numbers of recruits, some kind of group therapy may well be indicated.

A key feature of this study is the advocacy of a program for counseling and referral of recruits on individual problems and for family services, what might be termed the "psychosocial component" of the strategic plan. Recruits not only have vocational and educational deficiencies but also bring to the job-hunting situation family and personal problems that are amenable to support services. It is extremely difficult for an enrollee who is beset with personal problems to be concerned with vocational training. If product strategy for earnability could include help with child care and other family support services, the likelihood of regular job attendance would be increased.

Preliminary investigation in connection with the present study revealed enthusiastic support for a psychosocial program within the PSIP. One survey of business found that general orientation counseling could be the "most useful of all government-financed programs for providing stable employment for disadvantaged youth" (Carlson et al. 1978, pp. 18, 19). Reporting on a 15-year study, Milton Shore and Joseph Massimo (1979) assert: "Comprehensive vocationally-oriented psychotherapy continues to show promise as a technique for reaching so-called 'hard-to-reach' adolescents, influencing their adjustment positively even into mid-life" (p. 245). The PIC is in an enviable and timely position to consider arranging for such help as an integral component of its product mix. The concepts of caring and sharing enter into what might otherwise be considered the cold, inhumane aspects of industrialization.

This part of the plan has discussed design and improvement of the product offerings to the PIC's consumers. The first section focused upon productivity to industry and the second upon earnability to recruits. But the distinction between the two products was drawn only for expository purposes; the two are closely intertwined. A more productive worker enjoys better earnability, which, in turn, improves productivity. Many large firms, IBM, for example, maintain on-site staff to help employees with personal problems. But most businesses making up the PIC's primary market cannot afford to offer this service to their personnel. It seems reasonable that the PIC, in dealing with a constituency of small firms, can and should consider such programming to be within its scope and thereby fill an important need of its consumers. The idea should be of great interest to employers who in the past suffered because of poor work habits of CETA recruits, and employees as well.

Distribution: Parties to the Process

In the same way that the distribution system for a tangible product is made up of series of firms—producer, wholesaler, retailer, and so on—the channel of distribution—social marketers—are aware of a set of institutions involved in one way or another with the delivery of a social product such as the PSIP. Channel theory highlights the reality that the social marketer operates not in a vacuum, but within a network of other community-based organizations (CBOs).

The channel structure (Figure 8.3) for the distribution of the PSIP begins with the "prime sponsor," the regional CETA organization. Next, the PIC serves

FIGURE 8.3

A Channel of Distribution for Two CETA Products

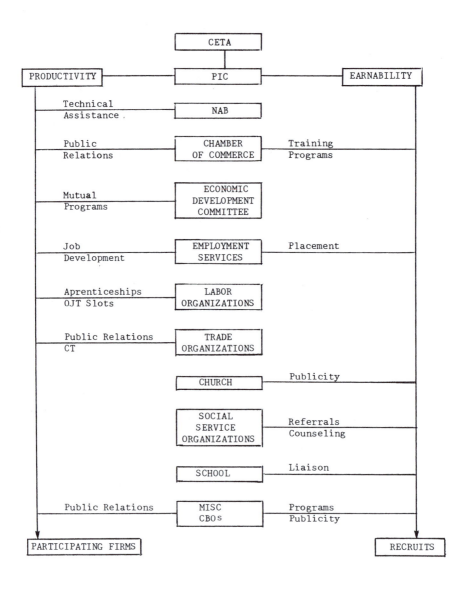

Source: Constructed by the author.

in an advisory capacity on PSIP matters. In terms of channel concepts the PIC is the "producer" or marketer of PSIP. Because the PIC has two consumers, the private sector and the disadvantaged unemployed, the channel presented in Figure 8.3 forks into two branches, one for each of the products/markets, although several channel members interact with both. The chart is self-explanatory and is not elaborated upon here.

The crux of this brief section is this: As with middlemen in conventional marketing, if each member of the channel contributes to the marketing process by performing its implicitly designated functions, effective delivery of the product to the consumer is facilitated.

Pricing Strategy for the Private Sector Initiative Program

Social prices, including time, effort, psyche, and changes in lifestyle (see Chapter 5), are taken into account in the design and promotion of social products such as productivity and earnability. A commercial marketer sets a price sufficiently high to ensure a profit and low enough to attract a sale. Somewhat similarly, the social marketer seeks to extract sufficient involvement or sacrifice from the adopter, to create respect for the social product, while keeping the extent of the commitment that the consumer must make low enough so as not to drive him or her away. If the price is too high, PSIP will not sell, but if the price is too low, it might be perceived as lacking credibility or importance.

The Price of the PIC Brand of Productivity

Client firms have become disenchanted with high prices they have paid for taking part in government-sponsored manpower programs. These high prices are just another way of viewing their complaints listed earlier, and correcting these ills may be seen as a price-reduction campaign. The marketing approach thus provides a double-barreled implement for planning promotion strategy.

The goodwill of participating firms must be regained by not only offering a high-quality brand of productivity but also at a reasonable social price. For example, not only must PSIP be associated with the better prepared recruit, but in addition, the amount of red tape expected of employees is to be demonstrably reduced and similarly for other points of contention. At the same time, the "contract" must not characterize Title VII or TJTC provisions as "giveaways," lest the program become suspect. The two-way nature of the exchange transaction must be upheld. Thus the tax credit is a product form offered in exchange for the price of training time, and Title VII subsidies are exchanged for time (and patience) required to break in a new recruit, and so on.

Participation is a price. The very name assigned to the primary market for the PSIP, that is, the participating firms, connotes a social price paid by these customers when they purchase the PIC brand of productivity. They participate by making training slots available and by interacting with job-development staff.

Moreover, the PSIP invites participation of private sector input into the planning process, the essence of the PSIP idea.

Social Price Paid by Recruits

These concepts also apply to recruits who purchase earnability. A commitment to the program must be elicited from all enrollees so that they too will have a sense of investment through participation in exchange for benefits that they derive.

Recruits sacrifice all four of the social prices—time, effort, psyche, and lifestyle change—in exchange for the PIC brand of earnability. Pricing strategy dictates that the program be so devised as to set systematically these prices at levels that will not be too high or too low. Thus complicated intake procedures might discourage enrollment. But if entry is made too simple, the program could appear superficial. The price must be right.

One of the first tasks asked of new employees is to fill out forms, which they often find difficult to do (frankly, I know a Ph.D. who finds most forms enigmatic). PIC could sponsor classes in the art of filling out forms, attendance being free but mandatory for all recruits. The time and effort of attendance are social prices to be paid in exchange for the product, earnability.

Summarizing, price tags bearing social prices like the few examples alluded to in this brief section, and fastened to PSIP products, have neither numbers nor dollar signs printed upon them. Instead, they signify certain nonmonetary sacrifices expected of consumers in exchange for productivity and earnability. These prices are part of the exchange process, and to the extent that they constitute fair payment in that exchange, they need to be considered in marketing planning.

Promotion

The promotion component of a marketing plan is sometimes known as the "advertising plan" and is all too often the only part of the marketing plan. However, by first examining the markets, products, distribution, and price factors, a broader background is obtained for campaign planning.

Promoting Productivity to Industry

An important communications objective is to instill in the private sector market the impression of a totally new and important source of manpower, reversing the poor image that firms have about workers supplied through government projects. The function of the promotion program is therefore to create awareness of the new product, create favorable association, and encourage switching from other "brands" of manpower sources. Copy strategy is to emphasize freedom from government interference, less competition from PSE, and quality in favor of subsidy. If PIC's workers will now have access to new forms of counseling, which will hopefully result in more diligent attendance on the job, then this serves as feed for ad message design. By broadcasting such aspects of the program, one hopes to restore employers' shattered confidence in CETA. The CETA brand having been disappointing, PIC will now offer a new improved brand of productivity to the private sector and will advertise it as such. Message themes could include:

> CETA Goes Private Sector
> The New CETA
> The Private Sector CETA

The product being innovative, it is necessary to build awareness through repeated exposure of the message. That is, strategy will emphasize frequency of ad placement, rather than broad reach across a wide market. Productivity messages will be carried in both print and broadcast media, and fullest advantage should be taken of opportunities for public service announcement (PSA) spot broadcasts. In addition, direct mail is a highly efficient medium for promoting the PSIP program. Direct mail permits pinpointing specific industries that can be reached at strategic points in time, that is, when hiring needs are greatest (see Figure 8.1). Such practice also reduces the possibility of heavy demand for workers, likely to result from a large general mailing. Brochures, booklets, Western Union Mailgrams, and flyers may be used as vehicles in direct-mail campaigns.

While mass media create awareness, industry involvement in PSIP will require interpersonal promotion as well. The new PIC brand of productivity will need one-to-one selling to stress its innovative aspects such as the new procedures under which recruits will be processed. Employers will likely be pleased to hear that their preferences for quality and long-term manpower commitment are to underlie the PIC program. It will be refreshing news to them that they, and not politicians, will now have first call upon well-prepared recruits.

Personal selling of "productivity through PIC" could also be affected through the medium of guest speakers at industrial organization meetings. Staff members and others well informed about the program may arrange to be invited to functions of various industrial groups where they can speak and answer questions about the advantages of the PIC as a source of manpower.

Other promotional and public relations techniques have been invoked by PICs around the country, including press announcements, luncheons and dinners with potentially concerned leaders, and well-publicized colloquia on structural employment and coordination of manpower programs (Summary Report October 1978, p. 41).

Promoting Earnability to Recruits

While there is general agreement that PSIP must be marketed to industry, promotion aimed at the recruit market appears to have been overlooked in PIC programs. The prevalent feeling is that potential recruits obtain manpower information automatically and are always ready to go to work, that PSIP does not have to be sold to them. Such an approach may adequately serve programs seeking to do nothing but place applicants into entry-level jobs, but it is inconsistent with the concept of earnability. The market for earnability consists of those who not only want jobs but who are willing to invest in self-betterment. If PSIP is to be an improvement over its predecessors, it must appeal to applicants interested in advancing their capacity to earn money, and not just to obtain jobs, a premise that guides copy strategy proposed in this section.

As an audience, recruits should be quite receptive to such message appeals. For they have had jobs, but still have little money. They have repeatedly experienced the pain of quickly losing jobs. Earnability is to be billed as more important than a job. Copy strategy is to convince recruits that while they are now job seekers, they must become job keepers, and that PSIP will show them the way.

Another message theme in the campaign to attract recruits concerns the status of manual work. Because society attaches greater dignity to white-collar jobs, schools herd youngsters into academic programs, and some vocationally oriented individuals develop low opinions of themselves. But not everyone is interested in, nor equipped to become, a so-called professional. Promotion messages should be structured about such values as the work ethic and build feelings in workers that they are valuable and needed. Respect for manual dexterity in technology should be emphasized and the "lowly trades" elevated: "It was soiled hands that built this country."

The hard-to-employ are not readers of newspapers, with the result that print ads for this market have a high "cost per thousand" (CPM), the yardstick of efficiency with which a medium reaches its audience. The aim of print campaigns is thus mainly to reach a "referring audience" of individuals and institutions, like welfare workers, schools, and churches, whence earnability messages will hopefully be relayed to target recruits.

Similarly, CPM is extremely high for reaching this market via radio stations serving wide areas. Even where a geographic match can be found between vehicle and audience, programming compatibility must be achieved, for example, with rock music. On the other hand, classical music is frequently piped in to waiting rooms in doctors' offices, and other such places where messages could reach recruits either directly or as a "pass-along" audience.

"Out-of-home" media, such as billboards and bus cards, should be considered. Some movie theaters show spot announcements, and one wonders why PIC should not advertise in the phone directory Yellow Pages under the employment heading. Earnability may well be promoted too by circulating handbills, brochures, and flyers at church and social functions, timing the distributions to coincide with the need for increased recruit enrollment.

As observed in discussing the campaign to promote productivity, mass media are useful principally to create awareness. Personal modes of communications are needed to bring recruits closer to actual adoption of earnability (enrollment). Posters placed in neighborhood shop windows serve this purpose and are quite inexpensive. Their cost effectiveness is extended still further as the very process of introducing them into the shops provides an opportunity for personal interaction between a PIC representative and a "middleman," the shopkeeper. They may, of course, also be placed on bulletin boards of schools, community centers, and so forth. An effective form for personal selling of earnability is the neighborhood sectarian church. The PIC could build relationships with key religious leaders in the community, who are generally quite receptive to the cause of improving the lot of the economically disadvantaged.

Scheduling

Promotion strategy (Figure 8.1) was planned for the fiscal year, which, for the PIC, runs from October 1 to September 30. The schedule provides for a "continuity program" of 20 newspaper ads during the year, 4 aimed at firms and 16 at recruits, although this proportion is readily modified to suit seasonal requirements. With both products, newspaper ad scheduling is pulsed for increased frequency at the start of the fiscal year and in advance of peak anticipated demand from firms. Trimonthly 250-line ads will gradually change to monthly appearances. Flyers are to be mailed according to the percentages indicated—about two to six per firm during the year. Extra mailings should go out to firms having a concentration of hiring patterns during the months listed in Figure 8.1. The pace of distribution of posters is such that promotion to recruits precedes promotion to industry.

The point here is that, ideally, if a job slot opens up, a recruit should be on hand to fill it. Fullest advantage will be taken of free local radio spots (PSAs). The 7:00 P.M. to midnight periods will do for earnability spots to the recruit audience, but the employer market may be reached during the more popular (and difficult to obtain) "drive times," 6:00 A.M. to 10:00 A.M. and 3:00 P.M. to 7:00 P.M.

In a postscript to the Special Report Number 31 (1978), Chairman Eli Ginsburg synthesized the thrust of the situation with respect to the structurally unemployed by observing: "The unemployed youth must become part of the job system or else we must accept the fact that they would become part of the crime system, or the welfare system." This is the awesome responsibility facing manpower planners.

SUMMARY

In this chapter vocational training of the economically disadvantaged was treated as a product to be marketed. A synopsis was presented of a strategic plan for the marketing program, illustrating the use of social marketing theory in the dissemination of ideas for societal benefit. Conceptual and methodological aspects of the plan ought to be readily generalizable to many other ideas and issues. The plan took into account the institution's background and objectives and proposed specific strategies and tactics for achieving those objectives. It employed the principal components of the marketing model as set forth in the preceding chapters. The actual plan has been implemented by a regional CETA agency, where it, at this writing, guides many of the organization's day-to-day activities.

PART III

9

CONSUMER RESEARCH IN
SOCIAL MARKETING

... The citizen did not so much vote for a candidate as make a
psychological purchase of him.

                              −Joe McGinniss (1969, p. 27)

Consumer behavior is a popular area of interest within marketing. In fact,
among all marketing topics, the number of volumes on consumer behavior (more
than 100) ranks second only to that of advertising books in print. For this book's
purpose, a fitting definition is: "behavior that consumers display in searching for,
purchasing, using, and evaluating products, services, and ideas, which they expect
will satisfy their needs" (Schiffman and Kanuk 1978, p. 4). In fact, consumer
behavior concerns the study of all consumer factors influencing decision-making
processes. The focus of this chapter is on those aspects of the consumer affecting
decision making in the adoption of concepts.

The first section of the chapter inquires into the possibility that the study
of social marketing warrants consideration of a "social" consumer behavior. The
inquiry continues in the second section discussing several factors typically subsumed under the consumer behavior rubric, but with emphasis on the adoption
of ideas. In the final section of the chapter, a study is described whose purpose
was to examine empirically the possibility raised above, by comparing consumer
characteristics in social marketing with those in conventional marketing.

Research into consumer behavior, a type of social research, can be thought
of in either of two general types.

One type, evaluative research, covers market studies undertaken after the
fact, that is, following introduction of a product, or to test effectiveness of a
promotion campaign. After a certain number of consumers have tried a product
(adopted a concept), it is useful to obtain feedback about product satisfaction
and similarly for feedback regarding response to promotion effort, ads, and so
on. Sponsors of ideas and issues, promoters of tangibles, and educators—the

145

parallels are striking—all want to know how well their audiences have learned and how much attitude and behavior have changed. In a sense, what is commonly known in marketing as testing advertising effectiveness differs very little from scholastic midterm exams.

A cogent argument for the use of evaluative research in social marketing was presented by Hans Zeisel (1980), in a plea for the polling of the "citizen's *considered* reaction" to social issues. He calls for such polls to be conducted after the marketing of current sociopolitical topics, during prime television time.

Another type of consumer research is conducted to learn about the needs and wants of a market in order to prepare for product design—to match the offering with consumer demand. One wants to know in advance how to engineer the offering so that it will best suit the audience for which it is intended. That type of research, often called exploratory or descriptive research, is also useful in planning promotional strategy. It could unearth valuable clues as to message design and media decisions. The investigation reviewed later in this chapter is exploratory in nature, seeking to unearth determinants of "social" consumption decisions.

IS THERE A "SOCIAL" CONSUMER BEHAVIOR?

As with marketing in general, the scope of consumer behavior appears to be broadening to include the study of choice processes for political candidates, health and safety considerations, aesthetic enrichment, and other ideas and information; consumer researchers now speak of voting behavior, safety behavior, and family planning behavior (Zaltman and Sternthal 1975). Does the psychology of the consumer differ according to the nature of the exchange, or is the process essentially invariant across all product types? Do people experience similar thought processes when they buy tangibles as when they buy concepts? If these processes differ, how do they differ? Is there a consumer behavior unique to social marketing?

Research into understanding the process by which concepts are absorbed has remained largely within the aegis of learning theory, where it enjoys an abundant literature. However, what is virtually nonexistent is formal examination, from a marketing viewpoint, of factors associated with idea adoption by consumers. With a few exceptions, notably the case of voting behavior, social scientists have given little attention to studies of markets for ideas and social issues. Another exception is an accumulation of empirical research by Father Andrew Greeley of the University of Chicago, whose work focuses on determinants of acceptance of religion. As these words are being written, the very first center for researching the contemporary market for Jewish ideas and issues is under way at Brandeis University. A news account of the event reports:

Such issues as intermarriage between Jews and non-Jews, the impact of religious cults on young Jews and the size and complexity of the Jewish population have received widespread and persistent attention, but there is little reliable information about these areas. . . . As a result, religious, educational and charitable groups have lacked basic facts that could help shape programs to needs and circumstances. (Briggs 1980, p. A16)

It seems natural that the study of the consumer in social marketing should seek to compare consumer behavior in the adoption of concepts with consumer behavior in the acquisition of ordinary goods and services. Calling the former social goods and the latter economic goods, Laczniak, Lusch, and Strang (1980) conducted such an investigation with respect to consumers' perceptions about the ethics of the marketing process. Earlier, Hupfer and Gardner (1971) inquired whether individuals were more involved with tangibles than with issues. They found that issues generally drew greater involvement than ordinary products and concluded that "once a product has been related in the consumer's mind to an issue, something important to him, the probability of this person's retaining knowledge of the product is increased" (p. 10).

But these writers made no attempt to relate consumer characteristics with such involvement differences. By contrast, the present study sets out to compare several factors about consumers of ordinary products with those of consumers (adopters) of ideas and issues.

Similarities

The adoption process for intangibles shares similarities with purchase decision making. For one thing, the human brain is finite in size and capacity. Whether acquiring goods or adopting ideas, there is no difference in the chemistry and physiology of the brain which accommodates seven "chunks" of information—plus or minus two (Miller 1956). Psychological concepts, such as memory, information overload (what marketers call "clutter," as in the proliferation of advertising), and receptivity of messages, all no doubt play similar roles in both types of decision making. The self-interests of individuals must be appealed to no matter what the product. Moreover, both product types are likely subjects of the fickle nature of consumer demand:

Both commercial and social action persuasion lead to a high proportion of shifted perceptions rather than changed attitudes. Whimsical decisions predominate, which are soon forgotten and have little carry-over to other situations. Lasting dedication to a cause is not a common consequence of social action campaigning. When an evangelist in a crusade welcomes many new converts to the altar, he knows that a large proportion of the penitent sinners will falter and require reconversion, again and yet again. (Brembeck and Howell 1976, p. 340)

Ninety-five percent of the respondents in a national sample stated they would accept usage of the $2 bill, but when it was issued it met with almost universal rejection.

Are devotees of causes as influenced by the semantics of brand names as are purchasers of products? One conjectures that in the same way a person learns to satisfy a need for flavor by seeking out Heinz's ketchup, another fulfills a yearning for socialization or altruism by taking up with one side of the issue to "Save Chrysler," the promotion of the idea of "UNICEF," or in the adherence to a cause such as "Save the Whales" or "Battered Wives." Brand names must play similar roles in both cases.

Differences

Quite apart from these similarities, what about *differences* between consumer decision processes in the adoption of ideas or social issues on the one hand, and the purchase of conventional products on the other? One difference lies in the nature of the forces motivating purchase behavior. The impulse to acquire something tangible usually stems from selfish, rather than societal interests. According to the marketing concept, people have needs, the product satisfies those needs, and repeat purchase produces personal reinforcement; this is behavior modification in practice.

In concept adoption, reinforcement through gratification is either delayed (this is the case with most ideas), or accrues not to the individual but to society (typical with social issues). The absence of immediate or personal reinforcement makes it difficult to obtain long-run or repeat behavior. "There is nothing in it for the individual; altruism, will only go so far. If I must walk around with a popsicle stick in my hand for an hour because I can't find a receptacle, my cost is very high and my benefit is virtually non-existent" (Rothschild 1980).

The perceived (and actual) consequences and benefits of the acceptance of an idea, or of a position on an issue, could be more far-reaching, more involving, than the effects of an ordinary purchase. The purchase of a product gives the user more control over the use of that product than is the case in social marketing. A vote for a candidate or a political issue may result in consequences completely unpredictable. In buying a product one might simply reinforce one's sense of identity as a result of the acquisition, but in joining a social movement, one is attaching part of oneself to a larger group. To say that I am a Chevy buyer is not as profound an observation as to say that I am a Democrat. At the same time, consequences and benefits of concept adoption are usually more difficult to comprehend. Thus Everett Rogers and F. F. Shoemaker (1971), describing rejection of the idea of boiling drinking water in a Peruvian village, reported:

Mrs. C. does not understand germ theory, in spite of Nelida's repeated explanations. How, she argues, can microbes survive in water which would drown people? Are they fish? If germs are so small that they cannot be seen or felt, how can they hurt a grown person? There are enough real threats in the world to worry about—poverty, hunger—without bothering with tiny animals one cannot see, hear, touch, or smell. Mrs. C's allegiance to traditional customs are at odds with the boiling water. A firm believer in the hot-cold superstition, she feels that only the sick must drink boiled water. (p. 4)

From the consumer's viewpoint, social marketing seems more complex than ordinary marketing: One becomes more deeply involved, for example, in joining a civil rights movement than in purchasing a commodity. Social marketing is probably more affected by group influence than is conventional marketing: When causes such as gay rights or capital punishment run counter to group norms, the group is more likely to ostracize a member adopting these ideas than one who wears clothing or takes food considered "different." Sometimes the adopter of an idea, and certainly the individual who joins a movement, is motivated by a need to counter authority.

It would seem that adoption behavior is based upon more subtle and indirect motivation than acquisition behavior. In committing oneself to follow a particular movement one probably undergoes a good deal of forethought. Impulse buying is not very prevalent in social marketing, with exceptions such as hot lines for suicide, VD, or mental health. The purchase of a tangible good is a trend phenomenon. No matter how expensive, one can later exchange a car, one can discard it when it has become rusty and useless, but the adoption of a concept often results in an enduring state of affairs. The idea to vote for tax reform, government subsidies, or nuclear energy, for example, has far-reaching and long-lasting consequences.

The price paid (usually some nonmonetary sacrifice) in exchange for the adoption of a concept is more difficult to understand than the stated cash price of an object. Different communication channels are sometimes employed to diffuse ideas than those used to sell goods—lobbying, newsletters, organizationally sponsored phone calls, and so forth. Finally, social marketers have discussed client participation in program development, a notion completely foreign in business transactions.

Questions relating to similarities and differences between consumption processes of acquiring traditional and social products are considered in the remainder of this chapter. Under the tacit assumption that one's propensity for social goods is identifiable and even measurable, the aim of the chapter is to compare characteristics of individuals more involved (in some sense) with social products than with ordinary goods and services. An ancillary aim is to attempt to isolate significant correlates of such involvement.

CONCEPTUAL FRAMEWORK

While it has no rigid pattern of discourse, consumer behavior is typically studied in terms of such components as perception, cultural values, attitudes, group influence, personality, learning, cognition, decision making, social class, and information processing. For present purposes, these are coalesced into the first five factors and are addressed with emphasis on the exchange of intangibles. The way is thus paved for an empirical exploration, described later in this chapter.

Perception

Perception is the ability with which an individual grasps a concept; it is a process of organizing a picture in one's mind about some situation, and at the same time a learning process that depends upon the experience and cognitive style the individual brings to the situation. Cognitive style is the degree of complexity with which mental processes occur. Of the many theories of learning and perception borrowed from the field of psychology for the study of consumer choice processes, the theory of cognitive style seems particularly relevant to the perception of social goods, in which mental processes would seem to be more dominant than sensory perception. For while the apparatus for perceiving a tangible object is brought into play very readily, perception of a concept requires primarily mental processes in which cognitive style becomes more important. Here the cognitively complex person is better equipped to perceive the ramifications and implications of abstract concepts than is the simple, concrete individual.

With social goods, perception stems from one's own picture rather than that presented by the product itself. (This argument has another side. While it is true that one views an object objectively and a concept subjectively, most phenomena are evaluated by a combination of objectivity and subjectivity. Both components of thought are realities of the human condition [Berkovitz 1980].) For example, the impact on perception of the assignment of an appropriate brand name to a concept was discussed in Chapter 4.

Perception was reported to be a significant factor in such issues as change to the metric system and decimalization of currency in England, because the marketing of these products poses complex learning problems. Another illustration is seen in the effort in 1968 by the city of New York to inaugurate the emergency phone number 911 for toll-free emergency calls to the police department. Unanticipated misperceptions on the part of the public resulted in a great number of calls that were not emergencies, but included requests for directions to one place or another, or for a police officer to repair a malfunctioning air conditioner. Because of such large-scale misperceptions by the market, a massive demarketing campaign was introduced in 1973 using the slogan "Save 911 for the Real Thing"; a modest reduction in nonemergency calls resulted.

Marketers of the idea of pursuing higher education have become aware during the 1970s that the youth market has modified its perceptions regarding that product. The 1970s introduced an era in which consumers making up this market were reassessing alternative ways of expending time, effort, and money in quest of career preparation.

A key reason for the marketer to understand the learning and perceptual capacities of the market for a social product stems from the nature of the exchange transaction itself, which in social marketing is always an educative process. In addition to the business role, the social marketer is also a teacher. Thus marketing strategy for child abuse prevention includes the establishment of workshops to aid abused children and abusive parents alike, as well as other educative devices.

Much has been written about the effect of information load supplied by the marketer and on the consumer's ability to process that information (see, for example, Wilkie 1977). Increasingly, marketers are becoming concerned with limitations on the amount of information that the consumer can process. Too much information may inhibit brand choice in consumer goods (Jacoby, Speller, and Kohn 1974) and similarly with social products. Zarrel Lambert (1977), for example, found that consumers experience substantial difficulty in translating large amounts of nutrition-label arguments into intelligent food shopping decisions. Information overload is no doubt an inhibiting factor in the absorption of such ideas as credit purchasing, franchising, and vegetarianism. Clearly, marketing strategy for ideational products calls for at least some inquiry into the perceptual capacities of the potential audience.

Attitudes

Of all consumer characteristics, none appears to have been more widely investigated and discussed in psychological and buyer behavior literature than attitudes, attitude change, and the relationship between attitudes and behavior. A concise synthesis, from a marketing viewpoint, of the debate over whether attitude change precedes behavior change or vice versa is given in James Taylor and Robert Jones (1978). Jagdish Sheth (1978) makes use of the reality that people's attitudes are often at odds with their actual behavior, by suggesting that a target market be segmented according to whether or not such discrepancy exists. Sheth illustrated with a social product—the idea of birth control.

In her fascinating conceptualization of the product, "a view of animals" marketed by zoos, Carol Kovach (1978) observed: "A visitor's attitude and receptiveness toward each animal needs to be assessed in order to determine whether it is worth packaging that animal in a new, perhaps costly exhibit . . ." (p. 353). Planning mass media campaigns for population control, Richard Manoff (1973) appealed to self-interests of target segments by taking attitudes into account: "The audience we had to deal with involved differences in religious views about conception, contraception, and birth control in general; political philosophies, such as the feeling on the part of some militant blacks that population control is basically genocidal" (p. 114). Examples of other social products toward which consumer attitudes have been explored are energy conservation (Milstein 1977), antismoking (O'Keefe 1971), the United Nations (Douglas et al. 1970), air pollution (Kassarjian 1971), and mass transit (Gilbert and Foerster 1977).

The failure of many information campaigns has been attributed to attitudinal barriers such as that which marketers call "selective perception." Mincing no words, psychologists Herbert Hyman and Paul Sheatsley (1947) described this phenomenon as a closed-minded or hard core of chronic "know-nothings" segment—people who are receptive only to information in which they are interested. ". . . People seek the sort of facts which are congenial to their existing attitudes" (p. 412), they argue, so why bother with elaborate campaigns. A generation earlier, Walter Lippmann (1922) expressed the same sentiment, but more kindly: "For the most part we do not first see, and then define, we define first and then see. In the great blooming, buzzing confusion of the outer world, we pick out what our culture has already defined for us, and we tend to perceive that which we have picked out in the form stereotyped for us by our culture" (p. 31).

Paul Bloom and William Novelli (1979) point out that social marketers face attitudes different from those confronting commercial marketers in one respect. Ordinarily, purveyors of goods and services plan appeals aimed at buyers, but the opposite is true with advocates of change. "Social marketers often face target markets who have the strongest *negative* predispositions toward their offerings" (p. 6). Examples include antilittering campaigns, value of education to dropouts, and metric measurements to those accustomed to English measures. However, one wonders. Are not all marketers, including those of tangible goods, confronted by consumers who are yet to be convinced? Otherwise what is meant by "brand switching"? Attitude (or habit) change occurs in individuals whether they change brands, quantities purchased, preconceived ideas, or voting preferences.

Cultural Values

Cultural values are social standards deemed desirable by a group. The impact of cultural values on consumption behavior has been examined in detail by Milton Rokeach (1973) and others. In an empirical study, W. H. Henry (1976) attempted to measure the actual extent of such impact, and D. L. Poston and Joachim Singelmann (1975) examined value orientations in fertility behavior. The Affirmative Action Movement and other such activities are virtually synonymous with changes in cultural values.

Because most issues are by definition two-sided, the concept market is dichotomized with each side likely to be characterized by a distinct value system and each side affected by different group influence. The issue of legalized gambling is a case in point. Consumers in favor of legalized gambling are likely to be made up of individuals whose value systems include a get-rich-quick component, while adherents of the work ethic probably are not favorably disposed toward this issue. The value of charity is evoked in appeals to blood donor, fund-raising drives, and so on.

Material and nonmaterial things are somehow related, and it is within such relationships that one may seek ties between the natures of the respective processes by which each is acquired. An early view by Ogburn (1922, in Etzioni and Etzioni-Halevy 1973, p. 477) sees the nonmaterial customs, beliefs, philosophies, mores, folkways, religion, laws, and so on—what may be subsumed under the culture rubric—as simply techniques for handling material things. He calls them the adaptive culture, because they are constantly adjusting to conform to new uses of material objects—the material culture. Ogburn's hypothesis of cultural lag suggests that the adaptive culture might lag behind the material culture "for varying lengths of time sometimes indeed for many years" (fifty years later Alvin Toffler referred to a similar phenomenon as future shock).

Ogburn illustrates by pointing to forests as material and conservation and reforestation as adaptive (ideas). Between change of the material culture (exploitation in this instance) and change in the adaptive culture, time lagged for many years. The theory of cultural lag introduces a temporal dimension into understanding the decision process in the adoption of social goods. One considers cultural values associated with physical goods that are related in some sense to the corresponding social good. The time lag itself could offer clues to decision-making differences.

Thus one could argue that the Women's Rights Movement lagged behind advances in kitchen appliances, the idea of Sunday closings (blue laws) followed the advent of suburban shopping centers, the euthanasia concept was given impetus by medical technology as it found new ways to keep the near-dead alive, and so on. For another example, compact automobiles and bicycles enjoyed wide use in most of the world long before American driving habits (adaptive culture) began to adjust to these materials. The material culture may be represented by the value of a comfortable and prosperous life. (Until early in the 1970s that value could typically be expressed by ownership of a large automobile, because for many years Americans were seduced into buying large cars.) After the thrill of high-speed driving is spent, a market is ready for appeals to the values of the pleasure of leisurely living, thrift through fuel economy, and compact-car ownership.

Individuals include ideas and social issues within their perceived assortments of commodities to be adopted only if it becomes culturally accepted to do so. This is because behavior is predicated to a large extent upon the value system of a society. It becomes important in the marketing of ideas and issues to determine not only the degree to which cultural values allow for change itself but also for change in emphasis from tangibles to abstract ideas.

There is some evidence that such a change appears to be current. This is not to say that Western society is ready, in the Thoreau spirit, to relinquish its preoccupation with technology, which is indeed on the rise. But that preoccupation is mediated by a hypothetical new ethic of consumption (Brown 1978) stressing loftier ideals than those available only from material goods. For example, the physical science disciplines are becoming "concerned with the social consequences of expanded technology and depletion of natural resources" (Sheth 1974, p. 404). Herbert Simons (1976) explained how this trend comes about:

> the quality of life issue could only have arisen in a society where technology had freed masses of people from the bondage of material necessity. If we are more openly critical of the way we live than we were a generation ago, it is because we now have the time to dream and the wherewithal to convert dreams into realities. Having satisfied biological and safety needs, to use Maslow's terminology, we now have the luxury of pursuing ego, belongingness, and self-actualization needs. Technology provided that extra into the system. . . . People are evincing greater interest in humanistic and spiritual values, and diminished interest in materialistic values, status goals, and unqualified economic growth. (p. 246)

Thus recent interest in social products stems directly from the technology with which that interest appears, at first glance, to be antithetical. As Simons points out, the technoculture and the socioculture (what Simons calls the counterculture) are related. For substantiation, Simons quotes Kenneth Burke: "the human being is distinguished from other animals, not by his capacity to make tools (including symbolic tools such as those employed in advertising), but by his capacity to make tool-making tools." To this Simons adds: "man also has tools for assessing the tools he has made. It is this gift of feedback which is our greatest hope for the future" (p. 246).

The new ethic of consumption has dual importance in consumer research. First, it evidences a trend toward concern for social products, itself a significant reality to social marketers. Second, it implies some evolutionary alterations of people's value systems and hence in consumer decision processes. Social marketers can be encouraged that receptivity to social reform is in keeping with current trends in cultural values. The populace is ripe for campaigns for the promotion of altruistic ideas.

Group Influence

Product offerings are supposed to be designed in such a manner as to render them capable of satisfying consumers' needs and desires. But it is useful to distinguish between needs and desires. In a very general way, the former is inherent in the individual; the latter is created by group norms: "In some societies, for example, there are norms or customs against husbands and wives discussing family-planning matters, despite an eagerness on the part of both parties to implement the family-planning concept" (Stycos in Zaltman and Lin 1971, p. 662).

All people are influenced by the standards of groups to which they belong (membership groups), peer groups, work groups, and so forth, as well as those to which they vicariously aspire (reference groups). Upholding group norms and standards yields rewards that include status, friendship, and recognition; deviants face ostracism or even expulsion from the group.

One way to demonstrate conformity is to acquire and exhibit possession of things held in high regard by other members, a habit inculcated into middle-class Americans at several ontological stages. Kindergarten children hold show-and-tell seisisions at which they share pride of ownership of new toys. Later on, boys in the Indian Guide movement are taught to relate various ways in which they were of service in the home: "I put the garbage out." Boy and Girl Scouting also generates pride in adherence to altruistic ideas such as the good deed and physical fitness. Historically, college youth have gained group acceptance from the espousal of timely social causes or political issues. One can go on and on.

In the marketing of such advocacy products as nutrition improvement and population control, many have advanced the principle of client participation in the planning process. The idea here is that those who are to be served or affected by an innovation should be given the opportunity to make known to the policy-makers their own ideas, felt needs, group standards, and suggestions for implementation. It has been argued that the practice should alleviate the alienation and sense of powerlessness usually characteristic of those in need. The planees thus represented are more likely to "buy" the social concept than if it were imposed upon them or even suggested to them entirely from outside their own group—as exemplified in the cry of "no taxation without representation" preceding the American Revolution. (In that severe case the entire social structure was predicated on opposition to social injustice, a rather extreme social marketing endeavor in its own right. There, group influence erupted into mob influence, typifying the point at which the marketing of ideas and social issues is transformed into a radical movement for social change, and similarly with the case of strikes by labor unions.)

Client participation has not proven to be a panacea. Matthew Cremson (1974) and others reported that rival factions and selfish concerns among participants themselves have undermined cooperative efforts and the potency of the entire group as an influence (p. 357). What results may be described as an "Animal Farm" situation (Orwell 1946) in which those who formerly bewailed exclusion from the group now exclude others. The issue remains an open question, with opinion divided between those who see client participation as an important factor in the decision process and others who argue that participation can impede rather than expedite consumption of social goods.

Ideas, like tangibles, are in style or out of style at varying times, depending upon the extent to which their adoption serves the desires of individuals to conform to norms established by membership as well as reference groups.

Personality

Personality is the set of characteristics determining the unique way that an individual reacts to the environment. These characteristics include sociability, self-acceptance, tolerance, introvertism, liberalism, dogmatism, and many others. Diffusion theorists (Rogers and Shoemaker 1971), amassing an impressive "tradition of research," have labeled personality types according to how readily individuals adopt innovations (Figure 9.1). Thus one who is usually quick to "buy" a new idea is called an innovator, while others may be early adopters, early and late majorities, and laggards. Innovators have been found to differ from laggards in that they are more open-minded, better educated, younger, enjoy higher socioeconomic status, and are better integrated into the fabric of society. Almost by definition they see less risk in adopting new ideas (and things).

Sociologists have isolated other personality types with reference to the diffusion of innovations. A large literature discusses the opinion leader, a most trusted carrier of information about new ideas (thorough treatments may be

FIGURE 9.1

Personality Types According to Adoption of Innovations

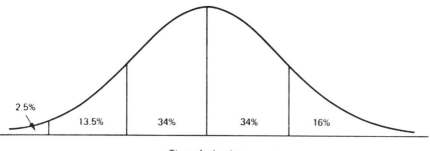

Time of adoption

Innovators	2.5%	Late majority	34.0%
Early adopters	13.5%	Laggards	16.0%
Early majority	34.0%		

Source: Robertson 1971, p. 90.

seen in Robertson 1971, ch. 7). If the opinion leader is a carrier, another person-ality type is situated at the other, the receiving, end of the message channel. This is the open-minded individual, who is highly prone to discuss an innovation (Jacoby 1976, p. 1042). Social marketers must rely on this type to try new things. The opinion leader transmits the idea and the open-minded continues the diffusion process. Steven Baumgarten (1975) and others found, not surprisingly, that the early adopter personality was likely to also be an opinion leader; they called such consumers innovative communicators (of fashion trends).

A classic framework for examining personality types is Abraham Maslow's (1970) hierarchy of needs model. This model is so very much a byword in the social sciences that it hardly needs elaboration here. To be sure, people whose physiological needs—food, shelter, sex—are not met can hardly be expected to allocate precious decision-making resources to the adoption of other social products. It seems reasonable to assume that as an individual climbs to higher socioeconomic levels, the consumption "shopping basket" contains an increasing proportion of ideas and issues over goods and services. On the other hand, individuals who have attained the lofty status of self-actualization in the Maslow model surely continue to acquire conventional goods. Are they then less involved with these goods than they were when positioned lower down the hierarchy? What is the relationship between tangibility of product and height of ascension on the Maslow model? The research described later in this chapter attempts to deal with such questions.

More generally, how do personality types, and innovativeness in particular, affect the types of product offerings on which this book focuses? Robertson (1970) found that innovativeness depends on product type. "A clearer innovative profile is obtained on a product category basis, instead of across all product cate-gories" (p. 137). An individual with an inclination for quick adoption for one kind of exchange may be slow to adopt another product type. If this is so with respect to differing traditional products, then it surely must apply to social products.

On the other hand it would not be surprising if a certain personality type consistently showed propensity for a "market basket" comprised of certain tra-ditional as well as social products. For example, adopters of the idea of personal-ized license plates could possess similar personality traits to those of consumers of optional chromium adornments on their vehicles.

Personality traits in social marketing were investigated by Ira Kaufman (1971), who set out to find which personality characteristics have greatest impact upon the degree with which individuals respond to communications re-garding the National Safety Council's Defensive Driving Course. A questionnaire was developed containing scales to measure dogmatism, internal-external control, self-esteem, social responsibility, values, anxiety, and other variables. The ques-tionnaire was personally administered to several hundred households in a middle-class area of Illinois. Following the survey, the experimental community was exposed to certain types of ads, via selected media, promoting the course.

Kaufman found, among other things, that more anxious people responded best to appeals low in fear arousal and that the image of the Defensive Driving Course as a product needed clarification in future advertising planning. The inquiry serves to illustrate how personality factors may be investigated and findings translated into marketing strategy in social marketing.

In some sense, a society also has a personality, a zeitgeist, or current trend of feeling. (At least a society is tagged with an anthropomorphised personality in the form of norms and pressures generated by the personalities embedded in individuals making up that society—something akin to Emile Durkheim's "collective conscience.") Earlier, a trend was described in consumer interest toward nonmaterial products, a phenomenon that may also be seen as a change in zeitgeist. Invoking David Riesman's typology of social character, Kassarjian and Robertson (1973) pointed out in that connection:

> A society of tradition-directed people . . . is characterized by general slowness of change, a dependence on kin, low social mobility, and a tight web of values. Inner-directed people are most often found in a rapidly changing, industrialized society with division of labor, high social mobility, and less security; these persons must turn to inner values for guidance. In contrast, other-directed persons depend upon those around them to give direction to their actions. The other-directed society is industrialized to the point that its orientation *shifts from production to consumption.* (Emphasis added. p. 138)

Implicit in this observation is further evidence of people's concern for ideas and social issues in their quest for success, as Kassarjian and Robertson (1973) argue, "not through production and hard work, but rather through one's ability to be liked by others, develop charm or 'personality,' and manipulate other people" (p. 138). But these abilities are enhanced by one's proclivity for the absorption of ideas and keeping abreast of current issues.

In this section five component topics in the study of consumer behavior were discussed from the standpoint of their relevance to the adoption of ideas. To be sure, an adoption process typically involves more than just one decision factor. For example, philanthropy, a social product (idea), is affected by group influence as well as by attitudes: "Individuals will donate to a charity only to avoid . . . social pressures, religious beliefs, and psychic unpleasantries" (Phelps 1975, p. 198). For another example of overlap of these factors, the other-directedness of industrialized society can just as well be seen as a cultural value, as collective personality. An attempt was made to relate these concepts to the decision processes involved in adopting ideas and to demonstrate their applicability to those processes. If they do indeed apply as well to the adoption process as to the acquisition process, then what may one assume about people's perceptions about these differences? Some of the premises explored above are examined empirically in the next section.

CONTRASTING PRODUCT BUYERS WITH IDEA ADOPTERS

This section reports the results and implications of a pilot study designed to investigate empirically perceived differences between the processes of acquisition of ordinary goods and services, and adoption of ideas. The purpose of the study was to compare characteristics of individuals more involved with social products than with ordinary goods; profiles of these two consumer types are developed.

Study Design

A questionnaire was administered to 247 students at Rutgers University in New Jersey so that respondents constitute a "convenience," nonrandom sample. Time constraints on the project precluded the use of probability sampling but nonresponse bias was diminished by obtaining a 100 percent return rate. The instrument was both structured and indirect in that it included specific items while purporting to uncover inferences, motivations, and subconscious feelings.

As a basis for analysis of comparative consumption decision making, a matrix (Appendix C) was prepared listing in its left-hand column 12 products—three each of tangibles, services, ideas, and issues. Thus the first six were conventional offerings and the other six were social products. Across the top of the matrix provision was made for five criterion measures to be scored by respondents on each of the 12 products. This arrangement made possible summative scores on each of the five criteria for conventional and for social transactions. Dividing the latter by the former yielded ratios representing relative values comparing social with traditional products.

Symbolically, if x_{ij} ($i = 1, 2, \ldots, 12$ and $j = 1, 2, \ldots, 5$) is the respondent's score on criterion j with respect to product i, then the five ratios are

$$r_j = \frac{\sum\limits_{i=7}^{12} x_{ij}}{\sum\limits_{i=1}^{6} x_{ij}}$$

These ratios constitute a set of indices whose construction was motivated by the earlier discussion of factors in the study of consumer behavior, although some have conceptual roots in other social science literature. The indices are:

The decision worth index: attempting to measure relative attitude toward the two focus product types by asking "How much time and effort is the purchase decision worth?"

The diffusion index: a measure of group influence asking for the number of people with whom the respondent would discuss the purchase decision.

Paul Placek (1974) used a similar measure in a family planning study (p. 555).

The confidence in judging index: appears in one form or another in most buyer behavior models. Respondents were asked for a self-rating of "your confidence in your ability to judge the product." It is thus also a measure of perception to discriminate between product types.

The opinion leadership index: follows Rogers and Shoemaker (1971, p. 217), asking whether "people seek out your opinions about the product."

The adoption index: obtained by asking whether the respondent is one of the last or one of the first to buy, that is, does he or she tend to be more of a "laggard" or an "innovator" personality type, a concept originating in rural sociological studies of diffusion of farm practices (North Central 1961).

In addition to these indices, an "importance" question (number 27) attempted to measure directly the respondent's perceived relative importance of the two product classes by requesting that subjects "divide ten points between them (constant sum scaling) according to how important they are to you." It was intended that this question would capture the respondent's perception of his or her concern for, or involvement with concept adoption as compared with product acquisition. The item was positioned within the instrument in such a way that by the time it appeared, the subject should have obtained some insight into the distinction between concepts and commodities. This "importance" question produced the criterion variable in the study. That is, all respondents were to be grouped either low or high on their relative involvement with concepts as products. Involvement as a construct in consumer behavior has been studied in detail by Herbert Krugman (1977) and Michael Rothschild (1978).

Two scales (groups of questions) were incorporated into the study. One was Srole's Anomie Scale, which measures self-to-others belongingness at one extreme and self-to-others distance or alienation at the other end. The scale consists of five items with which the respondent indicates disagreement/agreement. The scores therefore fall within the range of 0 to 5, with the higher score indicative of a greater manifestation of anomie. The other scale was the Citizen Political Action Scale, developed by the League of Women Voters to assess individual participation in community service. It is scored in a range from 1 to 12 as follows: 10-12, an outstanding citizen, 6-9, an average citizen, and 0-5, a citizen? (Miller 1970). These scales were selected to provide a larger base of information about respondents' personality traits (degree of introvertism) and values (concern for society). Their questions appear as items 1 through 5 and 6 through 17 respectively, in the questionnaire (Appendix C).

Other "psychographic" data were sought through questions about materialism, conservatism, and personal goals. Goals (or objectives) of the consumer are introduced here as a surrogate measure for values. While Rokeach (1973) and others have provided much raw material to consumer researchers with which to investigate values, there are precious few studies extant on consumer objectives (see Chapter 10). The usual gamut of demographic items completed the survey instrument.

Survey Results

One hundred and fifty-six respondents rated tangible goods and services as a more important product category than ideas and issues. The remaining 91 cases assigned higher ratings to the ideational than to the conventional product classes. Referring to individuals in the former group as materialists and those in the latter

TABLE 9.1

Group Means on Significant Variables in the Consumer Study

Characteristic	Materialists (n = 56)	Idealists (n = 91)	Significance
Demographics			
Household head, sex (percent female)	8.33	14.29	c
Family residence, percent owned (vs. rented)	83.33	76.82	c
Respondent's sex (percent female)	28.85	46.15	a
Respondent's age	21.78	22.46	b
Ever married (percent)	9.62	23.08	a
Race (percent nonwhite)	7.05	24.18	a
Employed, hours per week	21.67	18.46	c
Television viewing, hours per week	9.87	8.68	c
Radio listening, hours per week	12.21	10.77	c
Catholic (percent)	72.44	56.04	a
Protestant (percent)	9.62	20.88	a
Psychographics			
Decision worth index	0.92	0.97	c
Diffusion index	1.01	1.13	b
Opinion leadership index	0.94	1.02	c
Adoption index	0.91	0.99	c
Anomie (0–5, belonging–alienated)	1.55	1.14	a
Citizen political action (0–12, poor–good)	3.86	4.49	c
Materialistic–idealistic (1–5)	2.62	3.20	a
Goal in life is wealth (percent)	17.95	4.40	a
Goal in life is learning (percent)	8.33	19.78	a

Significant at: 0.01 (a), 0.05 (b), 0.10 (c).
Source: Fine (1980c).

as idealists, what follows are comparative descriptive consumer profiles to emerge from the study. (These labels are strictly for identification purposes and surely do not imply a respondent's lifelong commitment to either philosophy. Typical of any cross-sectional inquiry, all that can be claimed here is that at the time of the study the materialists, for example, professed greater interest or involvement in the six conventional offerings than in the social products listed in the matrix.) Table 9.1 lists within-group mean scores for materialists and idealists on those characteristics showing significant differences between the groups.

Not surprisingly, idealists again perceived themselves as more idealistic in response to a direct question (number 37). Furthermore the same sentiment consistently appeared in four out of the five matrix indices defined earlier in this section: the decision worth index, the diffusion index, the opinion leadership index, and the adoption index. Somewhat disappointing was the index measuring confidence in judging social products. Apparently, self-confidence, or its lack, transcends product type.

The idealist group included a significantly higher percentage of older, female, married, and racial minority individuals. Linkage of matriarchy with idealism appears again, in the result that a disproportionately large number of idealists came from homes where the head of the household was female. Religion appeared to be a significant characteristic in the study suggesting that Catholics are more likely to perceive themselves as materialistic and Protestants tending toward the idealistic. Other demographics, although somewhat less significant, portray idealists as less likely than materialists to own rather than rent their homes, spend less time attending to radio or television, and less time at their jobs.

Idealists are a gregarious group, with obviously higher interest in belongingness. On average, they scored significantly lower on the anomie scale and higher on the citizenship scale, revealing greater concern for community service and social action. These results are consonant with the manifestation for dominance in the spread of information that they revealed in their scores on the opinion leadership and diffusion indices. Not surprisingly, a greater percentage of materialists indicated wealth as a primary goal in life while wisdom dominated the goal choices of idealists.

Contrary to expectation, idealists and materialists demonstrated no significant differences in such socioeconomic factors as family income and education. The groups were also quite similar in volume of newspaper and magazine readership, although one can conjecture that their respective members read different material. Finally, respondents' self-designation on the conservative/liberal continuum was also unrelated to group separation.

One concludes that distinct differences as well as similarities may well be expected when comparing the concept adoption process with conventional purchase activity, at least with respect to certain characteristics of the consumer.

The pilot investigation reported in this chapter has barely scratched the surface of the complex problem undertaken. Yet it already seems clear that a consumer market for ideas and social issues must be examined through a different lens from that employed for purchases of commodities. Idealistic propensities exist and should be interesting to study. At the operational level, fullest use should be made of opinion leaders, adopters, and other personality types described by profiles like that drawn from this and similar studies. But this is easier said than done. In all marketing, whether for tangibles or concepts, precious little is known about how to locate, stimulate, or utilize word-of-mouth channels. It is an area in desperate need of research.

The choice of 12 products was restrictive. For the five indices to have been more meaningful, one could have randomly sampled from a larger assortment of offerings and results of the pilot project reported here are thus difficult to generalize. Nevertheless, the study suggests one method for further analysis.

SUMMARY

This chapter has attempted to demonstrate that a social consumer behavior may be pursued within the broader discipline of consumer psychology. Marketers have always been interested in the needs and desires of target groups and in characteristics affecting those needs and desires. For it is in their ability to develop and market products capable of satisfying customers that marketers earn their keep; this is true whether the product is a tangible good or a social cause. The purpose of the research discussed in this chapter will be well served if its results can be used to further the state of the art of consumer behavior, with respect to the process of adopting social products.

The idea of comparing consumer involvement with conventional and social offerings was explored. An "importance" variable was used as a proxy measure for involvement in the decision-making process for the adoption of ideas and social issues, on the one hand, and for the acquisition of conventional goods and services, on the other. Five determining factors of the choice process were discussed: perception, cultural values, group influence, attitudes, and personality. Another factor, consumers' goals, is taken up in Chapter 10.

Social marketing has established itself as a discipline with a growing body of knowledge and an awareness of its importance among theoreticians and practitioners alike. Most of its literature has to do with the standard marketing model—price, product, promotion, and distribution. The area of social consumer behavior is, as of this writing, virtually unexplored. Only a few topics believed to be among the more relevant were treated in this chapter, which, it is hoped, will spark further investigation into this fascinating and relatively untapped area of consumer research.

10

SEGMENTATION BY GOALS IN SOCIAL MARKETING

Like—but oh! how different!
—William Wordsworth, *Yes it was the Mountain Echo*

This chapter investigates a method of market segmentation based on the objectives and choice strategies of target consumption units. It is suggested that consumers' objectives and choice strategies are precursory to other variables—demographics, psychographics—(see Chapter 4) typically employed as segmenting criteria, and hence their use may result in more meaningful segmentation studies than have previously been common. That premise stems from the author's conviction that people's goals underlie their decisions to adopt ideas and to take positions on social issues, as well as other purchase decisions.

This is perhaps the most ambitious chapter of the book. For not only is segmentation by goals a new concept, but because goals are extremely difficult to measure (what researchers call the operationalization problem), a mathematical scheme is advanced as a possible step in the resolution of that dilemma. If the treatment in this chapter appears technical to the reader, it is because portions are, indeed, technical; that is the nature of social research technology. On the other hand, technical aspects and the mathematical formulations in particular, may be sidestepped with little, if any, loss of continuity.

The product studied as a case in point in this chapter is a social cause—malnutrition amelioration in a developing country. The social marketing approach to nutrition intervention, and the importance of market segmentation research in that approach, are presented. Consumers' objectives and choice strategies are

---

An earlier version of this chapter appeared in the *Journal of Consumer Research*, June 1980.

then discussed, and methodology centers about the specification of two models in terms of survey sample data. Both models are tested on these data and threats to validity and reliability are taken into account. The chapter concludes with a brief summary and some implications of the investigation.

It is particularly appropriate to exemplify an abstract concept such as segmentation by objectives, with a correspondingly impalpable social product, rather than with a conventional good or service. When considering the adoption of an idea as important as family nutrition, the consumer's decision process no doubt addresses internal psychic factors including very basic goals. By contrast, ordinary purchases are likely performed in a more surface manner.

Although the idea of nutrition intervention is used in this chapter merely as an example of a social product, that idea plays more than a passing role in the study's development. Intertwining illustrative cases with subject matter is common in social marketing, probably because writers experience a high degree of involvement with social products. For example, a recent inquiry into the marketing of zoos (Kovach 1978) was dominated by animal lore, which in no way detracted from the interest generated by that paper. The phenomenon of over-emphasis on illustrations imparts to social marketing an interdisciplinary flavor that, by its very definition, it deserves. Moreover, real-world examples hold an especially important place in a new and abstract discipline like social marketing, if only to facilitate familiarity with its precepts. On the other hand, it is hoped that a theory of segmentation by objectives, toward which this chapter is directed, will have generalizability to other social products.

BACKGROUND OF THE STUDY

In 1970, the U.S. Agency for International Development sponsored a major project, "An Operations Oriented Study of Nutrition as an Integrated System in the State of Tamil Nadu." Tamil Nadu is situated at the southern tip of the Indian subcontinent and occupies an area of 50,000 square miles with a population (1971) of 43 million. For various reasons, primarily political (for example, the outbreak of the Bangladesh war), work on the Tamil Nadu study was truncated shortly after data collection.

The problem of malnutrition, plaguing two thirds of the world's inhabitants, may be viewed from two possible vantage points. The first concerns actual food products—innovative enriched or fortified foods, modernization of food warehousing and distribution systems to reduce spoilage, and lowering of prices through more efficient operations (Sheth and Sudman in Sheth and Wright 1974). The second, which is highlighted in this chapter, deals with educative aspects of nutrition. It is aimed at strengthening nutrition programs through the diffusion of awareness about food/health relationships among target consumers and by disseminating information regarding particular foods that should be consumed for maximum nutritive benefits.

A (social) marketing approach to this problem considers malnourished individuals as comprising a market and malnutrition amelioration as a product to be marketed so as to satisfy the needs of the ill-fed. Specifically, the idea of a more healthful eating pattern within the home is to be marketed to a target audience. As with conventional product marketing, this approach would take into account such factors as price, promotion, and distribution in planning for the dissemination of nutrition programs, factors making up the four Ps marketing model. Because markets are heterogeneous, an early step in marketing strategy is to segment the market in some way so that product design and campaign planning may be somewhat individualized.

The need for segmentation in nutrition planning has been stressed by nutrition advocates (Berg, Scrimshaw, and Call 1973). Nutrition intervention must be preceded by identification of vulnerable target subgroups and isolation of the most important determinants of malnutrition. Such variables are components of a vector that A. Berg and R. Muscat (1972) suggest calling "an economic or *eco-nutritional profile* which would characterize the group . . . (and) serve as a kind of litmus paper against which any of the standard nutrition intervention programs could be tested" (p. 947).

Having selected the Tamil Nadu nutrition data with which to demonstrate the concept of segmentation by objectives, it seemed natural to designate the family as the unit of analysis. The family, and especially the extended family, is the focus in most sociological studies of preindustrial societies.

Objectives and Choice Strategies of the Consumer

Theoretical conceptualization stems from Charles Granger's (1964) hierarchy of objectives. While he admitted, "In reality we know very little about the nature of objectives" (p. 74), Granger's model demonstrated tnat objectives (goals) underlie choice strategies (decision rules), which, in turn, determine tactics (behavior). (Words in parentheses will be taken as synonymous, and used interchangeably, with Granger's.) The concept is schematized below:

Objectives (goals)
↓
Choice Strategies (decision rules)
↓
Behavior (adoption, purchase)

Subscribing to the logic of the Granger model, one would propose that marketers' concern with consumer behavior should be broadened to include consumer objectives and choice strategies, because these are hierarchically superordinate to behavior. Even if goal setting does not occur first, it might be coincident with other decision processes that are of interest to consumer theorists.

The aim in this section is to show that consumer objectives might constitute a useful characteristic to consider in the continuing effort to understand consumption decision making and behavior. That thesis, which is central to this chapter, has relevance whether the unit of analysis is the individual, the diad, the household, or any other social group. The suggestion applies particularly to market segmentation studies in which a first step must necessarily involve selection of a segmentation criterion.

The family as a decision-making unit is a widely discussed area of consumer research that has been reviewed in well-known works of Davis, Ferber, Hempel, Sheth, and others; most of the studies reviewed by those authors are based on husband-wife interaction in purchase decisions. Richard Bagozzi and Frances Van Loo (1978) review decision-process models that also consider household behavior as social exchange, or based on social judgment theory. However, as Jagdish Sheth (1979b) notes, "more research and theory are clearly needed" in household decision making (p. 6). In particular, household objectives have not been explored in spite of Robert Ferber's (1977) observation that family goals are a "major determinant of family marketing decisions" (p. 82).

This is no less true at the level of the individual consumer, where marketers have explored a full gamut of demographics as well as consumer activities, interests, and opinions—the psychographics (Wells 1975)—values, attitudes, and even the very structure of the decision process (Bettman 1971). Indeed, Herbert Krugman (1977) has gone so far as to examine different roles played in the purchase decision by the right and left lobes of the brain. Yet fundamental objectives that consumers set for themselves do not appear to have been examined as factors having impact upon purchase behavior. This is surprising because objectives must affect decision making as well as actions.

In fact, not to recognize goals as antecedent to behavior overlooks rationality in the choice process, a process that begins with objectives. People have goals and use these goals to determine the decision rules that they adopt: "One of the things that seems to distinguish man from other creatures is his ability to think, to reason, and to make decisions with respect to identifiable goals. Further, human beings seem to take the most logical means toward the achievement of these goals. We define this characteristic as rationality" (Stratmann 1975, p. 539).

With particular emphasis on developing society settings, D. W. Adams and A. D. Havens (1966) pointed out that an early step in strategy formulation for the marketing of social change is to identify the objectives of the target people (p. 281). So it is curious that, although most theories of social choice stem from such reasoning (Downs 1957), it does not seem to be more popular in the study of consumer behavior.

While neglecting objectives, consumer researchers have not overlooked choice strategies, the link in the chain between objectives and behavior (Bettman 1971; Hansen 1972). Peter Wright (1975) observed:

Different choice strategies can imply different marketing tactics. Once the likely choice strategy is predicted, marketing activity can (1) accept that as a given and adjust to accommodate it . . ., (2) try directly persuading the consumer to use another strategy more favorable to ultimate selection of the advocated product, or (3) try to help the consumer restructure his decision problem (e.g., reduce it to a simpler task) which in turn induces him into using a different choice rule. (p. 60)

Choice strategies (as well as their underlying objectives) regarding intrafamily distribution of inadequate food supplies must occupy a critical position in households of developing societies. Moreover, intrafamily food distribution behavior does not appear to be a widely explored area of nutrition study (Berg and Muscat 1972, p. 941). In a comprehensive report on the progress of third world development, the World Bank called for a program to increase "peoples' awareness of the nutrient needs of various family members (for example, the importance of breast feeding, and of introducing supplementary foods at the appropriate age), . . . to help improve their diets" (World Bank 1978, p. 35).

Toward a Theory

It is doubtful that families formally enunciate objectives or the decision rules by which they hope to attain those objectives. However, it seems reasonable to assume that the existence of goals is implicit in household structure and behavior—where the family resides, its size, its religion, the amount of education members obtain, its value orientations, and so on. A theory of consumption behavior as a function of household objectives should begin with an assumption of the degree of rationality attributed to individuals. According to the notion of economic man, people are utility maximizers and follow a rational choice process. For example, Bagozzi and Van Loo (1978) have explored fertility behavior as resulting directly from family choice processes "wherein overall household satisfaction is maximized subject to the constraints of income and prices" (p. 199). People seem to maximize perceived utilities of money, time convenience, form, and quality of products purchased.

Earlier, Wright (1975) examined the ways in which consumers select among alternative choice strategies. He assumed

. . . the output of a consumer's cognitive averaging of data on an option is his estimate of its global "utility" or "affect." Given that output, a common assumption has been that he picks the option offering highest utility, a BEST rule. Another plausible assumption is that he sets up a cutoff on his global utility dimension and uses this to discriminate "acceptable" options (via an ALL or FIRST rule). He is seen performing something akin to a mental discriminant analysis. (p. 61)

However as argued in Chapter 2, marketers believe that individuals settle for alternatives they deem good enough and not necessarily maximal. If so, how are objectives (or decision rules) related to behavior? As a first cut at theory building, this chapter explores observed behavior and posits inferences from that behavior about the decision rules that precede it. The investigation performs not mental but statistical discriminant analysis and then later examines the selected decision rules by means of multiple regression analysis.

METHOD

The purpose of this inquiry was to consider how consumer objectives and decision rules can be employed in segmentation research and to investigate how such research may be useful in programming nutrition intervention. To carry out that purpose, an eclectic approach to segmentation modeling was developed. The first stage is an inquiry into the goals that families implicitly set for themselves—goals underlying behavior patterns, including food distribution habits. In this stage, three decision rules are postulated a priori, and families are segmented according to how closely they seem to follow these rules. This is the decision-rule model.

The second stage examines the family as a decision-making system and identifies a set of criteria as dependent variables. Characteristics of nutritional behavior are posited as influencing these criteria and an econometric decision-process model is structured. Whereas the decision-rule model describes the family's behavior, the decision-process model attempts to explain that behavior.

Like those of many emerging societies, individuals in Tamil Nadu are "tradition directed" (Riesman 1950), in that they have low social mobility and adhere to conduct dictated by religion, fate, and social class. They place their greatest trust in opinion leaders whom they know personally and who live in their own villages. Forces outside the local setting encounter considerable difficulty in imposing social change (witness recent failures of the Indian government's vasectomy program). The family is typically "joint" or "extended," with elders and other relatives participating in decision making. The Tamil belief system does not relate food to health. Instead, eating has ritual, caste, symbolic, and religious implications. Thus white foods—eggs, milk, finely ground rice—assume high status and acceptance only because of their whiteness; any nutritive value is coincidental (indeed, unpolished rice is more nutritious). Many Indians believe that a full stomach implies a well-fed person; they do not understand the concept of nutrition (Sheth and Sudman 1974, p. 162).

The data used were obtained in a food-habits survey questionnaire administered to a two-stage, stratified random sample of 2800 families in Tamil Nadu in 1972. The first stage of sampling was village and urban blocks and the second stage was the household (Cantor 1973, vol. IIA, p. 3). From the data bank generated by that study, a purposive subsample of 668 cases was selected for

TABLE 10.1

Within-Group Mean Scores, Univariate F Values, and Standardized Discriminant Coefficients (Weights)

Variables and Units of Measurement	Within-Group Means					Discriminant	
	All Cases	DEQU	DPRO	DIAG	Endowed	F	Weights
Family health status (index 1 to 100)	44.75	44.09	46.06	47.06	44.37	1.46	0.149
Food expenditure pattern (percent of income)	73.29	73.58	72.14	73.13	73.67	0.67	0.071
Nutrition practice (index 0 to 50)	13.57	13.50	13.58	13.20	13.97	0.28	0.061
Percent caloric needs met	78.01	63.60	81.70	89.76	117.69	152.99	0.925
Food purchases per caloric need (rupees)	39.26	41.52	31.86	43.67	37.74	0.98	0.033
Vegetarianism (percent)	28.83	28.76	29.52	27.96	28.73	2.40	0.029
Weaned child's food cost (rupees)	15.49	15.33	14.13	15.98	17.32	0.46	0.044
Nutrition information sought (percent)	14.82	16.36	12.00	9.26	15.45	1.42	0.133
Distance to nearest medical aid (kilometers)	2.93	2.93	2.77	2.64	3.23	0.19	0.021
District food output per capita (pounds)	238.68	220.54	234.82	263.59	293.37	3.61	0.007
Village electrified (percent)	94.16	95.51	96.80	96.30	85.45	0.21	0.076
Land value (1000 rupees)	4.11	3.39	3.06	4.54	7.58	0.58	0.002
Village water source (quality category)	1.71	1.73	1.70	1.70	1.69	0.13	0.038
District population growth rate (percent)	7.27	6.68	7.38	7.35	9.10	1.69	0.005
District literacy rate (percent)	40.58	41.42	40.10	38.37	39.29	2.60	0.122
Family wealth (index)	60.13	57.97	58.83	63.56	67.37	0.33	0.142
Religion is Hindu (percent)	88.47	86.81	92.00	90.74	89.09	1.40	0.119
Family caste (index)	2.09	2.13	2.02	1.96	2.13	1.74	0.226
Age of infant (months)	8.34	8.47	8.33	7.41	8.37	0.82	0.120
Infant is female (percent)	51.80	53.83	52.80	51.85	43.64	0.05	0.062

Per capita income (rupees)	29.09	26.96	29.58	33.22	33.84	2.76	0.019
Family income in kind (percent)	12.52	11.00	16.16	12.78	13.45	2.54	0.051
Family size	6.76	7.06	6.49	5.81	6.49	10.79	0.226
Household head's age	39.83	39.78	39.37	38.24	41.32	0.49	0.065
Household head's occupation (index)	3.23	3.26	3.26	3.22	3.09	0.03	0.017
Spouse's education difference (years)	1.05	1.01	1.07	1.04	1.18	0.10	0.074
Spouse's age difference (years)	8.44	8.39	8.28	9.11	8.48	0.34	0.070
Mother's age	27.87	27.91	27.55	26.96	28.55	0.74	0.098
Mother's age at marriage	17.76	17.68	17.46	18.30	18.12	1.83	0.018
Weaned child's age (years)	4.55	4.46	4.69	4.80	4.56	3.16	0.131
Weaned child is female (percent)	49.10	49.34	43.20	55.56	51.82	1.29	0.001
Mother employed, hours weekly	5.21	5.11	5.17	3.81	6.25	0.22	0.019
Household help (1 if yes)	0.38	0.40	0.38	0.24	0.42	2.43	0.030
Family education (years for highest)	3.67	3.72	3.59	3.59	3.65	0.51	0.212
Household head's nutrition status	116.88	114.60	127.96	115.33	112.89	–	–
Mother's nutrition status	86.32	89.65	81.89	74.46	85.68	–	–
Weaned child's nutrition status	99.88	98.07	89.26	114.28	111.09	–	–
Infant's nutrition status	101.91	114.63	89.22	92.89	76.90	–	–

Source: Constructed by the author.

reanalysis on the criterion that each family include an infant, a weaning child, and a lactating mother.

Table 10.1 lists potential determinants of intrafamily food distribution patterns used in the model-building procedure. Although most measurements were taken directly from the questionnaire, some result from recalculations or were drawn from secondary sources. In addition, the following indices were constructed not only to reduce the data but also because multiple measures tend to cancel out errors that may be inherent in single items.

Family health status: a weighted composite of several illness and health items appearing in the survey instrument. These include symptoms of nutritional deficiencies in key members, mortality and morbidity, as well as interviewers' general impressions.

Food expenditure pattern: the proportion of total expenses allocated to food purchases. This variable has been shown to have analytic importance in nutrition studies (Nicol 1974, p. 76).

Nutrition practice: Combines data on breast feeding, weaning practices, and birth spacings in keeping with the Knowledge, Attitude, Practice (KAP) model.

Family wealth: a weighted composite of the value of the house, the source of water supply, and the value of family owned land, combined similarly to Levinson (1972, p. 108).

Nutrition status: calculated for four key members—household head, lactating mother, infant, and weaning child—as the quotient of the percent of caloric needs met for the member, divided by that for the entire household. Each indicates relatively how the individual member fares nutritionally within the home.*

Specification of the Decision-Rule Model

How may goals be postulated for a household? Intuitively, one can imagine a family in which a primary goal is the physical well-being of its members. In another, a harmonious home life is all-important. One household seems to work toward the achievement of high status, or amassing a great deal of wealth, or friends, or knowledge, and so forth. But model specification requires a more formal framework than that provided by heuristics alone. The concept that a household is a social system homologous to friendship groups, business organi-

---

*The four nutrition status measures are listed in Table 10.1 but were excluded from the discriminant and multiple regression analyses because their numerators were involved in calculations of the three decision-rule distance measures in expression (3). Their inclusion in the analyses might have upwardly biased the results.

zations, and churches (Levy and Zaltman 1975, p. 40) suggests borrowing from other disciplines. This led to Igor Ansoff (1976), whose three organizational objectives (p. 38) provided a point of departure for the present analysis. These objectives are:

- Equal responsibility to all members.
- Negotiated consensus among members.
- Survival of some members.

While Ansoff's focus in on the corporate organization, these objectives should be generalizable to any social system. Extrapolating Ansoff's objectives to the case of intrafamily food distribution, the following decision rules are postulated corresponding to those objectives:

Equality: food is distributed in equal proportion to need.
Proportionality: Allotments vary proportionally according to status within the household.
Triage: needs are fulfilled hierarchically until supplies are exhausted.

The aim of this analysis is to determine how closely each family in the sample appears to be following a decision rule dictated by one of the three objectives and then to establish characteristics that identify groups of families following each rule. The following notation is used in developing the formulation (Fine 1980a):

N_i = caloric needs of member i in units, where one unit equals the average daily caloric requirements of an adult.

D = $\sum_{i=1}^{k} N_i$ = total caloric needs for a family of k members.

M_i = percent caloric needs being met for member i.
F = percent caloric needs being met for the entire household.
Q_i = $M_i N_i$ = observed caloric intake for member i in units.
T = DF = observed total caloric intake for the household.
X_i = allotment under the equality decision rule.
Y_i = allotment under the proportionality decision rule.
Z_i = allotment under the triage decision rule.

R^{i-1} = the proportionality rate for member i.   (1)

By definition
$$\sum_{i=1}^{k} X_i = \sum_{i=1}^{k} Y_i = \sum_{i=1}^{k} Z_i = T \tag{2}$$

The equality decision rule is conceptually rooted in the work of Richard Pollay (1968), who stressed distributive justice in family decision making. Equality occurs where $X_i = N_i F$.

The proportionality rule. "Negotiated consensus among participants" might involve intrafamily negotiation based on the presumption that some members are more "important" than others and hence should be favored nutritionally. To define importance, a rank ordering was constructed of status priorities for members in the family based on norms prevailing in the Tamil culture (Table 10.2). Given the estimated priority ranking, this decision rule says that the highest ranking member will get all caloric requirements filled, that is, will have 100 percent of its needs met. The second ranking member will be allotted a lesser proportion of needs and so on for all members with the rate diminishing geometrically by powers of the rate R, where R is a proportionality rate estimated for each family (Appendix D):

$$Y_1 = N_1 \text{ units}$$
$$Y_2 = R N_2 \text{ units}$$
$$\vdots \qquad \vdots$$
$$Y_k = R^{k-1} N_k \text{ units}$$

and

$$\sum_{i=1}^{k} Y_i = \sum_{i=1}^{k} (R^{i-1} N_i) = T$$

TABLE 10.2

Priority Ranking of Family Members Used in Proportionality and Triage Rules

Rank	Member
1	Male head of household
2	Male, not head of household, aged 13 to 60
3	Single female aged 13 to 25
4	Infant less than 2
5	Elders, not head of household
6	Children 2 to 13
7	Single female 26 to 60: married female 13 to 60
8	Others

Source: Adapted from Montgomery 1972, pp. 3, 150.

The triage rule. A "survival" rule might maximize the chance that at least some members (probably the most "important") survive, although at the expense of other members. Under this rule, each member receives his or her full requirements until the supply is exhausted and then the remaining members go without. P. S. Heller has argued that the probability of nutritional survival of some family members "is itself parentally influenced, if not determined" (Heller and Drake 1979, p. 206, n. 10). Employing the notation listed in (1), the triage rule is formulated as follows:

$$Z_i = N_i \text{ units}$$

$$\vdots \quad \vdots$$

$$Z_j = N_j \text{ units}$$

$$\vdots \quad \vdots$$

$$Z_{j+1} = T - \sum_{i=1}^{k} N_i \text{ units}$$

$$Z_{j+2} = 0 \text{ units}$$

$$\vdots \quad \vdots$$

$$Z_k = 0 \text{ units}$$

"Conformity" to each rule is defined for each family in terms of deviation for each member between actual reported food distribution and predicted distribution under the rule. Summing squared deviations over family members and taking square roots yields a Euclidean distance measure for each rule for each family. Euclidean distance is appropriate here because the data are assumed to be intervally scaled:

Deviation from equality:
$$\text{DEQU} = \left(\sum_{i=1}^{k} (Q_i - X_i)^2 \right)^{1/2}$$

Deviation from proportionality:
$$\text{DPRO} = \left(\sum_{i=1}^{k} (Q_i - Y_i)^2 \right)^{1/2}$$

Deviation from triage:
$$\text{DIAG} = \left(\sum_{i=1}^{k} (Q_i - Z_i)^2 \right)^{1/2}$$

These three distance measures (DEQU, DPRO, and DIAG), whose acronyms also identify their respective food distribution strategies (the postulated decision rules), were calculated for each household, and a new (trichotomized) measure was constructed indicating which of the three distances has lowest value for each household. It thus tells whether the family most closely follows the equality, the proportionality, or the triage allocation strategies and also serves as the variable upon which segmentation is based. Because the segmentation criterion is pre-specified, discriminant analysis is used in the grouping process. If "natural" groupings were desired, cluster analysis would have been employed first.

Specification of the Decision-Process Model

For longer-term considerations and nutritional policymaking, it is also useful to amplify the meaning of segment characteristics by assessing their influence upon one or more consequences of household behavior. In this section an econometric decision-process model is specified in order to attempt to explain Tamil nutrition behavior. The model is estimated for each segment, providing deeper understanding of segment differences.

An important early step in the design of an econometric investigation is the identification of one or more appropriate dependent variables upon which the impact of explanatory variables may be assessed. The following indexes, defined above, were selected: family health status, nutrition practice, and food expenditure pattern. These are virtually independent of the decision-rule distance measure ($r = 0.03, 0.01$, and 0.05, respectively) and thus constitute new criteria that are hypothetically explained by exogenous factors. Because they represent unique operating properties of household process, each warrants a position as an endogenous or left-hand variable of an equation, and because these properties operate simultaneously within the household, a set of equations so formulated comprises a system of simultaneous equations. By assigning y_1, y_2, and y_3 to represent, respectively, health, practice, and expenditure patterns, the decision-process model takes the structural form:

$$y_1 = b_{11}y_{11} + b_{12}y_{12} + b_{13}y_{13} + c_{11}x_{11} + c_{12}x_{12} + \ldots + c_{1m}x_{1m} + u_1$$

$$y_2 = b_{21}y_{21} + b_{22}y_{22} + b_{23}y_{23} + c_{21}x_{21} + c_{22}x_{22} + \ldots + c_{2m}x_{2m} + u_2 \quad (4)$$

$$y_3 = b_{31}y_{31} + b_{32}y_{32} + b_{33}y_{33} + c_{31}x_{31} + c_{32}x_{32} + \ldots + c_{3m}x_{3m} + u_3$$

and in matrix notation:

$$y = Yb + Xc + u$$

in which

y is a 3×1 regressand vector of observations on the endogenous variables
Y is a 3×2 matrix of observations on the other endogenous variables

b is a 3×2 matrix of structural coefficients of the elements of y

X is a $3 \times m$ nonstochastic regressor matrix of observations on the exogenous variables, where m is the number of exogenous variables

c is a $3 \times m$ matrix of structural coefficients of the elements of x

u is a 3×1 vector of independent stochastic disturbance terms assumed to be distributed $N(0, \sigma^2)$

Some of the elements of matrices b and c will, of course, be zero.

With some Y_i inevitably situated among the X_i, the problem of reverse causality or simultaneity usually introduces bias and inconsistency in the estimation of structural parameters. This may be dealt with in any one of several ways, for example, by employing two-stage least squares for estimating parameters. In the present study, however, rank and order conditions for econometric identifiability were satisfied. That is, at least $n - 1 = 2$ system variables are absent from each equation ($n = 3 = $ the number of equations) in each system (Blalock 1969, p. 65; Farley 1967, p. 319). As such, ordinary least squares served to obtain coefficients.*

RESULTS

Segment Discrimination in the Decision-Rule Model

The postulated decision rules were fit to the Tamil Nadu data empirically by discriminant analysis to determine statistical uniqueness of the three segments and to develop consumer profiles in terms of the descriptive variables listed in Table 10.1. Of the 668 households, 558 (83.5 percent of the sample) were found to be in measured deficit in terms of calories and were assigned to the segments as follows:

Rule Used (Segment)		Families in Caloric Deficit
Equality	(DEQU)	379 (67.9%)
Proportionality	(DPRO)	125 (22.4%)
Triage	(DIAG)	54 (9.6%)

The remaining 110 households (16.5 percent of the sample) received as much or more caloric intake as they require. These are a special case that was termed the "endowed" group. They were omitted from the analyses because malnutrition should not be a problem in homes receiving sufficient food. But their characteristics and behavior are nevertheless of some interest and they are

---

*Bagozzi (1977) presents an illuminating explication of the causality issue.

included in Table 10.1. For example, some of these families distribute excessive amounts to some members while depriving others, a situation that cannot go unnoticed by the nutrition advocate.

The entire subsample of 558 families was used in the discriminant analysis because the objective was to identify the variables that best discriminate among the groups. Had the primary purpose been to determine the effectiveness of classification, more nearly equal group sizes would have been appropriate (Morrison 1969). Thus prior probabilities were proportional to the number of families actually in each segment.

The discriminating variables seem to have done an effective job of separating the groups as evidenced by a high value for Wilks' lambda (0.955) achieved by the first of two discriminating functions, the only one on which analysis was based. Its eigenvalue indicated 94 percent explained variation. The function correctly assigned 79 percent of the sample to the three decision-rule segments, compared with 57 percent and 68 percent, respectively, which would have been assigned employing the proportional chance and maximum chance criteria (by predicting all "equality" households) as formulated by Morrison (1969). These are both significant differences at the 0.01 level.

Pearson product moment correlations were calculated between all the discriminators to investigate their independence. Overall, correlations were quite low; practically all were less than 0.2, but even after data reduction through factor analysis, three correlations between 0.3 and 0.6 remained. Also, two secondary data relating to growth and literacy rates of districts showed $r = 0.7$; however both were included as important information. As a consequence, the independence assumption of the analyses was somewhat violated and results must be viewed in that light. Nonetheless, intergroup F statistics are significant at the 0.01 level. Subject to limitations posed by multicollinearity, the null hypothesis that the vectors of means are equal to one another is rejected; one may conclude that unique and distinct segments do exist.

Examination of the absolute values of the standardized discriminant coefficients* listed in Table 10.1 reveals that variables contributing most significantly to group separation are the percent caloric needs met, family size, family health status, family wealth, family caste, nutrition information sought, vegetarianism, and family education.

---

*The usual convention of considering standardized coefficients as measures of importance was followed. Their signs, however, were omitted. Compared with regression coefficients, signs of discriminant function coefficients are relatively unimportant. In fact, changing the sequence of insertion of variables might reverse the function's scale such that signs are exactly reversed, creating a mirror image of the original discriminant score plot.

Segment Profiles

Table 10.1 lists within-group mean values for all four groups. All segments share the characteristic that household heads are, on average, overfed, while the lactating or pregnant mother is deprived of adequate caloric sustenance. Also apparent from the table is a hierarchy of financial well-being, with the endoweds at the top, followed by the triages, the proportionalities, and the lowest economic rung, the equalities.

Equality segment families, which were postulated to allocate food equitably (according to members' needs), are significantly poorest in both per capita income and in percent caloric needs met. Yet only in this group are the infants well fed, too well, in fact. These families actively seek more nutrition information than those in the other two segments, a fact that should make them more receptive to promotional campaigns. Furthermore, these families are larger and have more children than the other groups, suggesting that nutrition programs and family-planning programs have especially common goals for this segment.

The proportionality segment had as a decision rule that all members participate to some extent in insufficient food supplies but that some members receive relatively more than others, provided all receive at least some sustenance. Yet, in this group we find the greatest disparity between benefits received by the household head and the young children. Not surprisingly, profiles of families most closely conforming to this rule lie between the other two groups, because the rule is midway between the two extremes in terms of behavior patterns.

Triage family members hypothetically receive "all or nothing" with the objective of ensuring benefits to at least those members most important for survival of the household. If one could imagine a triage family in the real world, then upon the demise of the sacrificed members, supplies would now suffice for those remaining and that family would join the endowed. In fact, by definition, each triage approaches the endoweds as a limit.

(A critic conjectured that this explained why triages most closely resembled the endoweds economically. It is a reasonable guess but one for which, alas, no support can be found in the data. From the data it appears that even in the poorest families no member is completely starved. In fact, no respondent household perfectly matched any of the three postulated strategies, which were hypothesized only as benchmarks. It is not uninteresting, however, to conjure up explanations for a triage/endowed linkage. Possibly, the most advantaged have the highest aspirations and the highest incentives to achieve survival, whereas the hopelessness of lowest class existence precludes hopes of survival. Perhaps poorer equalities have become accustomed to despair, including malnourishment. They are so far away from adequacy that they lack motivation to better themselves. The implication is that they prefer an intact undernourished household to the triage ideal of a healthy majority at the expense of deprived expendables.)

Empirical analysis of the decision-rule model indicates the apparent existence of three market segments that follow the postulated family objectives, and they are identified generally by vectors of characteristics listed in Table 10.1. According to market segmentation theory, differences in profiles of these three submarkets are to be taken into account when designing the product and in planning promotion campaigns. Ideally, one intervention program should be custom-tailored to suit the individual needs of each segment. Actual nutrition prescriptions are beyond the scope of this analysis, but if amelioration strategies can be framed in such a manner as to cater to differential characteristics of target submarkets, penetration of these groups should be facilitated.

Estimating the Decision-Process Model

The decision-process model is the second stage in the development of the segmentation modeling strategy evolving in this study. Having shown the existence of distinct segments, a logical next step is to explain the influence that the predictor set exerts upon the specified criterion variables—health, practice, and expenditure patterns. Some idea of differential impact of the predictors might be deduced from examination of discriminant function coefficients. But these weight the importance of the variables as discriminators only with respect to food distribution behavior and to no other criteria. More telling conclusions about the predictors' importance are obtained through multiple regression of the newly specified criteria on the predictors.

In the estimation phase, estimates are found for structural parameters, that is, coefficients for right-hand variables in the equations. The model contains a simultaneous three-equation system for the entire sample and one such system for each target segment. Although stepwise procedures are often employed in econometric model estimation, the entire variable set was "forced" into the analysis for two reasons: (1) It seemed important (in the sense of impact on the consequences) to compare the influence of the variables on the three behavioral consequences with their significance as discriminators found earlier, and (2) multicollinearity might cause the stepwise procedure to select the lesser important of a pair of highly correlated variables. Forcing all variables into a "specified" regression mitigates this possibility and tests the theory as formulated, although at a possible loss of some precision in estimation provided by stepwise selection. The sample being large, and degrees of freedom adequate, J. Johnston's admonition was followed, that "one should err on the side of including variables in the regression analysis rather than excluding them" (1972, p. 169).

In preparing variables for analysis, logarithmic transformations were performed to provide multiplicative exponential formulation for the regression equations. By structuring the equations multiplicatively, all predictor variables interact in producing the estimated values of an endogenous criterion. At the same time, the regression coefficients approximate elasticities in that they estimate the percentage change in a dependent variable for every 1 percent change in a particular independent variable (Farley 1967).

TABLE 10.3

Estimation of System Equations Using Ordinary Least Squares with Coefficients Expressed as Elasticities

	Entire Sample (n = 558)			Equality Segment (n = 379)		
	Health	Purchase	Practice	Health	Purchase	Practice
Family health status	-.264 (.077)[a]	-.083 (.024)[a]	-.058 (.027)[a]	-.261 (.096)[a]	-.078 (.029)[a]	-.034 (.032)
Food expenditure pattern	-.154 (.071)[a]	.078 (.040)[b]	.093 (.048)[b]	-.099 (.091)	.052 (.050)	.061 (.058)
Nutrition practice	-.067 (.055)	-.036 (.031)		-.172 (.070)[a]		
Percent caloric needs met		.094 (.016)[a]	-.054 (.018)[a]		.072 (.017)[a]	-.049 (.019)[a]
Food purchases per caloric need	.010 (.079)	.050 (.044)	.105 (.048)[a]	.034 (.032)		.099 (.055)[b]
Vegetarianism	.015 (.012)			.115 (.094)		
Weaned child's food cost		.007 (.007)	-.033 (.007)[a]			-.041 (.008)[a]
Nutrition information sought	-.025 (.018)	-.073 (.024)[a]			-.068 (.028)[a]	
Distance to nearest medical aid	-.024 (.013)[b]	.018 (.007)[a]	.023 (.011)[a]	.042 (.023)[b]	.019 (.009)[a]	.022 (.013)
District food output per capita			-.015 (.008)[b]	-.016 (.016)	.104 (.047)[a]	
Village electrified	-.016 (.014)	.056 (.041)			-.010 (.009)	
Land value	.092 (.056)[b]	.052 (.031)[b]				
Village water source	.037 (.028)	.042 (.015)[a]	-.072 (.034)[a]	.161 (.070)[a]	.101 (.038)[a]	-.094 (.041)[a]
District population growth rate			.040 (.017)[a]	.060 (.033)[b]	.040 (.018)[a]	
District literacy rate	-.058 (.021)[a]	-.067 (.052)	-.065 (.056)			-.035 (.016)[a]
Family wealth	.132 (.051)[a]		-.023 (.013)[b]	-.080 (.027)[a]	-.095 (.071)	
Religion is Hindu	-.112 (.100)			.143 (.060)[a]		
Family caste						
Age of infant			-.020 (.012)[b]			-.019 (.014)
Sex of infant is female			-.055 (.035)[b]			-.090 (.042)[a]
Per capita income	-.037 (.022)[b]		.136 (.014)	-.040 (.025)[b]	-.037 (.014)[a]	.020 (.015)
Family income in kind	.046 (.017)[a]	-.013 (.012)[a]	.171 (.010)[b]	.058 (.021)[a]	.021 (.012)[b]	.029 (.012)[a]

(continued)

TABLE 10.3 (continued)

	Entire Sample (n = 558)			Equality Segment (n = 379)		
	Health	Purchase	Practice	Health	Purchase	Practice
Family size		.082 (.042)[a]	-.134 (.045)[a]			-.124 (.051)[a]
Household head's age	-.103 (.082)		.090 (.050)[b]	-.122 (.102)		.134 (.060)[a]
Household head's occupation			-.056 (.033)[b]		.048 (.036)	
Spouse's education difference	.023 (.019)					
Spouse's age difference	.033 (.027)	.034 (.015)[a]				
Mother's age	.389 (.086)[a]		.408 (.051)[a]	.334 (.100)[a]		.392 (.056)[a]
Mother's age at marriage	-.156 (.074)[a]		-.191 (.044)[a]			-.188 (.047)[a]
Weaned child's age			-.075 (.034)[a]			.083 (.038)[a]
Weaned child is female			-.036 (.035)			
Mother employed, hours weekly	-.060 (.034)[b]	-.010 (.006)[b]		.074 (.041)[b]	-.008 (.007)	.008 (.006)
Household help		-.035 (.019)[b]	-.039 (.021)[b]		-.035 (.023)	.034 (.024)
Family education					.049 (.048)	
Constant	6.27	4.57	2.39	6.22	4.30	2.37
Coefficient of determination	.19	.25	.30	.22	.29	.37
Significant coefficients	11	12	20	11	9	12

	Proportionality Segment (n = 125)			Triage Segment (n = 54)		
	Health	Purchase	Practice	Health	Purchase	Practice
Family health status	-.403 (.150)[a]	-.182 (.068)[a]				
Food expenditure pattern			.121 (.105)			
Nutrition practice		.119 (.103)				
Percent caloric needs met						
Food purchases per caloric need		.216 (.064)[a]				.574 (.251)[a]
Vegetarianism		.036 (.021)[b]	.333 (.179)[b]		.086 (.049)[b]	-.095 (.086)
Weaned child's food cost					.219 (.124)[b]	

	(1)	(2)	(3)	(4)	(5)	(6)
Nutrition information sought		−.116 (.069)[b]			−.184 (.087)[a]	
Distance to nearest medical aid	.040 (.032)				.119 (.055)	
District food output per capita		−.023 (.022)			.036 (.028)	
Village electrified		−.153 (.120)				
Land value	−.041 (.036)				−.028 (.026)	
Village water source						
District population growth rate		.077 (.048)	.092 (.048)[b]	−.559 (.399)		
District literacy rate	−.178 (.162)					
Family wealth				−.148 (.144)		
Religion is Hindu					.168 (.104)	
Family caste	−.239 (.211)					
Age of infant			−.045 (.033)			
Sex of infant is female						
Per capita income		−.061 (.055)	.070 (.055)		−.052 (.039)	
Family income in kind			−.183 (.129)		.389 (.171)[a]	.056 (.035)
Family size					−.584 (.182)[a]	−.672 (.286)[a]
Household head's age			−.186 (.080)[a]	−.386 (.340)	.191 (.176)	
Household head's occupation					−.065 (.063)	
Spouse's education difference	.050 (.044)		.074 (.044)[b]			
Spouse's age difference					.242 (.062)[a]	
Mother's age	.594 (.207)[a]		.451 (.138)[a]	1.091 (.762)		.606 (.390)
Mother's age at marriage	−.744 (.229)[a]		−.185 (.163)		.327 (.313)	−1.070 (.485)[a]
Weaned child's age					−.135 (.099)	
Weaned child is female						
Mother employed, hours weekly					−.045 (.020)[a]	
Household help			.061 (.048)	.302 (.214)		.038 (.038)
Family education					−.291 (.100)[a]	
Constant	8.86	5.64	.90	8.89	2.68	.28
Coefficient of determination	.38	.37	.34	.56	.79	.76
Significant coefficients	4	5	4	0	8	4

Note: Standard errors of the estimates are in parentheses.
[a]Significant at .05.
[b]Significant at .10.
Source: Constructed by the author.

Overall, the same (discriminating) variables that proved to be important in assigning families to their respective segments appeared again as significant regressors (Table 10.3).* These include interest in nutrition as indicated by eagerness to search for information, family wealth, and size of the household. A notable disappointment was percent caloric needs met, which was so important before, yet only significant in 2 out of 12 possible occasions in the model. This supports findings in an earlier study that nutrition consequences are not based so much on availability of food as on cultural factors (Fine 1978). On the other hand, the importance of income is consistent with results of investigations in Calcutta (Reutlinger and Selowsky 1976) and Madras (Levinson 1972).

Three environmental factors emerge in this model as having important influence on nutritional outcomes: food output per capita, the type of water source available, and the growth rate of the district. Also, one sees the major role played in the home by the mother, who makes most of the crucial decisions in intrafamily food distribution and who will thus be an important audience in intervention planning. In fact, it is not uncommon for the mother secretly to put food aside for the child in anticipation of shortages.

R^2, the proportion of variability explained by the equations in the decision-process model, was high compared with marketing models in general and nutrition studies in particular. The average R^2 was 0.25 for the entire sample but rose to 0.45 for the segment models.

ERRORS AND THREATS TO VALIDITY
AND RELIABILITY

Sampling error is a lesser threat with a stratified random sample as selected in this study than it would have been for a corresponding simple random sample of the same size (Kish 1967, pp. 75-106) because the degree of dispersion within each stratum is less than that in the entire population. Then, too, the survey instrument was dominated by objective rather than open-ended items, which reduced interviewer and response bias, in spite of the fact that it was personally administered as is obviously necessary in a preliterate society.

But the important data relating to caloric need fulfillment were obtained by the method of 24-hour-recall. This is standard in nutrition surveys (ARC-MRC 1974), but the reliability of these data must be of serious question. Moreover, preexistence of the data precluded reliability testing by either test-retest or alternative forms methods, and none of the variables in the study was derived from a scale of survey items, thus obviating calculation of reliability coefficients such as Cronbach's alpha. Instead, a modified test of internal consistency relia-

---

*The relative number of significant estimates declined as sample sizes dropped across segments (see Table 10.3), probably reflecting losses in degrees of freedom.

bility was utilized in which the sample was divided into odd and even numbered cases to provide "split-half" samples whose means were compared. Similarity of the two sets of means provided good evidence of stability of the original survey and strengthened external validity or generalizability of the results.

Discriminant results were subjected to a double crossover validation procedure (Frank et al. 1965, p. 254). One half, the "analysis sample," was used to obtain coefficients of discriminant functions and to generate a classification table. These coefficients were then employed to predict group membership for cases in the other, the "validation sample." The process was then reversed using the function produced by the validation sample to assign analysis cases to groups.* The percentages of cases correctly classified were 71.48 and 66.79 percent, respectively, results that are not significantly different from each other, that is, whose similarity is not likely to be a chance occurrence (at the 0.01 level).

Harnessing the combined power of two models, each with different endogenous criteria and analyzed by different multivariate procedures, itself represents a multimethod testing process, somewhat analogous to the Campbell and Fiske device (1959). On the other hand, statistical validation notwithstanding, pitfalls mentioned earlier may not be lightly dismissed. Household behavior is inextricably linked with an historically specific social structure and culture; it cannot be presented as having universal applicability in terms of time and geography.

A methodological shortcoming in the decision-rule model stems from the dependency of the mode of intrafamily food allocation (the three decision rules) upon the percent of total caloric needs met (F), the respective correlations being $r = 0.35$, 0.44, and 0.12. For example, the functional relationship for the equality rule is, from (3):

$$\text{DEQU} = (\Sigma(Q_i - X_i)^2)^{\frac{1}{2}}$$
$$= (\Sigma(M_i N_i - N_i F)^2)^{\frac{1}{2}}$$

Indeed, one would have expected even greater dependency because if an equality family, for example, were to increase its food receipts, it would likely allocate according to one of the other two modes. That the correlations are still higher indicates that other characteristics of the family account for significant variability in food distribution behavior within the home, as discussed earlier in this chapter. Further research must guard against such intrusion of any predictors upon the independence of the segmenting criterion. A step in that direction will be to attempt to measure decision rules or objectives. This luxury was unavail-

*The author wishes to thank Benny Barak of Rutgers University for suggesting the cross-validation procedure.

able in the present inquiry, where specification could be carried out only with the preexisting Tamil Nadu data.

SUMMARY

This chapter examined the concept that the basic objectives consumers set for themselves play a role in consumption decision-making processes and therefore should be studied by consumer researchers. In the same vein, objectives of consumption units should plausibly make appropriate criteria upon which to segment target markets. A social marketing approach was employed; concepts were illustrated with a social product, the idea of nutrition improvement intervention in a developing society. The focus of analysis was the household. Data from a nutrition survey in Tamil Nadu, India, were used for empirical demonstration of one possible method for operationalizing consumer decision rules.

It was argued that the unique needs of social marketing indicate a broadened choice of criteria upon which prospective consumers should be partitioned. Among these criteria are the very basic goals that individuals set for themselves. A set of three goals was borrowed from the discipline of organizational behavior and was extrapolated to the case of intrafamily food distribution. (In a similar manner, other objectives could readily be extended to any day-to-day decision-making situation and to goals of consumption units in particular.) Corresponding to these objectives a set of intrafamily food allocation strategies (or decision rules) were postulated in a model that was then fit to the sample data. Significant differences were found between subgroups of the Indian market for nutrition intervention.

In an eclectic model-testing procedure, segment differences were first verified by discriminant analysis on respondents' deviations from the postulated strategies and then illuminated by multiple regression analysis of three nutrition behavior consequences upon a predictor set.

Implications

How would the analytic processes described here have differed if the sample was partitioned on family food distribution, per se, and not, as in this chapter, on food distribution as a proxy for household objectives? The answer is that the processes would be the same, but the interpretations would be different because purposes are different. In the former instance, the segmentation study could examine heterogeneity only with respect to distribution behavior as the sine qua non of the study. In the latter case, findings were immediately extended from behavior, upwards through Granger's hierarchy, into decision rules and goals, as a way of assessing the validity of the objectives that were postulated at the outset. Here, behavior is merely an intervening variable between consumer objectives and receptivity to nutrition intervention. Behavior is an indicator in the sense prescribed by Blalock (1969) and is employed as a proxy because goals either are too difficult to measure or simply have not been measured—the situation with the Tamil Nadu data. To study a lower-order characteristic of the consumer is to take a narrow view of the market, whereas beginning with superordinate objectives affords the marketer a broader look at target consumers.

If it were possible to make direct measurements on household objectives or on consumers' choice strategies, then analysis of such data might be useful in attempting to predict behavior. The converse seems also true: Observations made on behavior being followed reveals something about objectives underlying the behavior. Even if the reader adopts the basic idea that objectives make sense as segmentation criteria, still only the tip of the iceberg has been seen. What remains, among other things, is to find ways of operationalizing people's goals.

Segmentation by Objectives: A Methodology

Research into basic goals of the consumption unit might begin with some device for measuring these goals. One way could be directly, as with self-report items in a survey instrument. Another way is to plan for inferential quantification as suggested in this investigation. That is, a set of situationally relevant objectives is posited and a distance measure is calculated between the benchmark and each respondent's observed position (behavior). Either of these two methods provides a new vista for obtaining bases for segmentation, as well as criteria for multivariate analysis of data. What might result from this line of research is the possibility of forecasting adoption behavior merely from an understanding of goals that consumers set (explicitly or implicitly) for themselves. Alternatively, two or more sets of objectives could be hypothesized and modeled, and the rival models could then be tested to find the most robust in terms of internal reliability, goodness of fit, or other appropriate barometers.

With regard to nutrition, although the models structured in this study are still a long way from a practical planning device, they can already serve two useful functions. First, they can help both marketers and development planners to understand the structure of the problem of nutrition segmentation planning—the way in which sociodemographics, population structure, scarce resources, and environmental influences are interrelated in determining family nutrition behavior. For example, analysis of measures with potential for increasing families' caloric intake points to a combination of various social and economic programs as offering promise, including activities to increase food production, to increase per capita income growth, to limit family size, and to help develop social infrastructure in such areas as education and water supply. Second, they provide a basic framework around which to develop specific social marketing strategies. More study is needed to sketch the directions in which work can be done to improve the usefulness and applicability of this general approach in planning the allocation of social cause resources.

11

CONCLUDING OBSERVATIONS

This book has treated ideas and social issues as products that are traded in a marketplace—a concept industry. It is in order now to examine the extent to which the book's objective has been achieved. That objective was to consider ideas and social issues as marketable commodities and to show how they can be disseminated more effectively through the application of marketing theory and practice.

In point of fact, it is apparent from this inquiry that not only can concepts be marketed, but they *are* being marketed in very many cases. The activity goes under various other headings, such as education, gossip, rumor, public relations, public opinion, propaganda, lobbying, advocacy, and fund raising. But it is marketing nevertheless. It is called social marketing, idea marketing, or concept marketing, and its practitioners make up the concept sector within the economy. Concepts seem to fit the commodity role in every way. Virtually all of the marketing theoretical and methodological precepts seem to apply to ideas and issues just as they apply to conventional goods and services. That was repeatedly demonstrated in this book.

At least two tasks remain for further investigation. The first is to deal with the problem of evaluating the effectiveness of social marketing, an extremely difficult assignment. It may be consoling to observe that that task is, even in ordinary marketing, still in its infant and uncertain stage. Another is to treat in detail and with candor, the ethical dilemma posed by social marketing. Is intervention into idea dissemination justified by the "societally beneficial" expression employed in this book? Who is to define that term? Is it the interventionist or the consumer who knows better which ideas are best for individuals? Do we need a Consumers Union for concepts?

SYMBIOSIS IN SOCIAL AND TRADITIONAL MARKETING

The borrowing of thought and/or method from one social science and applying it to another is widely practiced; from an intellectual and scholarly viewpoint, this is as it should be. One may ask whether the loan must be repaid. Perhaps. Then what may be said about the large debt owed by social marketing to traditional marketing? Is knowledge and experience from the concept sector flowing back to marketing generalists?

It is too soon for a systematic proliferation of such feedback. But already it seems clear that if individuals purchase concepts as described in this book, then ideas pertaining to tangible goods are similarly adopted, probably in advance of the related product acquisitions. Before I buy something, I must first buy the idea that it is a good idea to buy the thing. The marketing of ideas gives rise to attitudes, interests, opinions, values, and beliefs, all of which underlie consumers' decision making in the purchase of goods and services. Before a traditional product, such as an automobile, is exchanged, the purchaser may "buy" the idea of a compact car, a five-speed transmission, and/or may take a position on the issue of inflatable collision bags, or the fairness of the 55-mile-per-hour speed limit.

Indeed, ideas and issues are inextricably bound up with products. As they are precursory to purchase, their role is crucial, and being intrinsic, is easily subordinated or overlooked in the marketing scenario. The marketing concept will have more depth if appeals about products are framed not directly about the products, per se, but about abstract ideas underlying the products—in the spirit of K. L. Lancaster's (1966) "bundle of attributes" suggestion.

In addition to concepts forming a basis for evaluating products, ideas and social issues are related in other ways to commercial interests. For example, consumerism and broad concern with product safety have had their impact on business policymaking and planning.

Other ideas and issues bear more directly on specific industries. Food producers find clues for product design and ad themes in social marketing programs for obesity prevention, and similarly with the apparel trades and "buy union label," accountants and tax reforms, universities and veterans' rights, real estate practitioners and fair housing, the petroleum industry and offshore drilling, purveyors of seafood and the 200-mile fishing limit, brewers and the drinking age; one may go on and on. Indeed, many effects of concept sector marketing are inextricably bound up with commercial enterprises. The potential, then, for repayment of the loan made by the latter to the former lies in business making conscious and systematic use of concept marketing. Again, the sporting goods firm cannot afford to stay aloof of the idea of PTAs if it markets equipment to schools. As Nancy Hupfer and David Gardner (1971) put it, "Once a product has been related in the consumer's mind to an issue, something important to him, the probability of this person's retaining knowledge of the product is increased" (p. 10). Then one of the benefits to accrue to traditional marketers from the advent of social marketing is that because ideas underlie ordinary products, the tenets of idea marketing may very well form a basis for an improved understanding of marketing in general.

With social marketing yet in its formative period, Harold Kassarjian (1971), writing about the incorporation of ecology into marketing strategy, observed: "The cause is what swings the sale" (p. 65). He will be followed, one anticipates, by other scholars who will find concept sector activity very much to be emulated in everyday marketing practice. Social and traditional marketers will enjoy a symbiotic relationship in the broadened discipline.

SOCIAL MARKETING: THE ULTIMATE MARKETING

A fascinating reality about social marketing is this: Social marketing is more inclusive and generalizable than traditional marketing, for to reiterate, ideas underlie all goods and services but the converse is not necessarily true. To market goods and services, it is usually necessary to employ ideas. On the other hand, one can promote an idea by focusing on the idea itself without consideration of any tangible good. For example, when designing promotion appeals in the marketing of tangibles, ideas are used to bolster the arguments presented. But concept marketers do not necessarily require actual products in message design, only ideas—words. One may speak of the steak without mentioning the sizzle. However, a sizzle's description that excludes the steak is without context. Therefore a study of social marketing necessarily also covers the traditional concepts of marketing itself. Again, the marketer calls upon the idea of energy conservation (efficiency) to market fuel oil, which, however, is not a vital ingredient in the framing of a conservation campaign. In fact, because social products enjoy a higher degree of independence than commercial goods and services, one may take the stance that social marketing is indeed the ultimate marketing. Moreover, the most potent products ever marketed were not goods or services but ideas such as those propounded by Marx, Freud, and Einstein.

The concept sector adds to the economy a dimension of caring about mental and social needs of the consuming populace. Marketing scholars and practitioners may look with pride at the acceptance of their discipline as a problem-solving forum. It is about time:

> Although recent years have seen an encouraging trend toward addressing important social issues with marketing tools, marketing research has concentrated in the past on the "cold sores" of society and ignored the "cancers." Few of the impressive analytical powers of market researchers have been applied to solving important social problems. (Rogers and Leonard-Barton 1978, p. 496)

The present volume, by drawing attention to many real-world problems from a marketing orientation, should encourage other researchers to become aware of the power of marketing technology as a tool in dealing with the roots of some of these issues.

A significant side benefit will likely be the improvement in perceptions of the marketing connotation itself. If, as the saying goes, the cure for the ills of democracy is more democracy, the wider (especially social) applications of marketing should tend to alleviate marketing's pejorative image.

As the concept sector materializes, one anticipates that marketers will engage in exciting joint ventures with social scientists and policymakers in such fields as ecology, social services, law, international development, education, and urban planning, to mention but a few.

APPENDIX A
Excerpt from John Dewey's
"The Origin and Nature of Ideas"

Something in an obscure situation suggests something else as its meaning. If this meaning is at once accepted, there is no reflective thinking, no genuine judging. Thought is cut short uncritically; dogmatic belief, with all its attending risks, takes place. But if the meaning suggested is held *in suspense*, pending examination and inquiry, there is true judgment. We stop and think, we *de-fer* conclusion in order to *in-fer* more thoroughly. In this process of being only conditionally accepted, accepted only for examination, *meanings become ideas. That is to say, an idea is a meaning that is tentatively entertained, formed, and used with reference to its fitness to decide a perplexing situation, a meaning used as a tool of judgment.*

Let us recur to our instance of a blur in motion appearing at a distance [mentioned earlier in Dewey's work]. We wonder what *the thing is*, i.e. what the *blur means*. A man waving his arms, a friend beckoning to us, are suggested as possibilities. To accept at once either alternative is to arrest judgment. But if we treat what is suggested as only a suggestion, a supposition, a possibility, it becomes an idea, having the following traits: (a) As merely a suggestion, it is a conjecture, a guess, which in cases of greater dignity we call a hypothesis or a theory. That is to say, it is a *possible but as yet doubtful mode of interpretation.* (b) Even though doubtful, it has an office to perform; namely, that of directing inquiry and examination. If this blur means a friend beckoning, then careful observation should show certain other traits. If it is a man driving unruly cattle, certain other traits should be found. Let us look and see if these traits are found. Taken merely as a doubt, an idea would paralyze inquiry. Taken merely as a certainty, it would arrest inquiry. Taken as a doubtful possibility, it affords a standpoint, a platform, a method of inquiry.

Ideas are not then genuine ideas unless they are tools in a reflective examination which tends to solve a problem. Suppose it is a question of having a pupil grasp *the idea* of the sphericity of the earth. This is different from teaching him its sphericity *as a fact*. He may be shown (or reminded of) a ball or a globe, and be told that the earth is round like those things; he may then be made to repeat that statement day after day till the shape of the earth and the shape of the ball are welded together in his mind. But he has not thereby acquired any idea of the earth's sphericity; at most, he has had a certain image of a sphere and has finally managed to image the earth after the analogy of his ball image. To grasp sphericity as an idea, the pupil must first have realized certain perplexities or confusing features in observed facts and have had the idea of spherical shape suggested to him as a possible way to accounting for the phenomena in question. Only by use as a method of interpreting data so as to give them fuller meaning does sphericity become a genuine idea. There may be a vivid image and no idea; or there may be a fleeting obscure image and yet an idea, if that image performs the function of instigating and directing the observation and relation of facts. (Dewey 1910, p. 108)

APPENDIX B
Questionnaire for the Institutional Study

SOCIAL MARKETING SURVEY. Please write a check (✔) in the appropriate space.

1. Type of institution:

   1 ( ) For-profit business firm
   2 ( ) Nonprofit organization
   3 ( ) Public (government) agency
   4 ( ) Other (specify)_____

2. Is your facility a

   1 ( ) Main office or
   2 ( ) a branch

3. What area is served by your facility

   1 ( ) City
   2 ( ) County
   3 ( ) Region
   4 ( ) State
   5 ( ) USA
   6 ( ) International
   7 ( ) Other _____

4. Age of your institution

   1 ( ) Less than 2 years
   2 ( ) 2-5 years
   3 ( ) 6-10 years
   4 ( ) 11-20 years
   5 ( ) More than 20 years

5. Annual budget of your facility

   1 ( ) Less than $10,000
   2 ( ) 10,000-25,000
   3 ( ) 25,001-100,000
   4 ( ) 100,001-500,000
   5 ( ) 500,001-1,000,000
   6 ( ) Over 1,000,000

6. If a nonprofit institution, what is
   your principal source of funds?

   1 ( ) Government
   2 ( ) Contributions
   3 ( ) Fee-for-service
   4 ( ) Other _____

7. Number of employees in the facility

   1 ( ) Under 20
   2 ( ) 21-40
   3 ( ) 41-60
   4 ( ) 61-100
   5 ( ) Over 100

8. You have considered the idea of
   _____ as
   a "product" to be marketed

   1 ( ) Never
   2 ( ) Rarely
   3 ( ) Sometimes
   4 ( ) Frequently
   5 ( ) Constantly

9. Does you institution have a marketing department or equivalent?

   1 ( ) Yes
   2 ( ) No

10. If no, briefly state a reason why
    _____
    _____

11. Age of your marketing department

    1 ( ) Less than 2 years
    2 ( ) 2-5 years
    3 ( ) 6-10 years
    4 ( ) 11-20 years
    5 ( ) More than 20 years

12. What is the name and title of the
    person(s) in your facility most
    closely involved with marketing or
    its equivalent?
    _____
    _____

13. How many staffers in your facility
    are directly concerned with mark-
    eting?

    0 ( ) None
    1 ( ) 1-3
    2 ( ) 4-10
    3 ( ) 11-20
    4 ( ) More than 20

14. Approximately what percent of your
    institution's overall budget is
    allocated to marketing or equivalent?

    0 ( ) 0%
    1 ( ) 1-20%
    2 ( ) 21-40%
    3 ( ) 41-60%
    4 ( ) 61-80%
    5 ( ) 81-100%

196

Following are some objectives (goals) which an organization might set for itself:

1. Maximization of return on available resources
2. Acquire additional resources
3. Short term survival (less than 5 years)
4. Long term survival (5 years or more)
5. Improve client satisfaction
6. Increase number of clients
7. Spread the message
8. Increase number of products offered
9. Increase utilization of existing products

While all are important, please force yourself to select the single most important by entering its number in the parentheses below:

15. ( ) According to your own feelings, and
16. ( ) According to your organizational policy.

Similarly, following are some terms one might associate with marketing:

1. Advertising
2. Propaganda
3. Public opinion
4. Persuasion
5. Public interest
6. Puffery
7. Education
8. Other (specify) _____

Please select the one you believe to be most descriptive of your marketing process and enter its number in the parentheses below:

17. ( ) According to your own feelings, and
18. ( ) According to your organizational policy.

As far as you know, which of the following marketing concepts are used by your organization in the marketing of _____?
(Enter one check for each concept):

	Unfamiliar concept 1	Never used 2	Sometimes used 3	Always used 4
19. Consumer orientation---------------- ( )		( )	( )	( )
20. Market segmentation------------------ ( )		( )	( )	( )
21. Product positioning----------------- ( )		( )	( )	( )
22. Product life cycle------------------- ( )		( )	( )	( )
23. Personal selling--------------------- ( )		( )	( )	( )
24. The "4 Ps"--------------------------- ( )		( )	( )	( )
25. New product strategy----------------- ( )		( )	( )	( )
26. Product differentiation-------------- ( )		( )	( )	( )
27. Channels of distribution------------- ( )		( )	( )	( )
28. Other (specify)_____ ( )		( )	( )	( )

Indicate the experience with each of the following in your promotion program. (Enter one check in each row):

		Perish the thought :	Never employed	Not effective	Moderately effective	Extremely effective
		1	2	3	4	5
29.	Television --------------- ( )		( )	( )	( )	( )
30.	Radio -------------------- ( )		( )	( )	( )	( )
31.	Magazines ---------------- ( )		( )	( )	( )	( )
32.	Newspapers --------------- ( )		( )	( )	( )	( )
33.	Direct Mail -------------- ( )		( )	( )	( )	( )
34.	Billboards --------------- ( )		( )	( )	( )	( )
35.	Word of mouth------------- ( )		( )	( )	( )	( )
36.	Sales representatives ---- ( )		( )	( )	( )	( )
37.	A marketing consultant --- ( )		( )	( )	( )	( )
38.	Yellow Pages ------------- ( )		( )	( )	( )	( )
39.	Ad agency ---------------- ( )		( )	( )	( )	( )
40.	Phone canvassing --------- ( )		( )	( )	( )	( )
41.	Consumer surveys --------- ( )		( )	( )	( )	( )
42.	Other (specify)					
	_____ ----- ( )		( )	( )	( )	( )

43. This questionnaire was administered;
    1 ( ) Personally
    2 ( ) By mail
    3 ( ) By phone

44. State what you perceive as the principal shortcoming in your promotion of

    _____

    _____

45. Would you like to add any comments?

    _____

    _____

Thank you for your time and cooperation.

APPENDIX C
Questionnaire for the Consumer Study

For each product listed at the left, please answer each question below by entering a number (1, 2, 3, 4, or 5) in the appropriate box. Work DOWN each column, answering each question for each of the 12 products, whether or not you had checked it as "purchased" in the first column.

"PRODUCTS"	In the column below, place a check (✓) in the box if you purchased the product in the past 12 months.*	How much time and effort is the purchase decision worth? 1 = little, to 5 = much	Number of people with whom you would discuss the purchase decision. 1 = few, to 5 = many	How would you rate your confidence in your ability to judge this product? 1 = poorly, to 5 = very well	Do people seek out your opinion on this product? 1 = hardly, to 5 = often	Among people you know, are you one of the last, or one of the first to buy this product? 1 = late to buy, to 5 = early to buy

*WITH THE FOLLOWING PRODUCTS, "PURCHASED" MEANS ACTUAL ACQUISITION OR SERVICE RENDERED TO YOU:

(tangibles)						
Automobiles	(1)	(13)	(25)	(37)	(49)	(61)
Jeans	(2)	(14)	(26)	(38)	(50)	(62)
Vitamins	(3)	(15)	(27)	(39)	(51)	(63)
(services)						
Medical care	(4)	(16)	(28)	(40)	(52)	(64)
Mass transit	(5)	(17)	(29)	(41)	(53)	(65)
Parcel delivery	(6)	(18)	(30)	(42)	(54)	(66)

*WITH THE FOLLOWING "PRODUCTS," PURCHASED MEANS YOU BECAME CONVINCED IT'S A GOOD IDEA OR AN IMPORTANT ISSUE:

(ideas)						
Physical fitness	(7)	(19)	(31)	(43)	(55)	(67)
Use of seat belts	(8)	(20)	(32)	(44)	(56)	(68)
Use of two-dollar bill	(9)	(21)	(33)	(45)	(57)	(69)
(issues)						
Legality of abortion	(10)	(22)	(34)	(46)	(58)	(70)
Buy union label	(11)	(23)	(35)	(47)	(59)	(71)
Abolish the death penalty	(12)	(24)	(36)	(48)	(60)	(72)

(PLEASE NOTE THAT YOU MUST ENTER A NUMBER IN EVERY BOX FROM 13 TO 72)

Please indicate whether you __agree__ or __disagree__ with each of the following statements by checking (✓) the line under the heading that best describes your feeling.

	Agree	Disagree
1. There's little use writing to public officials because they aren't really interested in the problems of the average man.	(1)	(0)
2. These days a person doesn't know who he can count on.	(1)	(0)
3. Nowadays a person has to live pretty much for today and let tomorrow take care of itself.	(1)	(0)
4. It's hardly fair to bring children into the world with the ways things look for the future.	(1)	(0)
5. In spite of what some people say, the lot of the average man is getting worse.	(1)	(0)

Each of the following statements can be answered __Yes__ or __No__. Please check (✓) the line under the appropriate heading which indicates your answer.

	Yes	No
6. Did you vote once in the last four years?	(1)	(0)
7. Did you vote two to five times in the last four years?	(1)	(0)
8. Did you vote six or more times in the last four years?	(1)	(0)
9. Do you inform yourself from more than one source on public issues?	(1)	(0)
10. Do you discuss public issues frequently with more than one person?	(1)	(0)
11. Did you write or talk to your Congressman or any other public official - local, state or national - to express your views once in the past year?	(1)	(0)

	Yes	No

12. Did you write or talk to your Congressman or any other public official - local, state or national - to express your views two or more times in the past year?

         (1)   (0)

13. Do you belong to one or more organizations that take stands on public issues?

         (1)   (0)

14. Did you discuss the qualifications needed for the offices on the primary election ballot?

         (1)   (0)

15. Did you work for the nomination of a candidate before the primary election once in the last four years?

         (1)   (0)

16. Did you work for the election of a candidate once in the last four years?

         (1)   (0)

17. Did you contribute money to a party or candidate once in the last four years?

         (1)   (0)

The following questions pertain to the most recent family household in which you are a member:

18. Number of members of the household   _____

19. Relationship of head of household to you   _____

20.   His or her occupation   _____

21. Family residence rented _____ or owned _____ (check one).
                           (0)   (1)

22.   Total number of rooms_____.

23. Total family income, most recent estimate (check one):

Less than $10,000	$10,000- 15,000	$15,001- 20,000	$20,001- 25,000	$25,001- 30,000	$30,001- 35,000	over 35,000
(1)	(2)	(3)	(4)	(5)	(6)	(7)

24. Level of schooling attained by most educated member of the household, including yourself (check one).

Grade school   high school   bachelors   masters   law   doctorate

   _____   _____   _____   _____   ____   _____
    (1)   (2)   (3)   (4)   (5)   (6)

25. Number of newspapers regularly read in the home _____

26. Number of magazines regularly read in the home _____

27. Divide ten points between each of the following two classes of "products" according to how important they are to you:

class 1) Tangible goods and services _____

class 2) Ideas and social issues   _____

(Note that the two figures must add up to: 10   )

Now a few questions about yourself:

28. Sex - male _____ (0); female _____ (1).
                (please check one)

29. Age - (check one) 18 & under   19-20   21-22   23-24   25 & over

                          _____   _____ _____ _____   _____
                           (1)   (2)   (3)   (4)   (5)

30. Were you born in continental USA ? _____ (1).

31. Status -   single   married   separated   divorced   widowed

             _____   _____   _____   _____   _____
              (1)   (2)   (3)   (4)   (5)

32. Religion -   Protestant   Catholic   Jewish   Atheist   other (specify)

                  _____   _____   _____   _____   _____
                   (1)   (2)   (3)   (4)   (5)

33. Race -   White   Black   Hispanic   Indian   other (specify)

           _____   _____   _____   _____   _____
            (1)   (2)   (3)   (4)   (5)

34. Number of hours per week employed -

	0	1-10	11-20	21-30	31-40	over 40
	(0)	(1)	(2)	(3)	(4)	(5)

35. About how many hours a week do you watch television?

	0	1-5	6-10	11-15	16-20	over 20
	(0)	(1)	(2)	(3)	(4)	(5)

36. About how many hours a week do you listen to the radio?

	0	1-5	6-10	11-15	16-20	over 20
	(0)	(1)	(2)	(3)	(4)	(5)

37. Do you consider yourself materialistic 1　2　3　4　5 idealistic?
    (please circle the most appropriate number on this scale)

38. Do you consider yourself conservative 1　2　3　4　5 liberal?
    (please circle the most appropriate number on this scale)

39. Following are some goals that one might set for one's self in life.
    Please check (✓) the one -- the only one -- which comes closest to:

    a) what you believe other people want for themselves, and
    b) what you want for yourself.

	a) What you believe others want	b) What you want
Achieve high status	___	___
Amass lots of money	___	___
Learn a great deal	___	___
Have a harmonious family life	___	___
Achieve physical well being	___	___
Have good friends	___	___

(PLEASE CHECK NO MORE THAN ONE GOAL IN COLUMN A AND ONE IN B)

Thank you very much.

APPENDIX D
Calculating R for the Proportionality Rule

The proportionality factor, R, is calculated for each family with the following algorithm:

a. $R^1 = 1$ by construction, as the first member's needs are filled.

b. To determine R for the family (and by implication R^i, $i = 2, \ldots, k$, for all remaining members), the computation scheme proceeds by assuming each member of the family receives F percent of his or her caloric needs met and then iteratively increases or decreases R in increments of 0.002 until the sum of the implied values for various family members is within 5 percent of the actual T for that family.

REFERENCES

Abler, Ronald, John S. Adams, and Peter Gould. 1971. *Spatial Organization.* Englewood Cliffs, N.J.: Prentice-Hall.

Adams, D. W., and A. D. Havens. 1966. "The Use of Socio-Economic Research in Developing a Strategy of Change for Rural Communities: A Columbian Example." *Economic Development and Cultural Change* 14, 204-16.

Allport, Gordon W., and Leo Postman. 1947. *The Psychology of Rumor.* New York: Holt, Rinehart and Winston.

Allvine, Fred C., and Fred A. Tarpley, Jr. 1977. *The New State of the Economy.* Cambridge, Mass.: Winthrop.

Alpert, Mark I. 1971. *Pricing Decisions.* Glenview, Ill.: Scott, Foresman.

Ansoff, H. Igor. 1976. *Corporate Strategy.* New York: Penguin.

ARC-MRC Committee. 1974. *Food and Nutrition Research.* New York: Elsevier.

Arensberg, C. M., and A. H. Niehoff. 1964. *Introducing Social Change: A Manual for Americans Overseas.* Chicago: Aldine.

Aspinwall, Leo V. 1962. "The Characteristics of Goods Theory." In William Lazer and Eugene J. Kelley (eds.), *Managerial Marketing: Perspectives and Viewpoints.* Homewood, Ill.: Irwin, 633-43.

Austin, Charles. 1980. "Churches Take to the Airways." (Bergen) *Record*, May 27, B-5.

Bagozzi, Richard P. 1977. "Structural Equation Models in Experimental Research." *Journal of Marketing Research* 14, 209-26.

——. 1975. "Marketing as Exchange." *Journal of Marketing* 39, 32-39.

——. 1974. "Marketing as an Organized Behavioral System of Exchange." *Journal of Marketing* 38, 77-81.

Bagozzi, Richard P., and M. Frances Van Loo. 1978. "Fertility as Consumption: Theories from the Behavioral Sciences." *Journal of Consumer Research* 4, 199-228.

Baumgarten, Steven A. 1975. "The Innovative Communicator in the Diffusion Process." *Journal of Marketing Research* 12, 12-18.

Beckman, Theodore N., William R. Davidson, and W. Wayne Talarzyk. 1973. *Marketing.* New York: Ronald Press.

Belk, Russell W. 1980. Personal communication.

———. 1976. "It's the Thought That Counts: A Signed Digraph of Gift-Giving." *Journal of Consumer Research* 3, 155–62.

Belshaw, Cyril S. 1965. *Traditional Exchange and Modern Markets.* Englewood Cliffs, N.J.: Prentice-Hall.

Berg, A., and R. Muscat. 1972. "Approach to National Planning." *American Journal of Clinical Nutrition* 25, 939–54.

Berg, A., Nevin S. Scrimshaw, and David L. Call. 1973. *Nutrition, National Development, and Planning.* Cambridge, Mass.: MIT Press.

Berkovitz, Harry. 1980. "Complementarity as a Means of Analysis in Philosophy." Unpublished.

Bernhardt, Kenneth L. 1979. "Consumer Research in Government." Paper presented at American Marketing Association Workshop on "Exploring and Developing Government Marketing," New Haven, Conn.

Bernstein, Sid R. 1973. "What Is Advertising?" *Advertising Age*, November 21, 8–18.

Bettman, James R. 1971. "The Structure of Consumer Choice Processes." *Journal of Marketing Research* 8, 465–71.

Blalock, H. M. 1969. *Theory Construction.* Englewood Cliffs, N.J.: Prentice-Hall.

Blau, Peter M. 1955. *The Dynamics of Bureaucracy.* Chicago: University of Chicago Press.

Bloom, Paul N., and William D. Novelli. 1979. "Problems in Applying Conventional Marketing Wisdom to Social Marketing Programs." Paper presented at the American Marketing Association Workshop, May 4, 1979, New Haven, Conn.

Bradshaw, B. R., and C. P. Mapp. 1972. "Consumer Participation in a Family Planning Program." *American Journal of Public Health* 62, 969–72.

Brembeck, Winston, L., and W. S. Howell. 1976. *Persuasion: A Means of Social Influence.* Englewood Cliffs, N.J.: Prentice-Hall.

Briggs, Kenneth A. 1980. "Brandeis Plans the First Center for Study of Jewish Life in U.S." *New York Times*, June 26, A16.

Brown, Daniel J., Philip B. Schary, and Boris W. Becker. 1978. "Marketing Down the Road: The Role of Marketing Analysis in Transportation Planning." In Subhash C. Jain (ed.), *Research Frontiers in Marketing: Dialogues and Directions*, 359–62.

Brown, Lester. 1978. "The Twenty-ninth Day." *Agenda* (June), 14–15.

Bryson, L., ed. 1948. *The Communication of Ideas*. New York: Harper & Row.

Campbell, D. T., and D. W. Fiske. 1959. "Convergent and Discriminant Validation by the Multitrait-Multirater Matrix." *Psychological Bulletin* 56, 81–105.

Cantor, Sidney M., Associates. 1973. *The Tamil Nadu Nutrition Study*. Haverford, Pa.

Carlson, Jack, et al. 1978. "A Survey of Federal Employment and Training Programs." Washington, D.C.: Chamber of Commerce of the U.S. (September).

Carlson, Robert O. 1975. *Communications and Public Opinion*. New York: Praeger.

Coleman, James, Herbert Menzel, and Elihu Katz. 1959. "Social Processes in Physicians' Adoption of a New Drug." *Journal of Chronic Diseases* 9, 1–19.

Commission on Freedom of the Press. 1947. *A Free and Responsible Press*. Chicago: University of Chicago Press.

Copeland, Melvin T. 1923. "Relation of Consumer's Buying Habits to Marketing Methods." *Harvard Business Review* 1, 282–89.

Cracco, Etienne, and Jacque Rostenne. 1971. "The Socio-Ecological Product." *MSU Business Topics* 19, 27–34.

Cremson, Matthew. 1974. "Organizational Factors in Citizen Participation." *Journal of Politics* 36, 356–78.

Daniels, L. N. 1973. "Everybody's Wonderful Gas-Powered Propaganda Machine." *Public Relations Journal* 29, 10–12.

DeFleur, Melvin L., and Sandra Ball-Rokeach. 1975. *Theories of Mass Communication*, 3rd ed. New York: McKay.

Demone, Harold E., Jr. 1978. *Human Services*. Washington, D.C.: HEW.

Department of Transportation. 1978. "55 mph Model Plan." HS 803 534 (September).

Dewees, Donald N. 1976. "Travel Cost, Transit and Control of Urban Motoring." *Public Policy* 24, 59–79.

Dewey, John. 1966. Quoted by Robert Park. In Bernard R. Berelson and Morris Janowitz (eds.), *Reader in Public Opinion and Communication*, 2nd ed. New York: Free Press.

———. 1939. *Freedom and Culture*. New York: Putnam.

———. 1910. *How We Think*. Boston: Heath.

Dionne, E. J., Jr. 1980. "The Mail-Order Campaigners." *New York Times*, September 7, F9.

Dixon, Donald F. 1978. "The Poverty of Social Marketing." *MSU Business Topics*, 50–56.

Douglas, Dorothy F., Bruce H. Westley, and Steven H. Chaffee. 1970. "An Information Campaign That Changed Community Attitudes." *Journalism Quarterly*, 479–92.

Downs, Anthony. 1957. *An Economic Theory of Democracy*. New York: Harper & Row.

Enis, Ben M. 1973. "Deepening the Concept of Marketing." *Journal of Marketing* 37, 57–62.

Etzioni, Amitai, and Eva Etzioni-Halevy. 1973. *Social Change*. New York: Basic Books.

Farley, John U. 1967. "Estimating Structural Parameters of Marketing Systems: Theory and Applications." *Proceedings of the American Marketing Association*, 316–21.

Ferber, Robert. 1977. "Applications of Behavioral Theories to the Study of Family Marketing Behavior." In Francesco M. Nicosia and Yoram Wind (eds.), *Behavioral Models for Market Analysis: Foundations for Marketing Action*. Hinsdale, Ill.: Dryden, 80–95.

Ferguson, John H., and Dean E. McHenry. 1973. *The American System of Government*, 12th ed. New York: McGraw-Hill.

Fine, Seymour H. 1981a. "Beyond Money: The Concept of Social Price." *Proceedings of the American Marketing Association Conference on Services Marketing*. Orlando, Florida, February 10.

———. 1981b. "A Concept Sector in the Economy." Paper presented at the joint conference of the American Marketing Association/European Society for Opinion and Marketing Research, Paris, France, March 30.

———. 1980a. "Toward a Theory of Segmentation by Objectives in Social Marketing." *Journal of Consumer Research* 7, 1–13.

———. 1980b. "The Idea of Energy Conservation Considered as a Product." *Proceedings of the Energy Conservation and Solar Public Awareness Conference*, Department of Energy, Silver Spring, Maryland, August 17.

———. 1980c. "Consumer Characteristics in Social Marketing." Working paper, Rutgers University.

———. 1979a. "A Strategic Plan for the Marketing of the Private Sector Initiative Program." Paper presented to the Employment and Training Administration, Passaic County, New Jersey.

———. 1979b. "A Broadened Typology of Exchange Transactions." *Proceedings of the Conference of the American Academy of Advertising*. East Lansing, Mich., 107–11.

———. 1978. "Segmentation Research in the Marketing of a Social Cause: Malnutrition in Developing Countries." Ph.D. diss., Columbia University.

Fox, Karen, and Philip Kotler. 1980. "The Marketing of Social Causes: The First Ten Years." Working paper, Northwestern University.

Frank, R. E., W. F. Massy, and Donald G. Morrison. 1965. "Bias in Multiple Discriminant Analysis." *Journal of Marketing Research* 2, 250–58.

Frank, R. E., W. F. Massy, and Y. Wind. 1972. *Market Segmentation*. Englewood Cliffs, N.J.: Prentice-Hall.

Fulbright, J. William. 1979. "The Legislator as Educator." *New York Times*, May 26, 19.

Gaedeke, Ralph M. 1977. *Marketing in Private and Public Nonprofit Organization*. Santa Monica, Calif.: Goodyear.

Gardner, John W. 1972. *In Common Cause*. New York: Norton.

Gilbert, Gorman, and James Foerster. 1977. "The Importance of Attitudes in the Decision to Use Mass Transit." *Transportation* 6, 321–32.

Gilbert, Neil. 1972. "Assessing Service Delivery Methods." *Welfare in Review* 10, 25–33.

Graham, Bradley. 1979. "Business Is Fighting for Its Right to Speak." *The Record*, April 2, A-8.

Granger, Charles B. 1964. "The Hierarchy of Objectives." *Harvard Business Review* 42, 63–74.

Greer, T. V., and W. G. Nickels. 1975. "The Advertising Council: A Model for Social Marketing?" *Marquette University Business Review* 19, 17–22.

Griff, Allen L., and Margaret Mead. 1978. *Handbook of Nutrition and Food.* Cleveland: CRC.

Gusfield, Joseph. 1963. *Symbolic Crusade: Status Politics and the American Temperance Movement.* Urbana: University of Illinois Press.

Gwyn, Robert J. 1970. "Opinion Advertising and the Free Market of Ideas." *Public Opinion Quarterly* 34, 246–55.

Haggerty, Brian A. 1979. "Public Relations in Direct Mail Political Fundraising." *Public Relations Review* 5, 10–19.

Haley, R. I. 1968. "Benefit Segmentation: A Decision-Oriented Research Tool." *Journal of Marketing* 32, 30–35.

Hansen, Flemming. 1972. *Consumer Choice Behavior: A Cognitive Theory.* New York: Free Press.

Heller, P. S., and W. D. Drake. 1979. "Malnutrition, Child Morbidity, and the Family Decision Process." *Journal of Development Economics* 6, 203–35.

Henry, W. A. 1976. "Cultural Values Do Correlate with Consumer Behavior." *Journal of Marketing Research* 13, 121–27.

Homans, George C. 1958. "Social Behavior as Exchange." *American Journal of Sociology* 63, 597–606.

Houston, Franklin S., and Richard E. Homans. 1977. "Public Agency Marketing: Pitfalls and Problems." *MSU Business Topics* 25, 36–40.

Howard, John A. 1977. *Consumer Behavior: Application of Theory.* New York: McGraw-Hill.

Howard, J. A., and J. N. Sheth. 1969. *The Theory of Buyer Behavior.* New York: Wiley.

Hunt, Shelby D. 1976. "The Nature and Scope of Marketing." *Journal of Marketing* 40, 17–28.

Hupfer, Nancy T., and David M. Gardner. 1971. "Differential Involvement with Products and Issues: An Exploratory Study." Paper presented at the Association for Consumer Research Annual Conference, September.

Hyman, Herbert H., and Paul B. Sheatsley. 1947. "Some Reasons Why Information Campaigns Fail." *Public Opinion Quarterly* 11, 412–23.

Isaacson, Larry, and Steven E. Permut. 1978. "Public/Private Marketing: Reflections on Recent Curricular Experience." *Proceedings, American Marketing Association Fall Conference*, 432–35.

Jacoby, Jacob. 1976. "Consumer and Industrial Psychology: Prospects for Theory Corroboration and Mutual Contribution." In M. D. Dunnette (ed.), *Handbook of Industrial and Organizational Psychology*. Chicago: Rand McNally, 1031–61.

Jacoby, Jacob, Donald E. Speller, and Carol A. Kohn. 1974. "Brand Choice Behavior as a Function of Information Load." *Journal of Marketing Research*, February, 63–69.

Johnston, J. 1972. *Econometric Methods*. New York: McGraw-Hill.

Kapp, K. W. 1971. *The Social Cost of Private Enterprise*. New York: Schocken.

Kassarjian, Harold H. 1971. "Incorporating Ecology into Marketing Strategy: The Case of Air Pollution." *Journal of Marketing* 35, 61–65.

Kassarjian, H. H., and T. S. Robertson. 1973. *Perspectives in Consumer Behavior*. Glenview, Ill.: Scott, Foresman.

Katz, Elihu, and Paul Lazarsfeld. 1955. *Personal Influence: The Part Played by People in the Flow of Mass Communications*. New York: Free Press.

Kaufman, Ira M. 1971. "A Microbehavioral Model of Social Marketing: A Field Test of Selected Psychosocial Variables in the Adoption of an Adult Education Course." Ph.D. diss., Northwestern University.

Kelman, Herbert C. 1965. "Manipulation of Human Behavior: An Ethical Dilemma for the Social Scientist." *Journal of Social Issues* (April), 31–46.

Kish, L. 1967. *Survey Sampling*. New York: Wiley.

Kisler, Charles A. 1975. "Conformity and Commitment." In Irving Louis Horowitz and Charles Nanry (eds.), *Sociological Realities II*. New York: Harper & Row, 63–65.

Kitaeff, Adrienne. 1975. "Public Service Television Spots: Avenue for Social Responsibility." *Public Relations Journal* 20, 10–11.

Klapper, Joseph T. 1965. *Effects of Mass Communication*. New York: Free Press.

Kornhauser, William. 1959. *The Politics of Mass Society*. Glencoe, Ill.: Free Press.

Kotler, Philip. 1980. Personal communication.

———. 1975. *Marketing for Nonprofit Organizations*. Englewood Cliffs, N.J.: Prentice-Hall.

———. 1972. "A Generic Concept of Marketing." *Journal of Marketing* 3, 46–54.

———. 1971. "The Elements of Social Action." *American Behavioral Scientist* 14, 691–717.

Kotler, Philip, and Sidney J. Levy. 1969. "Broadening the Concept of Marketing." *Journal of Marketing* 33, 10–15.

Kotler, Philip, and William Mindak. 1978. "Marketing and Public Relations." *Journal of Marketing* 42, 13–20.

Kotler, Philip, and Gerald Zaltman. 1971. "Social Marketing: An Approach to Planned Social Change." *Journal of Marketing* 35, 3–12.

Kovach, Carol. 1978. "A Hungry Problem for Zoos: In Search of New Prey." In Subhash C. Jain (ed.), *Proceedings of the Educator's Conference*. American Marketing Association, 350–54.

Krugman, Herbert. 1977. "Memory Without Recall, Exposure Without Perception." *Journal of Advertising Research* 17, 7–12.

Laczniak, Gene R., Robert F. Lusch, and William A. Strang. 1980. "Ethical Marketing: Perceptions of Economic Goods and Social Programs." Unpublished.

Lambert, Zarrel V. 1977. "Nutrition Information: A Look at Some Processing and Decision Making Difficulties." In William D. Perreault, Jr. (ed.), *Advances in Consumer Research*, 4. Atlanta: Association for Consumer Research, 126–32.

Lancaster, K. J. 1966. "A New Approach to Consumer Theory." *Journal of Political Economy* 74, 132–57.

Lazarsfeld, P. F., B. Berelson, and H. Goudet. 1944. *The People's Choice*. New York: Duell, Sloan and Pearce.

Lazer, William, and Eugene Kelley, eds. 1973. *Social Marketing: Perspectives and Viewpoints*. Homewood, Ill.: Irwin.

Leonard-Barton, Dorothy, and Everett M. Rogers. 1980. "Voluntary Simplicity in California: Precursor or Fad?" Paper presented at the American Institute for the Advancement of Science, San Francisco.

Levinson, F. J. 1972. "An Economic Analysis of the Determinants of Malnutrition Among Young Children in Rural India." Ph.D. diss., Cornell University.

Levy, S., and G. Zaltman. 1975. *Marketing, Society and Conflict*. Englewood Cliffs, N.J.: Prentice-Hall.

Lippmann, Walter. 1922. *Public Opinion*. New York: Harcourt Brace.

Long, Stephen H. 1976. "Social Pressure and Contributions to Health Charities." *Public Choice* 28, 55–56.

Lorimer, E. S., and S. W. Dunn. 1968. "Reference Groups, Congruity Theory, and Cross-Cultural Persuasion." *Journal of Communication* 18, 354–68.

Lovelock, Christopher H. 1975. "Decimalization of the Currency in Great Britain." Boston: Intercollegiate Case Clearing House, 9, 575–601.

Lovelock, Christopher H., and Jon Twichell. 1974. "Low Fare Transit Plans Gain Nationwide Trials." *Metropolitan* (May-June), 24–27.

Lovelock, Christopher H., and Charles B. Weinberg, eds. 1978. *Readings in Public and Nonprofit Marketing*. Stanford, Calif.: Scientific Press.

———. 1974. "Contrasting Public and Private Sector Marketing." *American Marketing Association, Combined Proceedings*, 242–47.

Lovelock, C., and R. H. Young. 1979. "Look to Consumers to Increase Productivity." *Harvard Business Review* (May-June), 168–78.

Luck, D. 1974. "Social Marketing: Confusion Compounded." *Journal of Marketing* 38, 70–72.

Lynn, Jerry R. 1974. "Effects of Persuasive Appeals in Public Service Advertising." *Journalism Quarterly* 51, 622–30.

McCarthy, E. Jerome. 1975. *Basic Marketing: A Managerial Approach*. Homewood, Ill.: Irwin.

McGinniss, Joe. 1969. *The Selling of the President*. New York: Trident.

McGuire, William J. 1976. "Some Internal Psychological Factors Influencing Consumer Choice." *Journal of Consumer Research* 21 (March), 302–80.

Mallen, Bruce. 1977. *Principles of Marketing Channel Management*. Lexington, Mass.: Lexington Books.

Manoff, Richard K. 1973. "The Mass Media Family Planning Campaign for the United States." *Using Commercial Resources in Family Planning Program: The International Experience*. Honolulu: East-West Center, 113-18.

Martin, N. A. 1968. "The Outlandish Idea: How a Marketing Man Would Save India." *Marketing Communications* (March), 54-60.

Maslow, A. H. 1970. *Motivation and Personality*, 2nd ed. New York: Harper & Row.

Mauss, Marcel. 1967. *The Gift*. New York: Norton.

Mead, M. 1955. *Cultural Patterns and Technical Change*. New York: Mentor Books.

Mendelsohn, Harold. 1973. "Some Reasons Why Information Campaign Can Succeed." *Public Opinion Quarterly* 37, 50-61.

Miller, C. Delbert. 1970. *Handbook of Research Design and Social Measurement*. New York: McKay.

Miller, George A. 1956. "The Magical Number Seven, Plus or Minus Two: Some Limits on Our Capacity to Process Information." *Psychological Review* 63, 81-97.

Milstein, Jeffrey S. 1977. "Consumer Behavior and Energy Conservation." *Advances in Consumer Research* 4, 315-21.

Mindak, W., and H. M. Bybee. 1971. "Marketing's Application to Fund-Raising." *Journal of Marketing* 35, 13-18.

Miracle, Gordon E. 1965. "Product Characteristics and Marketing Strategy." *Journal of Marketing* 29, 18-24.

Mishan, E. J. 1976. *Cost-Benefit Analysis*. New York: Praeger.

Montgomery, George E. 1972. "Stratification and Nutrition in a Population in Southern India." Ph.D. diss., Columbia University.

Morrison, D. G. 1969. "On the Interpretation of Discriminant Analysis." *Journal of Marketing Research* 6, 156-63.

Mushkin, Selma J., ed. 1972. *Public Prices for Public Products*. Washington, D.C.: Urban Institute.

Newell, Allen, and Herbert A. Simon. 1972. *Human Problem Solving*. Englewood Cliffs, N.J.: Prentice-Hall.

New York Times. 1978. May 24, 16.

Nicol, B. M. 1974. "Reasons for, and Methods in Dietary and Food Consumption Surveys." In J. C. Somogyi (ed.), *Assessment of Nutritional Status and Food Consumption Surveys.* Basel, Switzerland: S. Karger.

North Central Rural Sociology Subcommittee for the Study of Diffusion of Farm Practices. 1961. *How Farm People Accept New Ideas.* East Lansing, Mich.: North Central Regional Extension Service, Bulletin No. 13.

Novelli, William D. 1980a. "Toothpaste, Presidential Candidates and Good Health: Can Marketing Be Applied to All Three?" Paper presented at the Conference on the Selling of Health, Maryland Public Health Association.

———. 1980b. Personal communication.

O'Keefe, M. T. 1971. "The Anti-Smoking Commercials: A Study of Television's Impact on Behavior." *Public Opinion Quarterly* 35, 242–46.

Orwell, George. 1946. *The Animal Farm.* New York: Harcourt, Brace and World.

Palda, Kristian S. 1980. "The Public Sector and Marketing: Should the Twain Meet?" *Proceedings of the Second Annual Special Conference on Marketing Theory.*

Parameswaran, Ravi, Jac L. Goldstucker, and Barnett A. Greenberg. 1978. "A Market Opportunity Analysis for a Private Nonprofit Service Organization." *Proceedings of the Educator's Conference.* American Marketing Association.

Perry, Donald L. 1976. *Social Marketing Strategies: Conservation Issues and Analysis.* Santa Monica, Calif.: Goodyear.

Pessemier, Edgar A. 1972. "A Measurement and Composition Model for Individual Choice Among Social Alternatives." Working paper No. 348, Purdue University.

Petty, Richard E., et al. 1976. "Distraction Can Enhance or Reduce Yielding to Propaganda: Thought Disruption Versus Effort Justification." *Journal of Personality and Social Psychology* 34, 874–84.

Phelps, Edmund S., ed. 1975. *Altruism, Morality and Economic Theory.* New York: Basic Books (distributor for the Russell Sage Foundation).

Placek, Paul J. 1974–75. "Direct Mail and Information Diffusion: Family Planning." *Public Opinion Quarterly* 38, 548–61.

Polanyi, K., C. Arsenberg, and H. Pearson. 1957. *Trade and Market in the Early Empires*. Glencoe, Ill.: Free Press.

Pollay, Richard W. 1968. "A Model of Family Decision Making." *British Journal of Marketing* 33, 206-16.

Pool, Ithiel De Sola, ed. 1973. *Handbook of Communications*. Chicago: Rand McNally.

Poston, D. L., Jr., and Joachim Singelmann. 1975. "Socioeconomic Status, Value Orientations and Fertility Behavior in India." *Demography* 12, 417.

Quindlen, Anna. 1980. "The Image Makers: Five Busy Experts in Public Relations." *New York Times*, June 7, 21-24.

Ramond, Charles K., and Henry Assael. 1974. "An Empirical Framework for Product Classification." In Jagdish N. Sheth (ed.), *Models of Buyer Behavior*. New York: Harper & Row, 347-62.

Rathmell, John M. 1974. *Marketing in the Service Sector*. Cambridge, Mass.: Winthrop.

Reingen, Peter H. 1978. "On Inducing Compliance with Requests." *Journal of Consumer Research* 5, 96-97.

Reutlinger, S., and M. Selowsky. 1976. *Malnutrition and Poverty*. Baltimore: Johns Hopkins University Press.

Riesman, D. 1950. *The Lonely Crowd*. New Haven, Conn.: Yale University Press.

Robertson, T. S. 1971. *Innovative Behavior and Communication*. New York: Holt, Rinehart and Winston.

———. 1970. *Consumer Behavior*. Glenview, Ill.: Scott, Foresman.

Robinson, William A. 1978. "Promotion Through Good Deeds." *Advertising Age*, October 23, 72-74.

Rogers, Everett M. 1976. "New Product Adoption and Diffusion." *Journal of Consumer Research* 2, 190-301.

———. 1973. "Mass Media and Interpersonal Communication." In Ithiel De Sola Pool, *Handbook of Communications*. Chicago: Rand McNally.

Rogers, Everett M., and Dorothy Leonard-Barton. 1978. "Testing Social Theories in Marketing Settings." *American Behavioral Scientist* 21, 479-500.

Rogers, Everett M., and F. F. Shoemaker. 1971. *Communication of Innovations*. London: Collier-Macmillan.

Rokeach, M. 1973. *The Nature of Human Values*. New York: Free Press.

Rosenberg, Larry J. 1977. *Marketing*. Engelwood Cliffs, N.J.: Prentice-Hall.

Rosnow, Ralph L. 1977. "Gossip and Marketplace Psychology." *Journal of Communication* 27, 158–63.

Rosnow, Ralph L., and G. A. Fine. 1976. *Rumor and Gossip: The Social Psychology of Hearsay*. New York: Elsevier.

Rothschild, Michael L. 1980. Personal communication.

———. 1979. "Communications in Non-Business Situations—Or Why It's So Hard to Sell Brotherhood Like Soap." *Journal of Marketing* 43, 11–20.

———. 1978. "Political Advertising: A Neglected Policy Issue in Marketing." *Journal of Marketing Research* 15, 58–71.

Ryan, Bryce, and Neal C. Gross. 1943. "The Diffusion of Hybrid Seed Corn in Two Iowa Communities." *Rural Sociology* 13, 15–24.

Sanders, Irwin. 1969. "The Involvement of Health Professionals and Local Officials in Fluoridation Controversies." *American Journal of Public Health* 52, 1274–87.

"Save the Whales." 1979. WQXR, Sunday, June 10, 9:00 A.M.

Schiffman, Leon G., and Leslie L. Kanuk. 1978. *Consumer Behavior*. Englewood Cliffs, N.J.: Prentice-Hall.

Schneider, Benjamin. 1973. "The Perception of Organizational Climate." *Journal of Applied Psychology* 57, 242–56.

Schramm, Wilbur, and D. F. Roberts. 1971. *The Process and Effect of Mass Communication*. Chicago: University of Illinois Press.

Schwartzman, Helen B., Anita W. Kneifel, and Merton S. Krause. 1978. "Culture Conflict in a Community Health Center." *Journal of Social Issues* 34 (November 4), 93–110.

Sethi, S. Prakash. 1979. "Institutional/Image Advertising and Idea/Issue Advertising as Marketing Tools: Some Public Policy Issues." *Journal of Marketing* 43, 68–78.

Shapiro, Benson. 1973. "Marketing for Nonprofit Organizations." *Harvard Business Review* (September-October), 123-32.

Sheth, Jagdish N. 1980. Personal communication.

———. 1979a. "Psychology of Innovation Resistance: The Less-Developed Concept (LDC) in Diffusion Research." *Proceedings of the Association for Consumer Research.*

———. 1979b. "The Surpluses and Shortages in Consumer Behavior and Research." Working paper No. 573, University of Illinois at Urbana-Campaign.

———. 1978. "A Model of Strategy Mix for Planned Social Change." Unpublished, University of Illinois at Urbana-Champaign.

———, ed. 1974. *Models of Buyer Behavior.* New York: Harper & Row.

Sheth, Jagdish N., and Peter L. Wright, eds. 1974. *Marketing Analysis for Societal Problems.* Urbana-Champaign: University of Illinois.

Shibutani, T. 1966. *Improvised News: A Sociological Study of Rumor.* Indianapolis: Bobbs-Merrill.

Shore, Milton F., and Joseph L. Massimo. 1979. "Fifteen Years After Treatment: A Follow-up Study of Comprehensive Vocationally-Oriented Psychotherapy." *American Journal of Orthopsychiatry* 49:2 (April), 245.

Shostack, Lynn G. 1977. "Breaking Free from Product Marketing." *Journal of Marketing* 41, 73-80.

Sigal, Leon V. 1973. "Bureaucratic Objectives and Tactical Uses of the Press." *Public Administration Review* 33, 336-45.

Simon, Raymond, 1976. *Public Relations: Concepts and Practice.* Columbus, Ohio: Grid.

Simons, Herbert W. 1976. "Communication and Social Change: The Technoculture, the Counterculture and the Futureculture." *Vital Speeches* (February 1), 243-46.

Special Report No. 31. 1978. National Commission for Manpower Policy (November), Washington, D.C.

Star, Jack. 1973. "Why You Choose the Foods You Do." *Today's Health* 51, 31.

Stern, Louis W., and Adel I. El-Ansary. 1977. *Marketing Channels.* Englewood Cliffs, N.J.: Prentice-Hall.

Stratmann, William C. 1975. "A Study of Consumer Attitudes About Health Care: The Delivery of Ambulatory Services." *Medical Care* 8, 537–48.

Swagler, Roger M. 1979. "Information as Human Capital: Toward a Time-Use Approach." *Proceedings of the Association for Consumer Research.*

Takas, Andrew. 1974. "Societal Marketing: A Businessman's Perspective." *Journal of Marketing* 38, 2–7.

Taylor, James B. 1970. "Introducing Social Innovation." *Journal of Applied Behavioral Science* 6, 69–77.

Taylor, James W., and Robert B. Jones. 1978. "The Attitude Change—Behavior Change Problem." *Journal of Marketing* 42, 9.

Thompson, Wilbur. 1968. "The City as a Distorted Price System." In J. R. Wish and S. H. Gamble (eds.), *Marketing and Social Issues.* New York: Wiley, 79–88.

Tichenor, P. J., et al. 1970. "Mass Media Flow and Differential Growth in Knowledge." *Public Opinion Quarterly* 34, 159–70.

Titmuss, Richard M. 1972. *The Gift Relationship.* New York: Vintage.

Toffler, Alvin. 1980. "A New Kind of Man in the Making." *New York Times Magazine,* March 9, 24.

Turow, J. 1974. "Talk Show Radio as Interpersonal Communication." *Journal of Broadcasting* 18, 171–79.

Wedding, Nugent. 1975. "Advertising as a Method of Mass Communication of Ideas and Information." *Journal of Advertising,* Summer, 6–10.

Weiss, E. B. 1972. "New Life Styles of 1975–1980 Will Throw Switch on Ad-men." *Advertising Age,* September 18, 61–68.

Wells, William D. 1975. "Psychographics: A Critical Review." *Journal of Marketing Research* (May), 196–213.

Wharton, Clifford R., Jr. 1977. "The Role of the Professional in Feeding Mankind: The Political Dimension." *War on Hunger* (January).

White, Theodore H. 1973. *The Making of the President 1972.* New York: Atheneum.

Wiebe, G. D. 1951–52. "Merchandising Commodities and Citizenship on Television." *Public Opinion Quarterly* 15, 679–91.

Wilkie, William L. 1977. "Consumer Information Processing Issues for Public Policy Makers." Paper presented at the NSF Conference, MIT, July 28–29.

Wish, John R., and Stephen H. Gamble, eds. 1971. *Marketing and Social Issues*. New York: Wiley.

World Bank. 1978. *World Development Report*. Washington, D.C.

Wright, Peter. 1975. "Consumer Choice Strategies: Simplifying vs. Optimizing." *Journal of Marketing Research* 12, 60–67.

Yedvab, J. O. 1974. "Consumer's Role in Defining Goals, Structures, and Services." *Hospital Progress* 55, 56–60.

Zaltman, Gerald. 1979. "Knowledge Utilization as Planned Social Change." *Knowledge: Creation, Diffusion, Utilization* 1, 82–105.

——. 1973. *Process and Phenomena of Social Change*. New York: Wiley.

Zaltman, Gerald, and Robert Duncan. 1977. *Strategies for Planned Change*. New York: Wiley.

Zaltman, Gerald, and N. Lin. 1971. "On the Nature of Innovations." *American Behavioral Scientist*, 651–71.

Zaltman, Gerald, and Brian Sternthal, eds. 1975. *Broadening the Concept of Consumer Behavior*. Association for Consumer Research.

Zeisel, Hans. 1980. "Making Polls Count." *New York Times*, May 24, 23.

INDEX

constant sum scaling, 160
consumer cooperatives, 74
Consumer Reports, 115
consumers' surplus, 90
copy strategy, 138
counterculture, 154
credit purchasing, 151
crime prevention, 76
cultural values, 152
cultural lag hypothesis, 92, 153

D

debate, 43
decision worth index, 159
decision-rule model, 172
decision-process model, 176, 180
deductive reasoning, 8, 20
Delphi panel, 78
dependent variables, 176
diffusion effect, 99
diffusion index, 159
direct mail, 111, 138
distraction, 107
draft registration, 98
drilling, off-shore, 189
drinking age, 189
drug abuse control, 82
drunk driving, 69

E

economic man, 168
education, continuing, 73, 150
effort price, 84
electronic media, 111
emergency number, 69, 150
energy conservation, 152
Equal Rights Amendment, 53
ethic of consumption, new, 154

ethics, 188
ethos, 56, 101
euthanasia, 153
evaluative research, 145
evoked set, 25, 32
exchange, 62
exploratory research, 146

F

fair housing, 65
fairness and balance, 111
family planning, 14
fashion trend, 30, 47
FCC, 111
fear, 101
fire prevention, 26
fishing limits, 200 mile, 189
fluoridation, 107
food industry and nutrition, 117
foot-in-the-door, 41
foreign aid, 74
forest fire prevention, 10
foster parenthood, 76
franchising, 151
fraternal organizations, 117
free trade in ideas, 2
freedom of the press, 110
fundraising, 41
future shock, 153

G

gatekeepers, 109
gay rights, 149
gifts, 42
goals, 47
gossip, 84
gossipmongering, 35
government, 45

gun control, 111

H

halo effect, 100
health, value of, 107
Health Maintenance Organizations, 15
heuristics, 10
hierarchy of objectives, 166
hiking, walking, viii
hypodermic needle theory, 93

I

idealists, 162
ideas vs. issues, 11
image, 117
impalpable goods, 62
improvised news, 95
impulse buying, 149
inductive reasoning, 20
information and education, 34
information as a price, 84
information load, 151
inner- to other-directedness, 15
innovators, 156
intellectual goods, 62
introvertism, 160
involvement, 94, 147, 160

K

knowledge, 71

L

laggards, 156

leading national advertisers, 32
League of Women Voters, 53, 77
lefthandedness, 53
legalized gambling, 153
life style price, 85
listening station, 40
literacy, 73
littering prevention, 86
lobbying, 40
logos, 101

M

mainstreaming, 45
manpower programs, 70, 133
March of Dimes, 76
market segmentation, 131, 163
marketing concept, 20
marketing and public relations, 37
marketing functions, 19, 104
marketing plan, 127
marriage, 62
Maslow model, 157
mass media, 110
mass transit, 67, 83, 86
materialists, 154, 162
media, 109
mental health, 98
merit goods, 62
metric system, 73
middlemen, 104, 137
military recruiting, 74
minimum wage, 71
model specification, 172
motion pictures, 111
motorcycle helmets, use, 54, 68
multidimensional scaling, 68
Muscular Dystrophy Association, 113
museums, 78

N

National Rifle Association, 111
National Safety Council, 119
National Council of Jewish Women, 78
nature conservation, 100
New York City, 77
noise in the system, 37
nuclear energy, 73
nudism, 73
nutrition, 72

O

obesity prevention, 189
objectives, 49, 160
one dollar coin, 118
opinion leader, 114, 156
opinion leadership index, 160
organization goals, 49, 74, 76
other-directed society, 158
outdoor living, 17

P

packaging, 67
Parents Anonymous, 52
participation, 89, 118, 149, 155
pathos, 56, 101
peace, 77
Peace Corps, vii
perception, 150
personality, 156
pet responsibility, 21
philanthropy, 4, 158
physical fitness, 11
Plato, 8
poetry, 67
point of purchase, 120

police, support of, 67
political action committees, 115
political action, 160
politics, 45
pollution control, 152
population control, 151
posters, 141
prayer in schools, 71
preference map, 69
pressure groups, 115
price, 82
primacy, 101
print media, 110
prison reform, 17
problem-solving techniques, 20
product differentiation, 70
product form, 71
product life cycle, 72
product management, 61
product mix, 75
product positioning, 67
product space, 68
product safety, 189
productivity in industry, 46, 133
propaganda, vii
propagandizing, 39
psyche price, 85
psychic income, 83
psychographics, 160
psychological prices, 89
psychosocial component, 135
PTA, 189
public goods, 62
public opinion, 38, 108, 111
public price, 87
public relations, 37
public service announcement, 111, 139
publicity, 37
pull/push, merchandising, 20

ABOUT THE AUTHOR

SEYMOUR H. FINE is a member of the faculty at Rutgers University, where he teaches marketing management, advertising, and marketing for nonprofit institutions. Before entering the realm of scholarship, research, and writing, he started his business career in 1950 as founder and president of Fine Marketing Associates, wholesalers of decorative accessories for the home. He retired in 1975 at the age of 50 and for the next two years was a full-time student at Columbia's Graduate School of Business, receiving the Ph.D. in 1978 while already at Rutgers.

Professor Fine has published numerous papers on both conventional and social marketing topics. His research on market segmentation by consumer objectives received a national award in 1979 presented by the Association for Consumer Research. His book, *The Marketing of Ideas and Social Issues*, is the first to be written on the subject of a marketing approach to the dissemination of concepts. Its basic notion of the presence of a concept sector within the economy won for Dr. Fine an invitation to address the joint conference of the American Marketing Association and the European Society for Opinion and Marketing Research in Paris, in 1981.

Fine is a member of the American Marketing Association, The Association for Consumer Research, the American Academy of Advertising, the American Institute for Decision Sciences, and the Private Industry Council of Passaic County. He serves as consultant on strategic planning to private sector firms and institutions, as well as government.